P9-CQC-505

Reading and Study Workbook
Level B
With Math Support

Prentice Hall
Physical Science

Concepts in Action
With Earth and Space Science

SAVVAS
LEARNING COMPANY

Reading and Study Workbook
Level B
With Math Support

Prentice Hall

Physical Science

Concepts in Action
With Earth and Space Science

ISBN-13: 978-0-13-362832-6
ISBN-10: 0-13-362832-9
16 2022

How to use the *Reading and Study WorkBook Level B*

Did you know that learning to study more effectively can make a real difference in students' performance at school? Students who master study skills are more confident and have more fun learning. This book, the *Reading and Study Workbook Level B* for Prentice Hall Physical Science, is designed to help your students acquire the skills that will allow them to study Physical Science more effectively.

The *Reading and Study Workbook Level B* can be used to

- preview a chapter,
- learn key vocabulary terms,
- master difficult concepts, and
- review for chapter and unit tests.

The *Reading and Study Workbook Level B* concentrates on the Key Concepts presented in each chapter of the textbook. Each chapter in the *Reading and Study Workbook Level B* begins with a chapter summary. This review material stresses the Key Concepts and facts you should focus on in that particular chapter.

An alternate way of using the chapter summary is to assign students to read it before you cover the chapter in the textbook. In that way, students will be alerted to the important facts contained in the chapter. Used in this manner, the summary can be a prereading guide to the chapter material.

Following the chapter summary, you will find specific workbook activities designed to help students read and understand the textbook. Completing these worksheets will help students master the Key Concepts in each section.

The final part of each chapter consists of a WordWise vocabulary review. The WordWise vocabulary reviews take a variety of formats including crossword puzzles and matching exercises.

How to use the Reading and Study Workbook Level B

Did you know that learning to study more effectively can make a real difference in students' performance at school? Students who master study skills are more confident and have more fun learning. This book, the *Reading and Study Workbook Level B* for Prentice Hall *Physical Science*, is designed to help your students acquire the skills that will allow them to study Physical Science more effectively.

The *Reading and Study Workbook Level B* can be used to

- preview a chapter,
- learn key vocabulary terms,
- master difficult concepts, and
- review for chapter and unit tests.

The *Reading and Study Workbook Level B* concentrates on the Key Concepts presented in each chapter of the textbook. Each chapter in the *Reading and Study Workbook Level B* begins with a chapter summary. This review material stresses the Key Concepts and facts you should focus on in that particular chapter.

An alternate way of using the chapter summary is to assign students to read it before you cover the chapter in the textbook. In that way, students will be alerted to the important facts contained in the chapter. Used in this manner, the summary can be a prereading guide to the chapter material.

Following the chapter summary, you will find specific workbook activities designed to help students read and understand the textbook. Completing these worksheets will help students master the Key Concepts in each section.

The final part of each chapter consists of a WordWise vocabulary review. The WordWise vocabulary reviews take a variety of formats including crossword puzzles and matching exercises.

Contents

Chapter 1 Science Skills

Summary

1.1 What Is Science?

☞ Science begins with curiosity and often ends with discovery.

☞ Science and technology depend on each other. Advances in one lead to advances in the other.

- **Science** is a system of knowledge and the methods you use to find that knowledge.
- **Technology** is the use of knowledge to solve practical problems.

☞ Natural science is generally divided into three branches: physical science, Earth and space science, and life science.

- The two main areas of physical science are physics and chemistry.
- **Chemistry** is the study of the composition, structure, properties, and reactions of matter.
- **Physics** is the study of matter and energy and the interactions between the two through forces and motion.
- The foundation of Earth science is **geology,** the study of the origin, history and structure of Earth.
- The foundation of space science is **astronomy,** the study of the universe beyond Earth, including the sun, moon, planets and stars.
- The study of living things is known as **biology,** or life science.

1.2 Using a Scientific Approach

☞ The goal of any scientific method is to solve a problem or better understand an observed event.

- An organized plan for gathering, organizing, and communicating information is called a **scientific method.**
- An **observation** is information that you obtain through your senses.
- A **hypothesis** is a proposed answer to a question.
- A variable that causes change in another variable is called a **manipulated variable.**
- The **responding variable** is the variable that changes in response to the manipulated variable.
- A **controlled experiment** is an experiment in which only one variable, the manipulated variable, is deliberately changed at a time.
- A **scientific theory** is a well-tested explanation for a set of observations or experimental results.

☞ A scientific law describes an observed pattern in nature without attempting to explain it. The explanation of such a pattern is provided by a scientific theory.

☞ Scientific models make it easier to understand things that might be too difficult to observe directly.

1.3 Measurement

☞ **Using scientific notation makes very large or very small numbers easier to work with.**

☞ **Scientists use a set of measuring units called SI, or the International System of Units.**

- **Scientific notation** is a way of expressing a value as a product of a number between 1 and 10 and a power of ten.
- In SI, the base unit for **length,** or the straight-line distance between two points is the meter (m).
- The base unit for **mass,** or the quantity of matter in an object or sample, is the kilogram (kg).
- **Volume** is the amount of space taken up by an object.
- **Density** is the ratio of an object's mass to its volume.
- A **thermometer** is an instrument that measures temperature, or how hot an object is. The SI base unit for temperature is kelvin (K). A temperature of 0 K, or 0 kelvin, refers to the lowest possible temperature that can be reached.

☞ **The precision of a calculated answer is limited by the least precise measurement used in the calculation.**

- **Precision** is an assessment of how exact a measurement is.
- **Significant figures** are all the digits that are known in a measurement, plus the last digit that is estimated.
- Another important quality of measurement is **accuracy,** which is the closeness of a measurement to the actual value off what is being measured.

1.4 Presenting Scientific Data

☞ **Scientists can organize their data by using data tables and graphs.**

☞ **Scientists can communicate results by writing in scientific journals or speaking at conferences.**

- A bar graph is often used to compare a set of measurements, amounts, or changes.
- A circle graph shows how a part or share of something relates to the whole.
- A line graph shows changes that occur in related variables.
- A relationship in which the ratio of two variables is constant is called a **direct proportion.**
- A relationship in which the product of two variables is a constant is called an **inverse proportion.**
- Occasionally, the data points in a line graph produce a straight line. The steepness or **slope** of this line is the ratio of a vertical change to the corresponding horizontal change.

Chapter 1   Science Skills

Section 1.1 What Is Science?
(pages 2–6)

This section describes the characteristics of science and technology. It also discusses the big ideas of physical science.

Reading Strategy (page 2)

Previewing Skim the section to find out what the main branches of natural science are. Complete the concept map based on what you have learned. For more information on this Reading Strategy, see the **Reading and Study Skills** in the **Skills and Reference Handbook** at the end of your textbook.

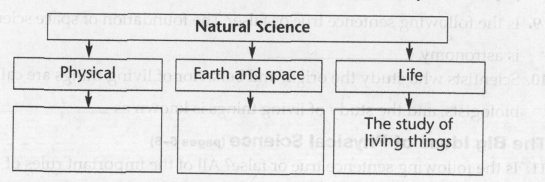

Science From Curiosity (pages 2–3)

1. Define science. _____

_____

2. What prompts the questions that lead to scientific discovery? Circle the correct answer.

   the library   your teacher   curiosity

3. Is the following sentence true or false? The results of every scientific

   experiment are quantitative. _____

Science and Technology (page 3)

4. Is the following sentence true or false? The use of knowledge to

   solve practical problems is known as curiosity. _____

Branches of Science (page 4)

5. The two main areas of physical science are chemistry and _____.

6. Circle the letters of each branch of natural science.

   a. physical science

   b. social science

   c. Earth and space science

Chapter 1   Science Skills

7. Circle the letter of each sentence that is true about the field of chemistry.

   a. Chemists study reactions involving matter.

   b. Chemists study the composition of matter.

   c. Chemists study the structure of matter.

8. What is the study of matter, energy, and the interactions between the two through forces and motion known as? Circle the correct answer.

   physics   chemistry   earth science

9. Is the following sentence true or false? The foundation of space science is astronomy. _____

10. Scientists who study the origin and behavior of living things are called biologists, and the study of living things is known as _____.

The Big Ideas of Physical Science (pages 5–6)

11. Is the following sentence true or false? All of the important rules of nature have already been discovered. _____

12. The two characteristics of matter are mass and _____.

13. What are the basic building blocks of matter called? Circle the correct answer.

    atoms   molecules   protons

14. Is the following sentence true or false? A force causes a change in time. _____

15. Define kinetic energy. _____

16. Two general types of energy are kinetic energy and _____ energy.

Science and Your Perspective (page 6)

17. Is the following sentence true or false? The scientific facts of today will not change in the future. _____

Chapter 1   Science Skills

Section 1.2 Using a Scientific Approach
(pages 7–11)

This section describes scientific methods and how they are used to understand the world around you.

Reading Strategy (page 7)

Using Prior Knowledge Before you read, add to the web diagram what you already know about scientific methods. After you read the section, revise the diagram based on what you have learned. For more information on this Reading Strategy, see the **Reading and Study Skills** in the **Skills and Reference Handbook** at the end of your textbook.

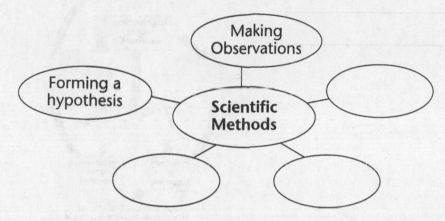

Scientific Methods (pages 7–9)

1. Name three types of variables in an experiment.

   a. Manipulated variable b. _____   c. _____

2. Is the following sentence true or false? If the data from an experiment do not support your hypothesis, you can revise the hypothesis or

   propose a new one. _____

Match the following vocabulary terms to the correct definition.

Definition	Vocabulary Terms
_____ 3. Information that you obtain through your senses	a. theory
_____ 4. A well-tested explanation for a set of observations	b. hypothesis
_____ 5. A proposed answer to a question	c. observation

Chapter 1   Science Skills

6. Complete the model of a scientific method by using the sentences in the box below to fill-in the missing steps.

> Test hypothesis with further experiments.
> Revise hypothesis.
> Analyze data and draw conclusions.
> Develop theory.

a. _____

b. _____

c. _____

d. _____

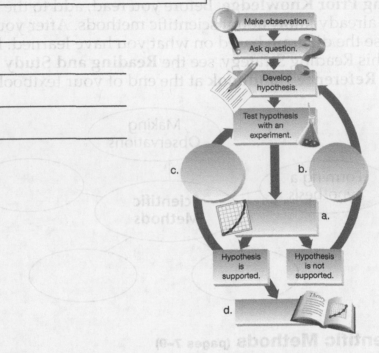

Scientific Laws (page 9)

7. All scientists may accept a given scientific law, but different scientists may have different _____ to explain it. Circle the correct answer.

models   scientific theories   hypotheses

Scientific Models (page 10)

8. Why are scientific models useful? _____
_____

Working Safely in Science (page 11)

9. Circle the letters of safety precautions to follow whenever you work in a science laboratory.

a. Study safety rules.

b. Never ask questions.

c. Read all procedural steps.

Chapter 1   Science Skills

Section 1.3 Measurement
(pages 14–20)

This section discusses units of measurement, making and evaluating measurements, and calculations with measurements.

Reading Strategy (page 14)

Previewing Before you read the section, draw a table like the one below in your notebook. Rewrite the green and blue topic headings in this section as questions in the table. As you read, write answers to the questions. For more information on this Reading Strategy, see the **Reading and Study Skills** in the **Skills and Reference Handbook** at the end of your textbook.

Measurement
Why is scientific notation useful? It makes very large or very small numbers easier to work with.

Using Scientific Notation (pages 14–15)

1. Scientific notation expresses a value as the product of a number between

   1 and 10 and _____.

2. Circle the letter of the value that is expressed as 3×10^8.

   a. 300

   b. 300,000

   c. 300,000,000

SI Units of Measurement (pages 16–18)

3. Is the following sentence true or false? Units in the SI system include

   feet, pounds, and degrees Fahrenheit. _____

Match the SI base unit with the quantity that is used to measure.

	SI Base Unit	Quantity
_____	4. meter	a. mass
_____	5. kilogram	b. time
_____	6. kelvin	c. length
_____	7. second	d. temperature

8. Use the terms in the box to complete the table of SI prefixes.

micro-	billion(10^9)	1,000,000	c
milli-	tenth(10^{-1})	1,000	n

SI Prefixes			
Prefix	**Symbol**	**Meaning**	**Multiply Unit By**
giga-	G		1,000,000,000
mega-	M	million (10^6)	
kilo-	k	thousand (10^3)	
deci-	d		0.1
centi-		hundredth (10^{-2})	0.01
	m	thousandth (10^{-3})	0.001
	μ	millionth (10^{-6})	0.000001
nano-		billionth (10^{-9})	0.000000001

9. A ratio of equivalent measurements that is used to convert a quantity expressed in one unit to another unit is called a(n) _____. Circle the correct answer.

fraction   conversion factor   proportion

Limits of Measurement (page 19)

10. Circle the letter of each expression that has four significant figures.

    a. 1.25×10^4

    b. 12.51

    c. 0.1255

11. Is the following sentence true or false? The precision of a calculated answer is limited by the least precise measurement used in the calculation. _____

Measuring Temperature (page 20)

12. Circle the letter of the base unit of temperature in SI.

    a. degree Fahrenheit (°F)

    b. degree Celsius (°C)

    c. kelvin (K)

Chapter 1   Science Skills

Section 1.4 Presenting Scientific Data
(pages 22–25)

This section describes how scientists organize and communicate data.

Reading Strategy (page 22)

Comparing and Contrasting After you read this section, compare the types of graphs by completing the table. For more information on this Reading Strategy, see the **Reading and Study Skills** in the **Skills and Reference Handbook** at the end of your textbook.

Type of Graph	Description	Used For
Line graph	A graph in which a line is plotted to describe changes that occur in related variables	Showing how a variable responds to changes in another
Bar graph		
Circle graph		

Organizing Data (pages 22–24)

1. Circle the letters of tools that scientists use to organize their data.

    a. the Internet   b. newspapers   c. graphs

2. The simplest way to organize data is to present them in a(n) _____. Circle the correct answer.

    line graph   bar graph   data table

3. Circle the letter of the place on a line graph where the manipulated variable is generally plotted.

    a. the y-axis

    b. the x-axis

    c. the run

4. On a line graph, the ratio of the vertical change to the corresponding horizontal change is called the line's _____. Circle the correct answer.

    rise   run   slope

Chapter 1   Science Skills

5. Use the words in the box to identify each data organizing tool shown below.

| line graph | bar graph |
| circle graph | data table |

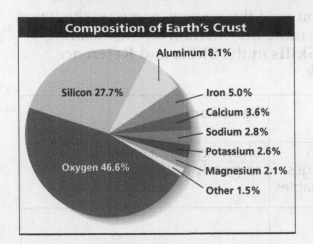

Composition of Earth's Crust

Aluminum 8.1%

Silicon 27.7%

Iron 5.0%

Calcium 3.6%

Sodium 2.8%

Potassium 2.6%

Oxygen 46.6%

Magnesium 2.1%

Other 1.5%

a. _____

Average Annual Precipitation for Selected U.S. Cities

City	Average Annual Precipitation (cm)
Buffalo, N.Y.	98.0
Chicago, Ill.	91.0
Colorado Springs, Colo.	41.2
Houston, Tex.	117.0
San Diego, Calif.	25.1
Tallahassee, Fla.	166.9
Tucson, Ariz.	30.5

b. _____

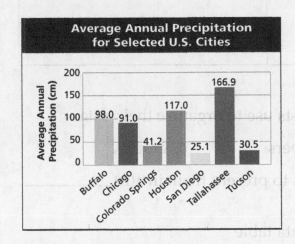

Average Annual Precipitation for Selected U.S. Cities

c. _____

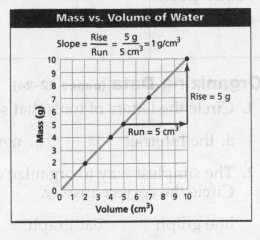

Mass vs. Volume of Water

$$\text{Slope} = \frac{\text{Rise}}{\text{Run}} = \frac{5\,g}{5\,cm^3} = 1\,g/cm^3$$

Rise = 5 g

Run = 5 cm^3

d. _____

Communicating Data (page 25)

6. Scientists can report results of their experiments by writing in _____ and by speaking at _____.

7. Why is peer review an important part of scientific research?

_____

_____

Chapter 1   Science Skills

WordWise

Use the clues and the words below to help you write the vocabulary terms from the chapter in the blanks. Use the circled letter in each term to find the hidden vocabulary word. Then write a definition for the hidden word.

slope	accuracy	technology
observation	physics	thermometer
model	precision	science
scientific law		

Clues

Vocabulary Terms

The study of matter, energy, and their interactions

Ⓞ _ _ _ _ _ _

The closeness of a measurement to the actual value of what is being measured

_ _ _ _ _ _ Ⓞ _

A gauge of how exact a measurement is

Ⓞ _ _ _ _ _ _ _ _

The ratio of a vertical change to the corresponding horizontal change in a line

_ _ Ⓞ _ _

An instrument used to measure temperature

_ _ _ _ _ _ _ Ⓞ _ _

The use of knowledge to solve practical problems

_ _ _ Ⓞ _ _ _ _ _

A representation of an object or event

_ _ _ Ⓞ _

A system of knowledge and the methods used to find that knowledge

Ⓞ _ _ _ _ _ _

A statement that summarizes a pattern found in nature

_ _ _ _ _ _ _ Ⓞ _ _ _ _ _ _ _

Information that you obtain through your senses

_ _ Ⓞ _ _ _ _ _ _ _ _

Hidden word: _ _ _ _ _ _ _ _ _ _ _

Definition: _____

Chapter 1   Science Skills

Using Scientific Notation

Calculate the density of a solid material if the mass is measured as 1.50×10^2 g and its volume is measured as 5.0 cm^3.

Math Skill:
Scientific Notation

You may want to read more about this **Math Skill** in the **Skills and Reference Handbook** at the end of your textbook.

1. Read and Understand

What information are you given?

Mass = 1.50×10^2 g

Volume = 5.0 cm^3

2. Plan and Solve

What unknown are you trying to calculate?

Density = ?

What formula contains the given quantities and the unknown?

$$\text{Density} = \frac{\text{Mass}}{\text{Volume}}$$

Replace each variable with its known variable and known value.

$$\text{Density} = \frac{1.50 \times 10^2 \text{g}}{5.0 \text{ cm}^3}$$

$$= \frac{1.50}{5.0} (10^2)(\text{g}/\text{cm}^3)$$

$$= 0.30 \times 10^2 \text{g}/\text{cm}^3$$

$$= 3.0 \times 10^1 \text{g}/\text{cm}^3$$

3. Look back and check

Is your answer reasonable?

Yes, the number calculated is the quotient of mass and volume, and the units (g/cm^3) indicate density.

Math Practice

On a separate sheet of paper, solve the following problems. Show your work.

1. The mass of a liquid is 8.03×10^4 kg. The liquid fills up a 100,000 L tank. What is the density of this liquid?

2. You measure the mass of a piece of iron to be 17.37 g on an electronic balance. You then measure the volume to 2.21 cm³. What is the density of the iron?

Chapter 2 Properties of Matter

Summary

2.1 Classifying Matter

☛ **Every sample of a given substance has the same properties because a substance has a fixed, uniform composition.**

☛ **An element has a fixed composition because it contains only one type of atom.**

- Matter that always has exactly the same makeup is classified as a **pure substance.**
- An **element** is a substance that cannot be broken down into simpler substances.
- An **atom** is the smallest particle of an element.

☛ **A compound always contains two or more elements joined in a fixed proportion.**

- A **compound** is a substance that is made from two or more simpler substances. It can be broken down into those simpler substances.
- The properties of a compound differ from those of the substances from which it is made.

☛ **The properties of a mixture can vary because the composition of a mixture is not fixed.**

- In a **heterogeneous mixture,** the parts of the mixture are noticeably different from one another.
- A **homogeneous mixture** appears to contain only one substance.

☛ **Based on the size of its largest particles, a mixture can be classified as a solution, a suspension, or a colloid.**

- A **solution** forms when substances dissolve and form a homogeneous mixture.
- A **suspension** is a heterogeneous mixture that separates into layers over time.
- A **colloid** contains some particles that are intermediate in size between the small particles in a solution and the larger particles in a suspension.

2.2 Physical Properties

☛ **Viscosity, conductivity, malleability, hardness, melting point, boiling point, and density are examples of physical properties.**

- A **physical property** is any characteristic of a material that can be observed or measured without changing the composition of the substances in the material.

- **Viscosity** is the tendency of liquid to keep from flowing.
- A material's ability for allowing heat to flow through it is called **conductivity**.
- **Malleability** is the ability of a solid to be hammered without shattering.
- The temperature at which a substance changes from solid to liquid is its **melting point.**
- The temperature at which a substance boils is its **boiling point.**
- Density is the ratio of the mass of a substance to its volume.

◉ **Physical properties are used to identify a material, choose a material for a specific purpose, or to separate the substances in a mixture.**

◉ **Filtration and distillation are two common separation methods.**

- **Filtration** is a process that separates materials based on the size of their particles.
- **Distillation** is a process that separates substances in a solution based on their boiling points.
- Filtration and distillation are physical changes. A **physical change** occurs when some of the properties of a material change, but the substances in the material remain the same.

2.3 Chemical Properties

◉ **Chemical properties can be observed only when the substances in a sample of matter are changing into different substances.**

- A **chemical property** is any ability to produce a change in the composition of matter.
- **Flammability** is a material's ability to burn in the presence of oxygen.
- **Reactivity** is the property that describes how readily a substance combines chemically with other substances.

◉ **Three common types of evidence for a chemical change are a change in color, the production of a gas, and the formation of a precipitate.**

- A **chemical change** occurs when a substance reacts and forms one or more new substances.
- A **precipitate** forms when a solid separates from a liquid during a chemical change.

◉ **When matter undergoes a chemical change, the composition of the matter changes. When matter undergoes a physical change, the composition of the matter remains the same.**

Chapter 2   Properties of Matter

Section 2.1 Classifying Matter
(pages 38–44)

This section explains how materials are classified as pure substances or mixtures. It discusses types of pure substances and mixtures.

Reading Strategy (page 38)

Summarizing As you read, complete the classification of matter in the diagram below. For more information on this Reading Strategy, see the **Reading and Study Skills** in the **Skills and Reference Handbook** at the end of your textbook.

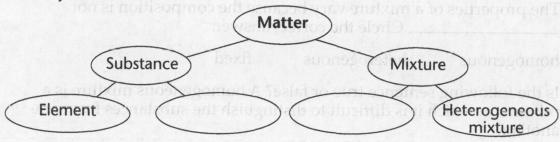

Pure Substances (page 39)

1. Is the following sentence true or false? Every sample of a pure substance has exactly the same composition and the same properties.

_____

2. The two categories of pure substances are _____ and compounds.

Elements (page 39)

3. What is an element? _____

_____

4. Is the following sentence true or false? The smallest particle of an

element is an atom. _____

Match each element to its correct symbol.

Element	Symbol
_____ 5. aluminum	a. C
_____ 6. gold	b. Al
_____ 7. carbon	c. Au

Compounds (page 40)

8. Circle the letter of each sentence that is true about compounds.

   a. A compound always contains at least two elements.

   b. The substances that make up a compound are always joined in a fixed proportion.

   c. A compound has the same properties as the elements from which it is formed.

Mixtures (pages 41–42)

9. The properties of a mixture vary because the composition is not _____. Circle the correct answer.

   homogenous   heterogenous   fixed

10. Is the following sentence true or false? A homogeneous mixture is a mixture in which it is difficult to distinguish the substances from one another.

   _____

Solutions, Suspensions, and Colloids (pages 42–44)

11. Circle the letter of the term that identifies the homogeneous mixture that forms when sugar is dissolved in a glass of hot water.

   a. solution   b. suspension   c. colloid

12. Use the terms in the box to complete the table about solutions, suspensions, and colloids.

Homogenous	Suspension	Yes
Small	Colloid	Heterogenous

Solutions, Suspensions, and Colloids			
Type of Mixture	Relative Size of Largest Particles	Homogeneous or Heterogeneous?	Do Particles Scatter Light?
Solution			No
	Intermediate	Homogeneous	
	Large		Yes

13. Circle the letter before each example of a colloid.

   a. windshield wiper fluid

   b. fog

   c. homogenized milk

Section 2.2 Physical Properties
(pages 45–51)

This section discusses physical properties and physical changes. It also explains how physical properties can be used to identify materials, select materials, and separate mixtures.

Reading Strategy (page 45)

Building Vocabulary As you read, write a definition for each term in the table below. For more information on this Reading Strategy, see the **Reading and Study Skills** in the **Skills and Reference Handbook** at the end of your textbook.

Defining Physical Properties	
Physical Property	**Definition**
Viscosity	The tendency of a liquid to resist flowing
Malleability	
Melting Point	

Examples of Physical Properties (pages 45–47)

1. A physical property is any characteristic of a material that can be observed or measured without changing the _____ of the substances in the material. Circle the correct answer.

   proportion   composition   definition

2. Is the following sentence true or false? A liquid with a high viscosity flows more slowly than a liquid with a low viscosity at the same temperature.

   _____

3. Is the following sentence true or false? Discovering which of two materials can scratch the other is a way to compare the hardness of the materials.

   _____

Match each term to its definition.

Term	Definition
_____ 4. conductivity	a. The ability of a solid to be hammered without shattering
_____ 5. malleability	
_____ 6. melting point	b. The temperature at which a substance changes from a liquid to a gas
_____ 7. boiling point	c. The ability to allow heat to flow
_____ 8. density	d. The ratio of the mass of a substance to its volume
	e. The temperature at which a substance changes from a solid to a liquid

Chapter 2   Properties of Matter

Using Physical Properties (page 48)

9. The box below contains three steps that can be used to identify a material. Put them in the correct order.

> Test a sample of the unknown.
> Compare the results with data for known materials.
> Decide which properties to test.

a. _____

b. _____

c. _____

10. Is the following sentence true or false? Usually, people consider only

one property when choosing a material. _____

Using Properties to Separate Mixtures (page 50)

11. Circle the letter for each process that is commonly used to separate mixtures.

a. filtration

b. distillation

c. precipitation

12. Distillation converts seawater into _____. Circle the correct answer.

small particles   fresh water   pure salt

Recognizing Physical Changes (page 51)

13. Is the following sentence true or false? In a physical change, some of the substances in a material change, but the properties of the material stay

the same. _____

14. Circle the letter for each process that is a reversible physical change.

a. wrinkling a shirt

b. freezing water

c. cutting hair

Chapter 2   Properties of Matter

Section 2.3 Chemical Properties
(pages 54–58)

This section discusses chemical properties and describes clues that may show that a chemical change has taken place.

Reading Strategy (page 54)

Relating Text and Visuals As you read, complete the table by finding examples of the clues for recognizing chemical changes in Figures 19 and 20. For more information on this Reading Strategy, see the **Reading and Study Skills** in the **Skills and Reference Handbook** at the end of your textbook.

Recognizing Chemical Changes	
Clue	Example
Change in color	Copper roof changing color from red to green when exposed to moist air
Production of gas	
Formation of precipitate	

Observing Chemical Properties (pages 54–55)

1. Circle the letters of the compounds formed when a candle burns.

   a. paraffin

   b. water

   c. carbon

2. What is a chemical property? _____

   _____

3. Is the following sentence true or false? Flammability is a material's

   ability to burn in the presence of carbon dioxide. _____

4. The property that describes how readily a substance combines chemically with other substances is _____. Circle the correct answer.

   reactivity   malleability   conductivity

5. Circle the letter of each property that is a chemical property.

   a. hardness

   b. density

   c. flammability

Chapter 2   Properties of Matter

Recognizing Chemical Changes (pages 56–57)

6. A _____ change occurs when a substance reacts and forms one or more new substances. Circle the correct answer.

   distillation   physical   chemical

7. Circle the letters of examples of evidence for a chemical change.

   a. a change in color

   b. a filter trapping particles

   c. the production of a gas

Match each example to evidence of a chemical change.

Example	Chemical Change
_____ 8. Lemon juice is added to milk.	a. the production of a gas
_____ 9. A silver bracelet darkens when exposed to air.	b. the formation of a precipitate
_____ 10. Vinegar is mixed with baking soda.	c. a change in color

Is a Change Chemical or Physical? (page 58)

11. Is the following sentence true or false? When iron is heated until it turns red, the color change shows that a chemical change has taken place.

   _____

12. During a chemical change the composition of matter _____, but during a physical change, the composition of matter

   _____.

13. Complete the following table about chemical changes.

Chemical Changes		
Type of Change	Are New Substances Formed?	Example
Chemical	Yes	
Physical		Sugar dissolving in water

Chapter 2   Properties of Matter

WordWise

Use the clues and the words below to help you write the vocabulary terms from the chapter in the blanks. Use the circled letter in each term to find the hidden vocabulary word. Then, write a definition for the hidden word.

boiling point	colloid	flammability
conductivity	precipitate	pure substance
physical change	compound	solution

Clues	Vocabulary Terms
A mixture that results when substances dissolve to form a homogeneous mixture	Ⓞ _ _ _ _ _ _ _
A substance that can be broken down into two or more simpler substances	_ _ _ _ _ Ⓞ _ _
A change in which the composition of matter stays the same	_ _ _ _ _ Ⓞ _ _ _ _ _ _ _
A solid that forms and separates from a liquid mixture	_ Ⓞ _ _ _ _ Ⓞ _ _ _ Ⓞ _
The ability of a material for allowing heat to flow	_ _ Ⓞ _ _ _ _ _ _ _ _
A classification for matter that always has the same composition	_ _ _ _ Ⓞ _ _ _ _ _ _ _
The ability of a material to burn	_ _ _ _ _ _ _ _ Ⓞ _ _ _
A homogeneous mixture containing particles that scatter light	_ Ⓞ _ _ _ _ _
The temperature at which a substance changes from a liquid to gas	_ _ _ _ _ _ Ⓞ _ _ _ _

Hidden Term: _ _ _ _ _ _ _ _ _ _

Definition: _____

_____

_____

Chapter 2   Properties of Matter

Melting and Boiling Points

Math Skill:
Data Tables

You may want to read more about this **Math Skill** in the **Skills and Reference Handbook** at the end of your textbook.

Melting and Boiling Points of Some Substances		
Substance	Melting Point	Boiling Point
Hydrogen	−259.3°C	−252.9°C
Nitrogen	−210.0°C	−195.8°C
Water	0.0°C	100.0°C
Acetic acid (found in vinegar)	16.6°C	117.9°C
Table salt	800.7°C	1465°C

Which of the substances in the table above are solids at a temperature of −40°C?

1. Read and Understand

What information are you given?

Temperature = −40°C

The melting and boiling points of five substances are listed in the table.

2. Plan and Solve

What unknown are you trying to find?

Which of the five substances are solids at −40°C?

What guideline can you use?

Any substance that is a solid at −40°C must have a melting point greater than −40°C.

Check the melting point of each substance in the table to find out whether it satisfies the guideline.

Water, acetic acid, and table salt are solids at −40°C.

3. Look Back and Check

Is your answer reasonable?

Because water, acetic acid, and table salt have melting points equal to or greater than 0°C, they will all be solids at a temperature well below 0°C.

Math Practice

On a separate sheet of paper, solve the following problems.

1. Which substance in the table is a liquid at 105°C? _____

2. Which substance in the table boils at the lowest temperature?

_____

Chapter 3 States of Matter

Summary

3.1 Solids, Liquids, and Gases

☞ **Materials can be classified as solids, liquids, or gases based on whether their shapes and volumes are definite or variable.**

- A **solid** is a material that has a definite shape and a definite volume.
- A **liquid** is a material that has a definite volume but not a definite shape.
- A **gas** is a material that has neither a definite shape nor a definite volume.

☞ **The kinetic theory of matter says that all particles of matter are in constant motion.**

- **Kinetic energy** is the energy an object has due to its motion.

☞ **There are forces of attraction among the particles in all matter.**

☞ **The constant motion of particles in a gas allows a gas to fill a container of any shape or size.**

☞ **A liquid takes the shape of its container because particles in a liquid can flow to new locations. The volume of a liquid is constant because forces of attraction keep the particles close together.**

☞ **Solids have a definite volume and shape because particles in a solid vibrate around fixed locations.**

3.2 The Gas Laws

☞ **Collisions between particles of a gas and the walls of the container cause the pressure in a closed container of gas.**

- **Pressure** is the result of a force distributed over an area. Pressure is measured in pascals.

☞ **Factors that affect the pressure of an enclosed gas are its temperature, its volume, and the number of its particles.**

☞ **Raising the temperature of a gas will increase its pressure if the volume of the gas and the number of particles are constant.**

☞ **Reducing the volume of a gas increases its pressure if the temperature of the gas and the number of particles are constant.**

- **Charles's law** states that the volume of a gas is directly proportional to its temperature in kelvins (K) if the pressure and number of particles of the gas are constant.
- A temperature of 0 K is called **absolute zero.**

- **Boyle's law** states that the volume of a gas is inversely proportional to its pressure if the temperature and the number of particles are constant.

☞ **Increasing the number of particles will increase the pressure of a gas if the temperature and the volume are constant.**

3.3 Phase Changes

☞ **Melting, freezing, vaporization, condensation, sublimation, and deposition are six common phase changes.**

- A **phase change** is the reversible physical change that occurs when a substance changes from one state of matter to another.

☞ **The temperature of a substance does not change during a phase change.**

☞ **Energy is either absorbed or released during a phase change.**

- During an **endothermic** change, the system absorbs energy from its surroundings.
- The amount of energy absorbed during melting is the **heat of fusion.**
- During an **exothermic** change, the system releases energy to its surroundings.
- **Vaporization** is the phase change in which a substance changes from a liquid into a gas. Vaporization is an endothermic process.
- The amount of energy water absorbs to vaporize is called the **heat of vaporization.**
- **Condensation** is the phase change in which a substance changes from a gas or vapor to a liquid. Condensation is an exothermic process.
- **Sublimation** is the phase change in which a substance changes from a solid to a gas or vapor without changing to a liquid first. Sublimation is an endothermic change.
- **Deposition** is the phase change in which a substance changes from a gas or vapor directly into a solid. Deposition is an exothermic change.

☞ **The arrangement of molecules in water becomes less orderly as water melts and more orderly as water freezes.**

☞ **Evaporation takes place at the surface of a liquid and occurs at temperatures below the boiling point.**

- **Evaporation** is the process that changes a substance from a liquid to a gas at temperatures below the substance's boiling point.
- The pressure caused by the collisions of vapor and the walls of a closed container is called **vapor pressure.**

Chapter 3   States of Matter

Section 3.1 Solids, Liquids, and Gases
(pages 68–74)

This section explains how materials are classified as solids, liquids, or gases. It also describes the behavior of these three states of matter.

Reading Strategy (page 68)

Comparing and Contrasting As you read about the states of matter, fill in the blanks in the diagram below with one of these phrases: *definite volume, variable volume,* or *variable shape.* For more information on this Reading Strategy, see the **Reading and Study Skills** in the **Skills and Reference Handbook** at the end of your textbook.

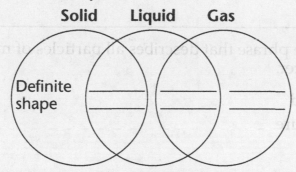

Describing the States of Matter (pages 68–70)

1. What are three common states of matter?

    a. Solids   b. _____   c. _____

2. Is the following sentence true or false? The fact that a copper wire can be bent shows that some solids do not have a definite shape._____

3. Circle the letter of each phrase that describes how particles at the atomic level are arranged within most solids.

    a. randomly arranged

    b. packed close together

    c. arranged in a regular pattern

4. Is the following sentence true or false? A liquid takes the shape of its

    container. _____

5. Is the following sentence true or false? A gas takes the shape and

    volume of its container. _____

6. On the sun, where temperatures are extremely high, matter exists in a state known as _____. Circle the correct answer.

    plasma   liquid   condensation

Chapter 3   States of Matter

7. Complete the table about states of matter.

States of Matter		
State	Shape	Volume
Solid	Definite	
Liquid		
		Not definite

Kinetic Theory (page 71)

8. Define kinetic energy. _____

_____

9. Circle the letter of the phrase that describes all particles of matter in the kinetic theory of matter.

   a. randomly arranged

   b. constant temperature

   c. in constant motion

Explaining the Behavior of Gases (pages 72–73)

10. Is the following sentence true or false? There are forces of attraction

among the particles in all matter. _____

11. Is the following sentence true or false? Because of the constant motion of the particles in a gas, the gas has a definite shape and volume.

_____

Explaining the Behavior of Liquids (page 73)

12. Do forces of attraction have a stronger effect on the behavior of the

particles in a gas or in a liquid? _____

13. Circle the letter of each factor that affects the behavior of liquids.

   a. fixed location of particles

   b. constant motion of particles

   c. forces of attraction among particles

Explaining the Behavior of Solids (page 74)

14. Solids have a definite volume and shape because particles in a solid vibrate in _____ locations. Circle the correct answer.

   orderly   several   fixed

Chapter 3   States of Matter

Section 3.2 The Gas Laws
(pages 75–81)

This section discusses gas pressure and the factors that affect it. It also explains the relationships between the temperature, volume, and pressure of a gas.

Reading Strategy (page 75)

Identifying Cause and Effect As you read, identify the variables that affect gas pressure. Write them in the diagram below. For more information on this Reading Strategy, see the **Reading and Study Skills** in the **Skills and Reference Handbook** at the end of your textbook.

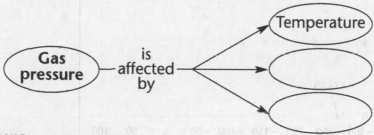

Pressure (pages 75–76)

1. What causes the pressure in a closed container of gas? _____

_____

2. Circle the letter of each unit used to express amounts of pressure.

    a. newton   b. joule   c. pascal

Factors That Affect Gas Pressure (pages 76–77)

3. Name the factors that affect the pressure of an enclosed gas.

    a. Its temperature   b. _____   c. _____

4. Is the following sentence true or false? In a closed container, increasing the temperature of a gas will decrease the force with which particles hit

    the walls of the container. _____

5. Raising the temperature of a gas will _____ its pressure, if the volume of the gas and the number of its particles are kept constant. Circle the correct answer.

    have no effect on   decrease   increase

6. Increasing the number of particles of a gas will _____ its pressure if the temperature and the volume are constant. Circle the correct answer.

    have no effect on   decrease   increase

Chapter 3   States of Matter

Charles's Law (page 78)

7. Jacques Charles recorded the behavior of gases on a graph like the one below. The data show that the volume of a gas increases at the same

    rate as the _____ of the gas.

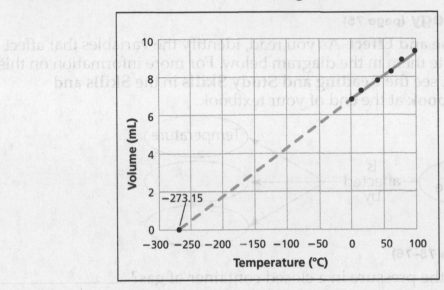

8. A temperature equal to 0 K on the Kelvin temperature scale is known as _____. Circle the correct answer.

    Kelvin zero   relative zero   absolute zero

Boyle's Law (page 79)

9. Boyle's law states that there is an inverse relationship between the pressure and volume of a gas. Circle the letter of the correct expression of this relationship.

    a. $P_1V_1 = P_2V_2$

    b. $\dfrac{P_1}{V_1} = \dfrac{P_2}{V_2}$

    c. $P_1P_2 = V_1V_2$

The Combined Gas Law (pages 80–81)

10. Circle the letters of the factors that are included in the expression of the combined gas law.

    a. temperature

    b. number of particles

    c. volume

Chapter 3   States of Matter

Section 3.3 Phase Changes
(pages 84–91)

This section explains what happens when a substance changes from one state of matter to another and describes six phase changes.

Reading Strategy (page 84)

Summarizing As you read, complete the description of energy flow during phase changes in the diagram below. For more information on this Reading Strategy, see the **Reading and Study Skills** in the **Skills and Reference Handbook** at the end of your textbook.

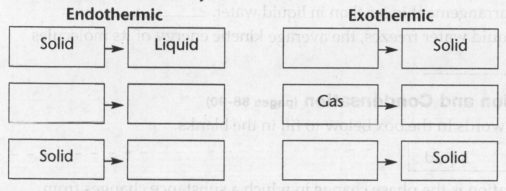

Characteristics of Phase Changes (pages 84–86)

1. A _____ is the reversible physical change that takes place when a substance changes from one state of matter to another.

Match each term with the letter of the phase change that best describes it.

Term	Phase Change
_____ **2.** freezing	a. Solid to gas
_____ **3.** sublimation	b. Liquid to gas
_____ **4.** condensation	c. Gas to solid
_____ **5.** melting	d. Liquid to solid
_____ **6.** deposition	e. Gas to liquid
_____ **7.** vaporization	f. Solid to liquid

8. Does the temperature of a substance increase, decrease, or remain constant during a phase change?

_____

9. A substance absorbs energy from its surroundings during a(n) _____ change. Circle the correct answer.

exothermic   endothermic   hydrothermic

10. The energy absorbed by one gram of ice as it melts is known as the _____ for water. Circle the correct answer.

    heat of fusion   heat of condensation   heat of vaporization

11. As water freezes, it releases heat to its surroundings. Freezing is an

    example of a(n) _____ change.

Melting and Freezing (page 88)

12. Is the following sentence true or false? Water molecules have a more

    orderly arrangement in ice than in liquid water. _____

13. When liquid water freezes, the average kinetic energy of its molecules

    _____.

Vaporization and Condensation (pages 88–90)

14. Use the words in the box below to fill in the blanks.

    | gas   liquid |

    Vaporization is the phase change in which a substance changes from

    a(n) _____ into a(n) _____.

15. The energy absorbed by one gram of water as it changes from its liquid

    phase into water vapor is known as the _____ for water.

16. Is the following sentence true or false? When water vapor collects above
    the liquid in a closed container, the pressure caused by the collisions of
    this vapor and the walls of the container is called

    vapor pressure. _____

17. The phase change in which a substance changes from a gas into a liquid

    is called _____.

18. Is the following sentence true or false? A gas absorbs energy as it

    changes into a liquid. _____

Sublimation and Deposition (page 91)

19. Dry ice can change directly from a solid to a gas without forming

    a liquid first. This process is an example of _____.

20. _____ is the phase change in which a substance changes
    directly from a gas to a solid without changing to a liquid first.

Chapter 3   States of Matter

WordWise

Use the clues and the words below to help you write the vocabulary terms from the chapter in the blanks. Use the circled letter in each term to find the hidden vocabulary word. Then, write a definition for the hidden word.

endothermic	evaporation	exothermic
Charles's law	condensation	deposition
solid	sublimation	

Clues

Vocabulary Terms

The process that changes a substance from a liquid to a gas below the substance's boiling point

_ _ _ _ ◯ _ _ _ _ _ _

A gas law that states that the volume of a gas is directly proportional to its temperature

_ _ _ _ _ ◯ _ _ _ ' _ _ _ _ _

The phase change in which a substance changes directly from a gas to a solid

_ ◯ _ _ _ _ _ _ _ _

The state in which matter has both a definite shape and a definite volume

◯ _ _ _ _

The phase change in which a substance changes from a gas to a liquid

_ _ _ _ _ _ _ ◯ _ _ _ _

The phase change in which a substance changes directly from a solid to a gas

_ ◯ _ _ _ _ _ _ _ _ _

The type of phase change in which a substance releases energy to its surroundings

_ _ _ _ _ _ _ ◯ _ _ _

The type of phase change in which a substance absorbs energy from its surroundings

◯ _ _ _ _ _ _ _ _ _ _

Hidden Term: _ _ _ _ _ _ _ _ _

Definition: _____

_____

Chapter 3   States of Matter

The Gas Laws

A gas in a cylinder has a pressure of 235 kPa at a volume of 5.00 L. The volume drops to 1.25 L. The temperature does not change. Find the new pressure of the gas.

Math Skill:
Calculating With
Significant Figures

You may want to read more about this **Math Skill** in the **Skills and Reference Handbook** at the end of your textbook.

1. **Read and Understand**

   What information are you given?

   $V_1 = 5.00$ L $V_2 = 1.25$ L $P_1 = 235$ kPa

2. **Plan and Solve**

   What unknown are you trying to calculate? P_2

   What expression can you use?

   $P_1 V_1 = P_2 V_2$

   Rearrange the expression to solve for P_2.

   $P_1 V_1 = P_2 V_2$ $P_2 = \dfrac{P_1 V_1}{V_2}$

   Replace each variable with its known value.

   $P_2 = 235 \text{ kPa} \times \dfrac{5.00 \text{ L}}{1.25 \text{ L}} = 940 \text{ kPa}$

3. **Look Back and Check**

   Is your answer reasonable?

   The volume of a gas is inversely proportional to its pressure if the temperature and number of particles are constant. The volume decreased by a factor of 4, from 5.00 L to 1.25 L. The answer, 940 kPa, is 4 times the original pressure, 235 kPa.

Math Practice

On a separate sheet of paper, solve the following problems. The number of particles remains constant for all problems.

1. A gas has a pressure of 340 kPa at a volume of 3.20 L. What happens to the pressure when the volume is increased to 5.44 L? The temperature does not change.

2. A gas has a pressure of 180 kPa at a temperature of 300 K. At what temperature will the gas have a pressure of 276 kPa? The volume does not change.

Chapter 4 Atomic Structure

Summary

4.1 Studying Atoms

- The ancient Greek philosopher Democritus believed that all matter consisted of extremely small particles that could not be divided.
- Aristotle did not think there was a limit to the number of times matter could be divided.

◔ **Dalton proposed the theory that all matter is made up of individual particles called atoms, which cannot be divided.**

- Dalton developed this theory to explain why the elements in a compound always join in the same way.
- In Dalton's model, the atom looks like a solid sphere.

◔ **Thomson's experiments provided the first evidence that atoms are made of even smaller particles.**

- In Thomson's model, electrons are scattered evenly in a positive mass of matter.

◔ **According to Rutherford's model, all of an atom's positive charge is concentrated in its nucleus.**

- The **nucleus** is a dense, positively charged mass located in the center of the atom.

4.2 The Structure of an Atom

◔ **Protons, electrons, and neutrons are subatomic particles.**

- A **proton** is a positively charged subatomic particle that is found in the nucleus of an atom. It has a charge of 1+.
- An **electron** is a negatively charged subatomic particle that is found in the space outside the nucleus. It has a charge of 1–. The mass of about 2000 electrons would equal the mass of a proton.
- A **neutron** is a neutral subatomic particle that is found in the nucleus of an atom. It has a mass almost equal to that of a proton.

◔ **Protons, electrons, and neutrons can be distinguished by mass, charge, and location in an atom.**

◔ **Atoms of different elements have different numbers of protons.**

- The **atomic number** of an element equals the number of protons in an atom of that element.
- The **mass number** of an atom is the sum of the protons and neutrons in the nucleus of that atom.

◒ **Isotopes of an element have the same atomic number but different mass numbers because they have different numbers of neutrons.**

- **Isotopes** are atoms of the same element that have different numbers of neutrons and different mass numbers.
- It is hard to notice any differences in the properties of different isotopes of an element.

4.3 Modern Atomic Theory

◒ **An electron in an atom can move from one energy level to another when the atom gains or loses energy.**

- The possible energies that electrons in an atom can have are called **energy levels**.

◒ **Scientists use the electron cloud model to describe the possible locations of electrons around the nucleus.**

◒ **An electron cloud is a good approximation of how electrons behave in their orbitals.**

- An **electron cloud** is a visual model of the most likely locations for electrons in an atom.
- The electron cloud is denser where the chances of finding an electron are high.
- An **orbital** is a region of space around the nucleus where an electron is likely to be found.

◒ **The most stable electron configuration is the one in which the electrons are in orbitals with the lowest possible energies.**

- A configuration is an arrangement of objects in a given space.
- An **electron configuration** is the arrangement of electrons in the orbitals of an atom.
- When all the electrons in an atom have the lowest possible energies, the atom is said to be in its **ground state**.

Chapter 4   Atomic Structure

Section 4.1 Studying Atoms
(pages 100–105)

This section discusses the development of atomic models.

Reading Strategy (page 100)

Summarizing As you read, complete the table about atomic models. For more information on this Reading Strategy, see the **Reading and Study Skills** in the **Skills and Reference Handbook** at the end of your textbook.

Atomic Models		
Scientist	**Evidence**	**Model**
Dalton		Indivisible, solid spheres
	Deflected beam	Negative charges evenly scattered through positively charged mass of matter (plum pudding model)
	Deflection of alpha particles passing through gold foil	

Ancient Greek Models of Atoms (page 100)

1. Democritus named the smallest particles of matter _____ because they could not be divided.

Dalton's Atomic Theory (page 101)

2. Is the following sentence true or false? John Dalton gathered evidence for the existence of atoms by measuring the masses of elements that

   reacted to form compounds. _____

3. Dalton's theory suggests that all matter is made up of individual

   particles called _____, which cannot be _____.

4. Circle the letters of the sentences that represent main points of Dalton's theory of atoms.

   a. All elements are composed of atoms.

   b. In a particular compound, atoms of different elements always combine the same way.

   c. All atoms have the same mass.

Chapter 4   Atomic Structure

Thomson's Model of the Atom (pages 102–103)

5. Use the words in the box below to fill in the blanks. Objects with like electric charges _____, and objects with opposite electric charges _____.

attract	deflect
reflect	repel

6. Thomson concluded that the particles in the glowing beam had a(n) _____ charge because they were attracted to a positive plate.

7. Circle the letter of the sentences that describe Thomson's model of the atom.

   a. An atom is filled with positive matter.

   b. An atom is mostly space with a small nucleus.

   c. Negative charges are scattered throughout an atom.

Rutherford's Atomic Theory (pages 104–105)

8. An _____ is a fast-moving particle that carries a positive charge.

9. Circle the letters of the sentences that describe what happened when Marsden directed a beam of particles at a piece of gold foil.

   a. More alpha particles were deflected than expected.

   b. None of the alpha particles were deflected.

   c. Some alpha particles bounced back toward the source.

10. Circle the letter of the sentence that states what Rutherford concluded from the gold foil experiment.

   a. An atom's negative charge is concentrated in its nucleus.

   b. An atom's positive charge is concentrated in its nucleus.

   c. An atom's positive charge is spread evenly throughout the atom.

Chapter 4 Atomic Structure

Section 4.2 The Structure of an Atom
(pages 108–112)

This section compares the properties of three subatomic particles. It also discusses atomic numbers, mass numbers, and isotopes.

Reading Strategy (page 108)

Monitoring Your Understanding Before you read, list in the table shown what you know about atoms and what you would like to learn. After you read, list what you have learned. For more information on this Reading Strategy, see the **Reading and Study Skills** in the **Skills and Reference Handbook** at the end of your textbook.

What I Know About Atoms	What I Would Like to Learn	What I Have Learned
Most students will know that atoms are the "building blocks" of matter, and some may know that atoms contain subatomic particles.	Based on the title of the section, students may say that they want to learn more about the structure of atoms.	

Properties of Subatomic Particles (pages 108–109)

1. What are three subatomic particles?

   a. _____ b. _____ c. _____

2. Circle the letter that identifies a subatomic particle with a positive charge.

   a. nucleus

   b. proton

   c. neutron

Comparing Subatomic Particles (pages 109–110)

3. Circle the letters of properties that vary among subatomic particles.

   a. color

   b. location in the atom

   c. charge

4. Circle the letter of the expression that accurately compares the masses of neutrons and protons.

   a. mass of 1 neutron = mass of 1 proton

   b. mass of 2000 neutrons = mass of 1 proton

   c. mass of 1 electron = mass of 1 proton

Atomic Number and Mass Number (page 110)

5. Is the following sentence true or false? Two atoms of the same element can have different numbers of protons. _____

6. The _____ number of an element equals the number of protons in an atom of that element.

7. Is the following sentence true or false? Two different elements can have the same atomic number. _____

8. The _____ number of an atom is the sum of the protons and neutrons in the nucleus of that atom.

9. Complete the equation in the table below.

Number of neutrons = Mass number − _____

Isotopes (page 112)

Use the words in the box below to fill in the blanks in questions 10–12.

electrons	isotopes
neutrons	protons

10. Every atom of a given element has the same number of _____ and _____.

11. Every atom of a given element does not have the same number of _____.

12. _____ are atoms of the same element that have different numbers of neutrons and different mass numbers.

13. All oxygen atoms have 8 protons. Circle the letter of the number of neutrons in an atom of oxygen-18.

a. 8

b. 10

c. 18

14. Is the following sentence true or false? Isotopes of oxygen have different chemical properties. _____

Chapter 4   Atomic Structure

Section 4.3 Modern Atomic Theory
(pages 113–118)

This section focuses on the arrangement and behavior of electrons in atoms.

Reading Strategy (page 113)

Sequencing After you read, complete the description in the flow chart below. Write how the gain or loss of energy affects electrons in atoms. For more information on this Reading Strategy, see the **Reading and Study Skills** in the **Skills and Reference Handbook** at the end of your textbook.

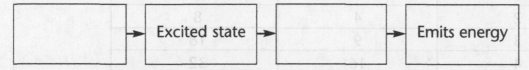

Bohr's Model of the Atom (pages 113–116)

1. Circle the letter of the sentence that tells how Bohr's model of the atom differed from Rutherford's model.

    a. Bohr's model focused on the nucleus.

    b. Bohr's model focused on the protons.

    c. Bohr's model focused on the electrons.

2. What can happen to an electron in an atom when the atom gains or loses

    energy? _____

    _____

3. Is the following sentence true or false? When electrons release energy,

    some of the energy may be released as visible light. _____

Electron Cloud Model (page 116)

4. Is the following sentence true or false? Bohr's model was correct in

    assigning energy levels to electrons. _____

5. When trying to predict the locations and motions of electrons in atoms, scientists must work with _____. Circle the correct answer.

    precision   probability   accuracy

6. An _____ is a visual model of the most likely locations for the electrons in an atom.

Chapter 4   Atomic Structure

Atomic Orbitals (page 117)

7. Is the following sentence true or false? An orbital is a region of space around the nucleus where an electron is likely to be found.

_____

Use this table to answer questions 8 and 9.

Energy Level	Number of Orbitals	Maximum Number of Electrons
1	1	2
2	4	8
3	9	18
4	16	32

8. Higher energy levels have _____ orbitals than lower energy levels do.

9. The maximum number of electrons in an energy level is _____ times the number of orbitals.

Electron Configurations (page 118)

10. Circle the letter of the number of energy levels needed for a lithium atom's three electrons when the atom is in its ground state.

   a. one

   b. two

   c. three

11. Is the following sentence true or false? An excited state is less stable than a ground state. _____

12. Circle the letters of each sentence that is true when all of the electrons in an atom are in orbitals with the lowest possible energies.

   a. The electrons are in the most stable configuration.

   b. The electrons are in an unstable configuration.

   c. The atom is in its ground state.

Chapter 4   Atomic Structure

WordWise

Use the clues and the words below to help you write the vocabulary terms from Chapter 4 in the blanks. Then find and circle the terms in the puzzle. The terms may occur vertically, horizontally, or diagonally.

atomic number	energy levels	isotopes
neutron	nucleus	orbital
proton		

```
m  a  l  s  n  a  m  b  u  r  u  n
l  o  r  b  i  t  a  l  x  a  p  i
e  f  n  a  t  p  t  s  p  b  k  s
n  a  c  t  s  r  d  c  r  h  l  o
e  l  d  o  g  o  f  l  s  g  a  t
r  t  s  m  r  t  g  r  n  b  t  o
g  z  b  i  o  o  p  l  q  d  c  p
y  n  p  c  l  n  n  m  a  s  s  e
l  u  e  n  n  n  u  c  l  e  u  s
e  c  l  u  i  r  i  o  s  k  m  r
v  l  x  m  t  v  a  b  t  o  p  k
e  e  m  b  a  r  c  s  r  n  r  e
l  a  q  e  b  z  o  e  t  a  b  d
s  s  i  r  e  h  j  n  m  r  n  k
```

Clues   **Hidden Words**

Dense, positively charged mass in the
center of an atom   _____

Positively charged subatomic particle found
in the nucleus   _____

Neutral subatomic particle found in the nucleus   _____

Number of protons in an atom of an element   _____

Atoms of the same element having different numbers
of neutrons   _____

Possible energies that electrons in an atom can have   _____

Region of space where an electron is likely to be found   _____

Chapter 4 Atomic Structure

Atomic Orbitals

Math Skill:
Ratios and Proportions

You may want to read more about this **Math Skill** in the **Skills and Reference Handbook** at the end of your textbook.

Refer to the table on page 117 of your textbook. Find the ratio of the maximum number of electrons to the number of orbitals for each of 4 energy levels.

1. Read and Understand

What information are you given?

The number of orbitals and the maximum number of electrons per energy level

2. Plan and Solve

What unknown are you trying to calculate?

The ratio of the maximum number of electrons to the number of orbitals in energy levels 1 through 4

What mathematical expression can you use to calculate the unknown?

$$\frac{\text{maximum number of electrons}}{\text{number of orbitals}}$$

Level 1: $\frac{2}{1} = \frac{2}{1}$ Level 3: $\frac{18}{9} = \frac{2}{1}$

Level 2: $\frac{4}{2} = \frac{2}{1}$ Level 4: $\frac{32}{16} = \frac{2}{1}$

3. Look Back and Check

Is your answer reasonable?

The ratio is the same for all four energy levels. Also, each orbital can contain only two electrons.

Math Practice

On a separate sheet of paper, solve the following problems.

1. Calculate the maximum number of electrons for energy level 5. Energy level 5 contains 25 orbitals.

2. A sodium atom has 11 electrons. How many orbitals in a sodium atom contain electrons?

Chapter 5 The Periodic Table

Summary

5.1 Organizing the Elements

☞ **Mendeleev arranged the elements into rows in order of increasing mass so that elements with similar properties were in the same column.**

- A **periodic table** is an arrangement of elements in columns, based on a set of properties that repeat from row to row.
- Within a column, the masses of elements increase from top to bottom.
- You can use the gaps in a periodic table to predict what undiscovered elements would be like.

☞ **The close match between Mendeleev's predictions and the actual properties of new elements showed how useful his periodic table could be.**

5.2 The Modern Periodic Table

☞ **In the modern periodic table, elements are arranged by increasing atomic number (number of protons).**

☞ **Properties of elements repeat in a predictable way when atomic numbers are used to arrange elements into groups.**

- Each row in the periodic table is called a **period.**
- Each column in the periodic table is called a **group.** The elements within a group have similar properties.
- The pattern of repeating properties is the **periodic law.**
- There are four pieces of information for each element on the periodic table: name, symbol, atomic number, and atomic mass.

☞ **Atomic mass is a value that depends on the distribution of an element's isotopes in nature and the masses of those isotopes.**

- An **atomic mass unit** (amu) is defined as one twelfth the mass of a carbon-12 atom.

☞ **Elements are classified as metals, nonmetals, and metalloids.**

- **Metals** are elements that are good conductors of electric current and heat. Almost all metals are solids at room temperature. Most are malleable and many are ductile.
- **Transition metals** are elements that form a bridge between the elements on the left and right sides of the periodic table. Many transition metals can form compounds with distinctive colors.

- **Nonmetals** are elements that are poor conductors of heat and electric current. They have low boiling points, so many are gases at room temperature.
- **Metalloids** are elements with properties that fall between those of metals and nonmetals.

☞ **Across a period from left to right, the elements become less metallic and more nonmetallic in their properties.**

5.3 Representative Groups

☞ **Elements in a group have similar properties because they have the same number of valence electrons.**

- A **valence electron** is an electron that is in the highest occupied energy level of an atom.
- The number of valence electrons increases from left to right in the periodic table.

☞ **The reactivity of alkali metals increases from the top of Group 1A to the bottom.**

- **Alkali metals** are elements in Group 1A.
- The alkali metals include lithium, sodium, potassium, rubidium, cesium, and francium.
- Alkali metals are extremely reactive. They have one valence electron.

☞ **Differences in reactivity among the alkaline earth metals are shown by the ways they react with water.**

- **Alkaline earth metals** are elements in Group 2A.
- All alkaline earth metals have two valence electrons.
- The alkaline earth metals include beryllium, magnesium, calcium, strontium, barium, and radium.

☞ **Aluminum is the most abundant metal in Earth's crust.**

- Aluminum often combines with oxygen. It is found in a mineral called bauxite.
- Aluminum, boron, gallium, indium, and thallium are in the boron family, Group 3A.

☞ **Except for water, most of the compounds in your body contain carbon.**

- Carbon is in Group 4A. It is a nonmetal.
- Other members of the group are metalloids (silicon and germanium) and metals (tin and lead). All have four valence electrons.

◉ Besides nitrogen, fertilizers often contain phosphorus.

- Nitrogen and phosphorus are both in Group 5A. They are nonmetals.
- Other members of the group include two metalloids (arsenic and antimony) and one metal (bismuth). All have five valence electrons.

◉ Oxygen is the most abundant element in Earth's crust.

- Oxygen is in Group 6A. Other nonmetals in the group are sulfur and selenium.
- Other members of the group are metalloids (tellurium and polonium). All have six valence electrons.

◉ Despite their physical differences, the halogens have similar chemical properties.

- **Halogens** are elements in Group 7A.
- The halogens include four nonmetals (fluorine, chlorine, bromine, and iodine) and one metalloid (astatine).
- Each halogen has seven valence electrons.

◉ The noble gases are colorless and odorless and extremely unreactive.

- **Noble gases** are elements in Group 8A. They include helium, neon, argon, krypton, xenon, and radon.
- Helium has two valence electrons. All the other noble gases have eight valence electrons.

Chapter 5   The Periodic Table

Section 5.1 Organizing the Elements
(pages 126–129)

This section explains how Mendeleev organized elements into a periodic table. It also discusses the predictions he made about undiscovered elements and how the discovery of those elements supported his version of the table.

Reading Strategy (page 126)

Identifying Main Ideas As you read, complete the table by identifying the main idea for each topic. For more information on this reading strategy, see the **Reading and Study Skills** in the **Skills and Reference Handbook** at the end of your textbook.

Topic	Main Idea
Mendeleev's proposal	
Mendeleev's prediction	The properties of existing elements will help predict properties of undiscovered elements.
Evidence supporting Mendeleev's table	

The Search for Order (page 126)

1. Is the following sentence true or false? The first elements to be identified were mainly gases. _____

2. As the number of known elements grew, so did the need to organize them into groups based on their _____. Circle the correct answer.

   phase state   color   properties

3. Circle the letter of each category that the French chemist Antoine Lavoisier used to classify elements.

   a. gases
   b. metals
   c. liquids

Mendeleev's Periodic Table (pages 127–129)

4. Circle the letter of each type of information Mendeleev knew about each element.

   a. name
   b. number of protons
   c. relative mass

5. Mendeleev arranged the elements into rows in order of _____ so that elements with similar properties were in the same column. Circle the correct answer.

increasing mass   atomic number   decreasing mass

6. Is the following sentence true or false? A periodic table is an arrangement of elements in columns, based on a set of properties that repeat from row to row. _____

7. Mendeleev published the table below in 1872. Mendeleev left some locations in his periodic table blank for _____ elements.

Group I	Group II	Group III	Group IV	Group V	Group VI	Group VII	Group VIII
H = 1							
Li = 7	Be = 9.4	B = 11	C = 12	N = 14	O = 16	F = 19	
Na = 23	Mg = 24	Al = 27.3	Si = 28	P = 31	S = 32	Cl = 35.5	Fe = 56, Co = 59,
K = 39	Ca = 40	— = 44	Ti = 48	V = 51	Cr = 52	Mn = 55	Ni = 59, Cu = 63.
(Cu = 63)	Zn = 65	— = 68	— = 72	As = 75	Se = 78	Br = 80	Ru = 104, Rh = 104,
Rb = 85	Sr = 87	Yt = 88	Zr = 90	Nb = 94	Mo = 96	— = 100	Pd = 106, Ag = 108.
(Ag = 108)	Cd = 112	In = 113	Sn = 118	Sb = 122	Te = 125	I = 127	
Cs = 133	Ba = 137	Di = 138	Ce = 140	—	—	—	— — — —
(—)	—	—	—	—	—	—	Os = 195, Ir = 197,
—	—	Er = 178	La = 180	Ta = 182	W = 184	—	Pt = 198, Au = 199.
(Au = 199)	Hg = 200	Tl = 204	Pb = 207	Bi = 208			
			Th = 231	—	U = 240		

8. Circle the letters of two elements that have similar properties.

    a. zinc (Zn)

    b. chlorine (Cl)

    c. bromine (Br)

9. Is the following sentence true or false? Mendeleev was the first scientist to arrange elements in a periodic table. _____

10. Mendeleev used the properties of _____ located near the spaces in his table to predict properties for undiscovered elements.

11. Circle the letter of each element that was discovered after Mendeleev published his periodic table and that supported Mendeleev's predictions.

    a. gallium

    b. scandium

    c. aluminum

Chapter 5   The Periodic Table

Section 5.2 The Modern Periodic Table
(pages 130–138)

This section explains the organization of the modern periodic table and discusses the general properties of metals, nonmetals, and metalloids.

Reading Strategy (page 130)

Previewing Before you read, complete the table by writing two questions about the periodic table on pages 132–133. As you read, write answers to your questions. For more information on this reading strategy, see the **Reading and Study Skills** in the **Skills and Reference Handbook** at the end of your textbook.

Questions About the Periodic Table	
Question	**Answer**

The Periodic Law (pages 131–133)

1. Is the following sentence true or false? In the modern periodic table,
   elements are arranged by increasing number of protons. _____

2. Properties of elements repeat in a predictable way when atomic numbers are used to arrange elements into groups. This pattern of repeating
   properties is called the _____ law.

Atomic Mass (page 134)

3. Label the four types of information supplied for chlorine in the diagram.

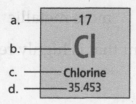

a. ___ — 17
b. ___ — Cl
c. ___ — Chlorine
d. ___ — 35.453

   a. Atomic number   b. _____

   c. _____ d. _____

Chapter 5   The Periodic Table

4. Define atomic mass. _____

_____

5. Circle the letter of each sentence that is true about a carbon-12 atom.

   a. It has 6 protons and 6 neutrons.
   b. Scientists assigned a mass of 6 atomic mass units to the carbon-12 atom.
   c. It is used as a standard for comparing the masses of atoms.

6. Is the following sentence true or false? Most elements exist as a mixture

   of two or more isotopes. _____

Classes of Elements (pages 135–136)

7. Name the three categories into which elements are classified based on their general properties.

   a. Metals
   b. _____
   c. _____

8. Is the following sentence true or false? All metals react with oxygen in

   the same way. _____

9. Circle the letter of each sentence that is true about nonmetals.

   a. Nonmetals are poor conductors of heat and electric current.
   b. Many nonmetals are gases at room temperature.
   c. Nonmetals that are solids tend to be malleable.

Variation Across a Period (page 138)

10. Across a period from left to right, the elements become _____.
    Circle the correct answer.

    less metallic   less nonmetallic   more metallic

11. Circle the letter of each Period 3 element that is highly reactive.

    a. sodium
    b. silicon
    c. chlorine

Chapter 5   The Periodic Table

Section 5.3 Representative Groups
(pages 139–145)

This section discusses how the number of valence electrons affects the properties of elements. It also describes properties of elements in Groups 1A through 8A.

Reading Strategy (page 139)

Monitoring Your Understanding As you read, record an important fact about each element listed in the table. For more information on this reading strategy, see the **Reading and Study Skills** in the **Skills and Reference Handbook** at the end of your textbook.

Element	Important Fact
Magnesium	Magnesium plays a key role in the process that uses sunlight to produce sugar in plants.
Aluminum	
Chlorine	

Valence Electrons (page 139)

1. An electron that is in the highest occupied energy level of an atom is a(n)

   _____ electron.

2. Elements within a group have the _____ number of valence electrons.

The Alkali Metals (page 140)

3. The reactivity of alkali metals _____ from the top of Group 1A to the bottom. Circle the correct answer.

   decreases   increases   stays the same

The Alkaline Earth Metals (page 141)

Find and match two properties to each element listed.

Alkaline Earth Metal   **Property**

____ 4. magnesium   a. Helps build strong teeth and bones

____ 5. calcium   b. Helps plants produce sugar

                              c. Is used to make lightweight bicycle frames

                              d. Is the main ingredient in limestone

Chapter 5   The Periodic Table

The Boron Family (page 142)

6. List the four metals in Group 3A.

   a. Aluminum   b. _____

   c. _____   d. _____

The Carbon Family (page 142)

7. List the two metalloids in Group 4A.

   a. Silicon   b. _____

8. Except for water, most of the compounds in your body contain

   _____ .

The Nitrogen Family (page 143)

9. List the nonmetals in Group 5A.

   a. Nitrogen   b. _____

10. Name two elements in the nitrogen family that are contained
    in fertilizer.

    a. Nitrogen   b. _____

The Oxygen Family (page 143)

11. List the nonmetals in Group 6A.

    a. Oxygen   b. _____   c. _____

12. Name the most abundant element in Earth's crust. _____

The Halogens (page 144)

13. List the four nonmetals in Group 7A.

    a. Fluorine   b. _____

    c. _____   d. _____

14. Halogens have similar _____ properties but different

    _____ properties. Use the words in the box to fill in the blanks.

chemical	electric
physical	reactive

The Noble Gases (page 145)

15. Name three characteristics of noble gases.

    a. Colorless   b. _____   c. _____

Chapter 5   The Periodic Table

WordWise

Match each definition with the correct term by writing the definition's number in the grid. When you have filled in all the boxes, add up the numbers in each column, row, and the two diagonals. Hint: The sum should be 15 in each case.

Definitions

1. An arrangement of elements in columns based on a set of properties that repeat from row to row

2. A pattern of repeating properties that occurs when atomic numbers are used to arrange elements into groups

3. One twelfth the mass of a carbon-12 atom

4. Elements that are good conductors of heat and electric current

5. Elements that form a bridge between the elements on the left and right sides of the periodic table

6. Elements that are poor conductors of heat and electric current

7. Elements with properties that fall between those of metals and nonmetals

8. An electron that is in the highest occupied energy level of an atom

9. Colorless, odorless, and extremely unreactive gases

			diagonal = _____
nonmetals _____	periodic table _____	valence electron _____	= _____
metalloids _____	transition metals _____	atomic mass unit _____	= _____
periodic law _____	noble gas _____	metals _____	= _____
= _____	= _____	= _____	diagonal = _____

Chapter 5   The Periodic Table

Calculating Average Atomic Mass

Carbon has two stable isotopes. Carbon-12 has an assigned atomic mass of 12.0000. Its percentage in nature is 98.93%. The atomic mass of carbon-13 is 13.0034. Its percentage in nature is 1.070%. What is the average atomic mass for carbon?

Math Skill:
Percents and Decimals

You may want to read more about this **Math Skill** in the **Skills and Reference Handbook** at the end of your textbook.

1. Read and Understand

What information are you given?

carbon-12: atomic mass = 12.0000, % in nature = 98.93
carbon-13: atomic mass = 13.0034, % in nature = 1.070

2. Plan and Solve

What unknown are you trying to calculate?

Average atomic mass for carbon = ?

What equation can you use?

(atomic mass C-12) (% C-12) + (atomic mass C-13) (% C-13)
= average atomic mass of C

Convert the percentages to decimals and multiply the atomic mass of each isotope by the decimal representing its percentage in nature.

(12.0000) (0.9893) = 11.8716 rounded to 11.87
(13.0034) (0.01070) = 0.1391364 rounded to 0.1391

Add the products of the two multiplications to find the average atomic mass for carbon.

11.87 + 0.1391 = 12.0091 rounded to 12.01

3. Look Back and Check

Is your answer reasonable?

Because almost all the carbon atoms in nature are carbon-12 atoms, the average atomic mass of carbon (12.01) is close to the atomic mass of carbon-12 (12.0000).

Math Practice

On a separate sheet of paper, solve the following problem.

1. Nitrogen has two stable isotopes, nitrogen-14 and nitrogen-15. Nitrogen-14 has an atomic mass of 14.0031. Its percentage in nature is 99.63%. What is the percentage in nature of nitrogen-15?

Chapter 6 Chemical Bonds

Summary

6.1 Ionic Bonding

⊜ **When the highest occupied energy level of an atom is filled with electrons, the atom is stable and not likely to react.**

- The chemical properties of an element depend on the number of valence electrons.
- An **electron dot diagram** is a model of an atom in which each dot represents a valence electron.

⊜ **Some elements achieve stable electron configurations through the transfer of electrons between atoms.**

- When an atom gains or loses an electron, the number of protons is no longer equal to the number of electrons. The atom is not neutral.
- An atom that has a net positive or negative electric charge is called an **ion.**
- An ion with a negative charge is an **anion.**
- An ion with a positive charge is a **cation.**
- A **chemical bond** is the force that holds atoms or ions together as a unit.
- An **ionic bond** is the force that holds cations and anions together.
- The amount of energy used to remove an electron is called ionization energy. The lower the ionization energy, the easier it is to remove an electron from an atom.
- A **chemical formula** is a notation that shows what elements a compound contains and the ratio of the atoms of ions of these elements in the compound.

⊜ **The properties of an ionic compound can be explained by the strong attractions among ions within a crystal lattice.**

- Solids whose particles are arranged in a lattice structure are called **crystals.**
- The shape of an ionic crystal depends on the arrangement of ions in its rigid framework, or lattice. Crystals are classified into groups based on their shape.

6.2 Covalent Bonding

☞ **The attractions between the shared electrons and the protons in each nucleus hold the atoms together in a covalent bond.**

- A **covalent bond** is a chemical bond in which two atoms share a pair of valence electrons.
- When two atoms share one pair of electrons, the bond is called a single bond. When two atoms share two pairs of electrons, the bond is called a double bond.
- A **molecule** is a neutral group of atoms that are joined together by one or more covalent bonds.

☞ **When atoms form a polar covalent bond, the atom with the greater attraction for electrons has a partial negative charge. The other atom has a partial positive charge.**

- A covalent bond in which electrons are not shared equally is called a **polar covalent bond.**
- One atom in a polar covalent bond has a greater attraction for electrons than the other atom. The atom with greater attraction has a partial negative charge. The other atom has a partial positive charge.

☞ **The type of atoms in a molecule and its shape are factors that determine whether a molecule is polar or nonpolar.**

☞ **Attractions between polar molecules are stronger than attractions between nonpolar molecules.**

6.3 Naming Compounds and Writing Formulas

☞ **The name of an ionic compound must distinguish the compound from other ionic compounds containing the same elements. The formula of an ionic compound describes the ratio of the ions in the compound.**

- A compound made from only two elements is a binary compound.
- The name of a binary compound is the name of the cation followed by the name of the anion. Salt is a binary compound made of sodium and chlorine. Its name is sodium chloride.
- The name of the cation is simply the name of the metal. The name of the anion uses part of the name of the nonmetal with the suffix *-ide.*
- A covalently bonded group of atoms that has a positive or negative charge and acts as a unit is a **polyatomic ion.**
- If you know the name of an ionic compound, you can write its formula. Write the symbol of the cation first, and follow that with the symbol of the anion. Use subscripts to show the ratio of the ions in the compound.

The name and formula of a molecular compound describe the type and number of atoms in a molecule of the compound.

- The general rule in naming molecular compounds is that the most metallic element appears first. The name of the second element is changed to end in the suffix *-ide*, as in carbon dioxide. The prefix *di-* shows that there are two carbon atoms in the molecule.
- When writing molecular formulas, write the symbols for the elements in the order the elements appear in the name.
- The prefixes in the compound name indicate the number of atoms of each element in the molecule. The prefixes appear as subscripts in the formula.

6.4 The Structure of Metals

- In a metal, valence electrons are free to move among the atoms. The metal atoms act as though they are cations surrounded by a pool of shared electrons.

The cations in a metal form a lattice that is held in place by strong metallic bonds between the cations and the surrounding valence electrons.

- A **metallic bond** is the attraction between a metal cation and shared electrons that surround it.
- The more valence electrons an atom can contribute to the shared pool of electrons, the stronger the metallic bonds will be.

The mobility of electrons within a metal lattice explains some of the properties of metals.

Scientists can design alloys with specific properties by varying the types and amounts of elements in an alloy.

- An **alloy** is a mixture of two or more elements, at least one of which is a metal. Alloys have the same kinds of properties as metals.
- Bronze was an early alloy made of copper and tin. It is harder and stronger than each element alone.
- Steel is an alloy of iron and small quantities of carbon. The carbon atoms form bonds that help make a stronger lattice than iron bonds alone.

Chapter 6   Chemical Bonds

Section 6.1 Ionic Bonding
(pages 158–164)

This section describes the formation of ionic bonds and the properties of ionic compounds.

Reading Strategy (page 158)

Sequencing As you read, complete the concept map to show what happens to atoms during ionic bonding. For more information on this Reading Strategy, see the **Reading and Study Skills** in the **Skills and Reference Handbook** at the end of your textbook.

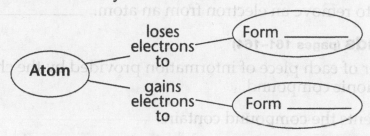

Stable Electron Configurations (page 158)

1. Circle the letter that describes the type of electron configuration that makes an atom stable and not likely to react.

   a. The lowest energy level of an atom is filled.

   b. The highest energy level of an atom is filled.

   c. All the energy levels of an atom are filled.

2. Define an electron dot diagram. _____

   _____

Ionic Bonds (pages 159–161)

3. Some elements achieve stable electron configurations through the

   transfer of _____ between atoms.

4. Circle the letter that states the result of a sodium atom transferring an electron to a chlorine atom.

   a. Each atom ends up with a more stable electron arrangement.

   b. The sodium atom becomes more stable, but the chlorine atom becomes less stable.

   c. The chlorine atom becomes more stable, but the sodium atom becomes less stable.

5. Is the following sentence true or false? An ion is an atom that has a net

   positive or negative electric charge. _____

6. An ion with a negative charge is called a(n) _____.

7. An ionic bond forms when _____ are transferred from one
   atom to another. Circle the correct answer.

   electrons   protons   ions

8. Is the following sentence true or false? The lower the ionization energy,

   the easier it is to remove an electron from an atom. _____

Ionic Compounds (pages 161–164)

9. Circle the letter of each piece of information provided by the chemical
   formula of an ionic compound.

   a. which elements the compound contains

   b. the charge on each ion in the compound

   c. the ratio of ions in the compound

10. Circle the letter of the correct answer. The formula for magnesium
    chloride is $MgCl_2$. The charge on the magnesium ion is 2+. What is the
    charge on each chloride ion?

    a. 2−

    b. 1−

    c. 1+

11. Circle two factors that determine the arrangement of ions in an ionic
    crystal.

    a. The ratio of ions

    b. The size of the ion charge

    c. The relative sizes of the ions

12. Is the following sentence true or false? The attractions among ions

    within a crystal lattice are weak. _____

Chapter 6   Chemical Bonds

Section 6.2 Covalent Bonding
(pages 165–169)

This section discusses the formation of covalent bonds and the factors that determine whether a molecule is polar or nonpolar. It also discusses attractions between molecules.

Reading Strategy (page 165)

Relating Text and Visuals As you read the section, look closely at Figure 9. Complete the table by describing each type of model shown. For more information on this Reading Strategy, see the **Reading and Study Skills** in the **Skills and Reference Handbook** at the end of your textbook.

Molecular Models	
Model	**Description**
Electron dot diagram	Dots represent valence electrons
Structural formula	
Space-filling	
Electron cloud	

Covalent Bonds (pages 165–167)

1. Define a covalent bond. _____

_____

2. A molecule is a _____ group of atoms that are joined together by one or more covalent bonds. Circle the correct answer.

   negative   neutral   positive

3. Is the following sentence true or false? In a covalent bond, the atoms are held together by the attractions between the shared electrons and the

   protons in each nucleus. _____

4. Circle the correct answer. Nitrogen has five valence electrons. How many pairs of electrons must two nitrogen atoms share in order for each atom to have eight valence electrons?

   a. one

   b. two

   c. three

Chapter 6   Chemical Bonds

Unequal Sharing of Electrons (pages 167–168)

5. Use the words in the box to fill in the blanks.

> chlorine   hydrogen   oxygen

In a hydrogen chloride molecule, the shared electrons spend more time

near the _____ atom than near the _____ atom.

6. Define a polar covalent bond. _____

_____

_____

7. When atoms form a polar covalent bond, the atom with the greater attraction for electrons has a partial _____ charge. Circle the correct answer.

neutral   positive   negative

8. Is the following sentence true or false? In a molecule of a compound,

electrons are always shared equally by both atoms. _____

9. Circle the letter of each factor that determines whether a molecule is polar or nonpolar.

a. the number of atoms in the molecule

b. the type of atoms in the molecule

c. the shape of the molecule

10. Compare the shapes of carbon dioxide and water molecules. Circle the letter of the polar molecule.

a. carbon dioxide   b. water

CO_2 H_2O

Attraction Between Molecules (page 169)

11. Water has a higher boiling point than carbon dioxide because

attractions between polar molecules are _____than attractions between nonpolar molecules.

12. Is the following sentence true or false? Attractions among nonpolar molecules explain why nitrogen can be stored as a liquid at low

temperatures and high pressures. _____

Section 6.3 Naming Compounds and Writing Formulas
(pages 170–175)

This section explains how to name and write formulas for ionic and molecular compounds.

Reading Strategy (page 170)

Predicting Before you read, predict the meaning of the term *polyatomic ion*, and write your prediction in the table. After you read, if your prediction was incorrect, revise your definition. For more information on this Reading Strategy, see the **Reading and Study Skills** in the **Skills and Reference Handbook** at the end of your textbook.

Vocabulary Term	Before You Read	After You Read
Polyatomic ion		

Describing Ionic Compounds (pages 171–173)

1. Is the following sentence true or false? The name of an ionic compound must distinguish the compound from other ionic compounds containing the same elements. _____

2. Circle the letter(s) of the information provided by the formula for an ionic compound.

   a. number of bonds in the compound

   b. ratio of ions in the compound

   c. elements in the compound

3. Is the following sentence true or false? Names of ions are formed by placing the suffix *-ide* after part of the name of the nonmetal. _____

4. When a metal forms more than one ion, the name of the ion contains a Roman numeral to indicate the _____ on the ion.

5. A _____ is a covalently bonded group of atoms that has a positive or negative charge and acts as a unit. Circle the correct answer.

   charged particle   molecule   polyatomic ion

6. Circle the letter that identifies the number of ammonium ions needed to form a compound with one phosphate ion. Use the table to help you.

   a. one

   b. two

   c. three

Some Polyatomic Ions

Name	Formula	Name	Formula
Ammonium	NH_4^+	Acetate	$C_2H_3O_2^-$
Hydroxide	OH^-	Peroxide	O_2^{2-}
Nitrate	NO_3^-	Permanganate	MnO_4^-
Sulfate	SO_4^{2-}	Hydrogen sulfate	HSO_4^-
Carbonate	CO_3^{2-}	Hydrogen carbonate	HCO_3^-
Phosphate	PO_4^{3-}	Hydrogen phosphate	HPO_4^{2-}

Describing Molecular Compounds (pages 174–175)

7. Circle the letter(s) of the information provided by the name and formula of a molecular compound.

   a. number of atoms in the compound

   b. number of bonds in the compound

   c. elements in the compound

8. What appears first in the name of a molecular compound? Circle the correct answer.

   a. the least metallic element

   b. the most metallic element

   c. the polyatomic ion

9. Is the following sentence true or false? The formula for a molecular compound is written with the symbols for the elements in the same order as the elements appear in the name of the compound.

   _____

10. Circle the letter that identifies the method of naming the number of atoms in molecular compounds.

   a. prefix

   b. suffix

   c. number

Chapter 6   Chemical Bonds

Section 6.4 The Structure of Metals
(pages 176–181)

This section discusses metallic bonds and the properties of metals. It also explains how the properties of an alloy are controlled.

Reading Strategy (page 176)

Relating Cause and Effect As you read, complete the concept map to relate the structure of metals to their properties. For more information on this Reading Strategy, see the **Reading and Study Skills** in the **Skills and Reference Handbook** at the end of your textbook.

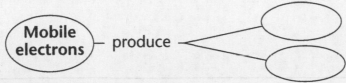

Metallic Bonds (pages 176–177)

1. Circle the letter of the metal with the highest melting point.

   a. gold

   b. titanium

   c. tungsten

2. Is the following sentence true or false? The properties of a metal are

   related to bonds within the metal. _____

3. Define a metallic bond. _____

   _____

4. Use the words in the box below to fill in the blanks.

anions	orbitals
cations	valence electrons

   The cations in a metal form a lattice. The lattice is held in place by strong

   metallic bonds between the _____ and the _____
   surrounding them.

5. Is the following sentence true or false? The more valence electrons a

   metal has, the stronger its metallic bonds will be. _____

Chapter 6   Chemical Bonds

Explaining Properties of Metals (page 177)

6. Some of the properties of metals can be explained by the _____ of the electrons within a metal lattice. Circle the correct answer.

   mobility   malleability   conductivity

7. Circle important properties of metals that can be explained by metallic bonding.

   a. ability to conduct electric current
   b. malleability
   c. ductility

Alloys (pages 178–181)

8. Define an alloy. _____

_____

9. Circle the letter of the sentences that correctly compare the hardness and strength of bronze to the hardness and strength of copper alone and tin alone.

   a. Copper is stronger than bronze.
   b. Tin is stronger than bronze.
   c. Bronze is stronger than copper.

10. Circle the factor(s) that scientists can vary to design alloys with specific properties.

    a. the types of elements in the alloy
    b. the amounts of elements in the alloy
    c. the temperature of elements in the alloy

11. When carbon is added to iron, the lattice becomes _____ and _____ than a lattice that contains only iron.

12. Circle the letters of the elements that all types of steel contain.

    a. carbon   b. chromium   c. iron

13. Circle the letter(s) of each correct description of stainless steel.

    a. Stainless steel contains more carbon than chromium.
    b. Chromium forms an oxide that protects stainless steel from rusting.
    c. Stainless steel is more brittle than steels that contain more carbon.

Chapter 6   Chemical Bonds

WordWise

Use the terms from the following list to fit each of the clues given below.

molecule	covalent	polyatomic
crystals	anion	polar
ionic	alloy	metallic
formula	bond	cation

Clues   **Vocabulary Terms**

A type of bond that holds cations and anions together   _____

A type of bond in which two atoms share a pair of   _____
valence electrons

A neutral group of atoms that are joined together by   _____
one or more covalent bonds

A term describing a covalent bond in which electrons   _____
are not shared equally

An ion that contains a covalently bonded group   _____
of atoms

An ion with a negative charge   _____

An ion with a positive charge   _____

A notation that shows what elements a compound   _____
contains and the ratio of the atoms or ions of these
elements in the compound

Solids whose particles are arranged in a lattice structure _____

A mixture of two or more elements, at least one   _____
of which is a metal

A type of bond that exists between a metal cation   _____
and the shared electrons that surround it

The force that holds atoms or ions together   _____

Chapter 6   Chemical Bonds

Writing Formulas for Ionic Compounds

Math Skill: Ratios and Proportions

You may want to read more about this **Math Skill** in the **Skills and Reference Handbook** at the end of your textbook.

What is the ratio of the ions in magnesium iodide?
What is the formula for magnesium iodide?

1. Read and Understand

What information are you given?

The name of the compound is magnesium iodide.

2. Plan and Solve

List the symbols and charges for the cation and anion.

Mg ion has a charge of 2+. I ion has a charge of 1−.

Determine the ratio of ions in the compound.

Mg with a 2+ charge needs two I ions, each with a charge of 1−. The ratio of the ions in the compound is 1 to 2.

Write the formula for magnesium iodide.

MgI_2

3. Look Back and Check

Is your answer reasonable?

Each magnesium atom loses two electrons and each iodine atom gains one electron. So there should be a 1-to-2 ratio of magnesium ions to iodide ions.

Math Practice

On a separate sheet of paper, solve the following problems.
Refer to Figures 16, 17, and 19 to help you solve the problems.

1. What is the formula for iron(III) chloride?

2. What is the formula for barium nitrate?

Chapter 7 Chemical Reactions

Summary

7.1 Describing Reactions

- In a chemical reaction, the substances that undergo change are called **reactants.**
- The new substances formed as a result of that change are called **products.**
- A **chemical equation** is a representation of a chemical reaction in which the reactants and products are expressed as formulas.

☞ **The law of conservation of mass states that mass is neither created nor destroyed in a chemical reaction.**

- During a chemical reaction, the mass of the products is always equal to the mass of the reactants.

☞ **In order to show that mass is conserved during a reaction, a chemical equation must be balanced.**

- In a balanced chemical equation, the number of atoms on the left side of the equation equals the number of atoms on the right.
- You can balance a chemical equation by changing the coefficients.
- **Coefficients** are the numbers that appear before the formulas.

☞ **Because chemical reactions often involve large numbers of small particles, chemists use a counting unit called the mole to measure amounts of a substance.**

- A **mole** (mol) is an amount of a substance that contains approximately 6.02×10^{23} particles of that substance. This number is known as Avogadro's number.
- The mass of one mole of a substance is called a **molar mass.** For an element, the molar mass is the same as its atomic mass expressed in grams.

☞ **In chemical reactions, the mass of a reactant or product can be calculated by using a balanced chemical equation and molar masses of the reactants and products.**

7.2 Types of Reactions

☞ **Some general types of chemical reactions are synthesis reactions, decomposition reactions, single-replacement reactions, double-replacement reactions, and combustion reactions.**

- A **synthesis reaction** is a reaction in which two or more substances react to form a single substance. The general equation for a synthesis reaction is $A + B \longrightarrow AB$.

- A **decomposition reaction** is a reaction in which a compound breaks down into two or more simpler substances. The general equation for a decomposition reaction is $AB \longrightarrow A + B$.
- A **single-replacement reaction** is a reaction in which one element takes the place of another element in a compound. The general equation for a single-replacement reaction is $A + BC \longrightarrow B + AC$.
- A **double-replacement reaction** is one in which two different compounds exchange positive ions and form two new compounds. The general equation for a double-replacement reaction is $AB + CD \longrightarrow AD + CB$.
- A **combustion reaction** is one in which a substance reacts rapidly with oxygen, often producing heat and light.

◉ **The discovery of subatomic particles enabled scientists to classify certain chemical reactions as transfers of electrons between atoms.**

- A reaction in which electrons are transferred from one reactant to another is called an **oxidation-reduction reaction,** or redox reaction.
- Any process in which an element loses electrons during a chemical reaction is called oxidation.
- Any process in which an element gains electrons during a chemical reaction is called reduction.

7.3 Energy Changes in Reactions

◉ **Chemical reactions involve the breaking of chemical bonds in the reactants and the formation of chemical bonds in the products.**

◉ **During a chemical reaction, energy is either released or absorbed.**

- **Chemical energy** is the energy stored in the chemical bonds of a substance.
- A chemical reaction that releases energy to its surroundings is called an **exothermic reaction.**
- A chemical reaction that absorbs energy from its surroundings is called an **endothermic reaction.**
- In both exothermic reactions and endothermic reactions, the total amount of energy before and after the reaction is the same. This principle is known as the law of conservation of energy.

7.4 Reaction Rates

Reaction rates tell you how fast a reaction is going.

- A **reaction rate** is the rate at which reactants change into products over time.
- Chemical reactions involve collisions between particles of reactants. If collisions occur more frequently, the reaction rate increases.

Factors that affect reaction rates include temperature, surface area, concentration, stirring, and catalysts.

- An increase in temperature will usually increase the reaction rate. A decrease in temperature will usually decrease the rate.
- An increase in surface area increases the exposure of reactants to one another. As a result, the reaction rate tends to increase with surface area.
- Stirring also increases the exposure of reactants to each other. As a result, the reaction rate tends to increase with stirring.
- *Concentration* refers to the number of particles in a given volume. More particles in the same volume means more frequent collisions. As a result, the reaction rate increases as concentration increases.
- A **catalyst** is a substance that affects the reaction rate without being used up in the reaction. Catalysts speed up reactions by lowering the energy barrier to the reaction.

7.5 Equilibrium

When a physical change does not go to completion, a physical equilibrium is established between the forward and reverse changes.

When a chemical reaction does not go to completion, a chemical equilibrium is established between the forward and reverse reactions.

- **Equilibrium** is a state in which the forward and reverse paths of a change take place at the same rate.
- A **reversible reaction** is a reaction in which the conversion of reactants into products and the conversion of products into reactants can happen simultaneously.

When a change is introduced to a system in equilibrium, the equilibrium shifts in the direction that relieves the change.

Chapter 7   Chemical Reactions

Section 7.1 Describing Reactions
(pages 192–198)

This section discusses the use of chemical equations and how to balance them. It also demonstrates the use of calculations in chemistry.

Reading Strategy (page 192)

Monitoring Your Understanding Preview the Key Concepts, topic headings, vocabulary, and figures in this section. List two things you expect to learn. After reading, state what you learned about each item you listed. For more information on this Reading Strategy, see the **Reading and Study Skills** in the **Skills and Reference Handbook** at the end of your textbook.

What I Expect to Learn	What I Learned

Chemical Equations (pages 192–193)

1. Is the following sentence true or false? The new substances formed as a result of a chemical reaction are called products. _____

2. Circle the letter of each sentence that is a correct interpretation of the chemical equation $C + O_2 \longrightarrow CO_2$.

   a. Carbon and oxygen react and form carbon monoxide.

   b. Carbon and oxygen react and form carbon dioxide.

   c. Carbon dioxide yields carbon and oxygen.

3. Is the following sentence true or false? The law of conservation of mass states that mass is neither created nor destroyed in a chemical reaction.

   _____

4. Circle the letter of the correct answer. According to the equation $C + O_2 \longrightarrow CO_2$, how many carbon atoms react with 14 molecules of oxygen to form 14 molecules of carbon dioxide?

   a. 1

   b. 7

   c. 14

Chapter 7   Chemical Reactions

Balancing Equations (pages 194–195)

5. Is the following sentence true or false? A chemical equation must be balanced in order to show that mass is conserved during a reaction.

   _____

6. Circle the letter of the name given to the numbers that appear before the formulas in a chemical equation.

   a. subscripts

   b. mass numbers

   c. coefficients

Counting With Moles (pages 195–196)

7. Chemists use a counting unit called a(n) _____ to measure amounts of a substance because chemical reactions often involve large numbers of small particles.

8. Circle the letter of the correct answer. One carbon atom has an atomic mass of 12.0 amu. One oxygen atom has an atomic mass of 16.0 amu. What is the molar mass of carbon dioxide?

   a. 28.0 amu

   b. 28.0 g

   c. 44.0 g

Chemical Calculations (pages 197–198)

9. Complete the table.

Formation of Water				
Equation	$2H_2$	+	O_2 $\longrightarrow$	$2H_2O$
Amount	2 mol		1 mol	
Molar Mass	2.0 g/mol			18.0 g/mol
Mass (Moles × Molar Mass)			32.0 g	36.0 g

10. Circle the letter of the correct answer. One mole of oxygen has a mass of 32 grams. What is the mass of 4 moles of oxygen?

    a. 128 g

    b. 128 amu

    c. 144 g

Chapter 7   Chemical Reactions

Section 7.2 Types of Reactions
(pages 199–205)

This section discusses how chemical reactions are classified into different types.

Reading Strategy (page 199)

Previewing Skim the section and begin a concept map like the one below that identifies types of reactions with a general form. As you read, add the general form of each type of reaction. For more information on this Reading Strategy, see the **Reading and Study Skills** in the **Skills and Reference Handbook** at the end of your textbook.

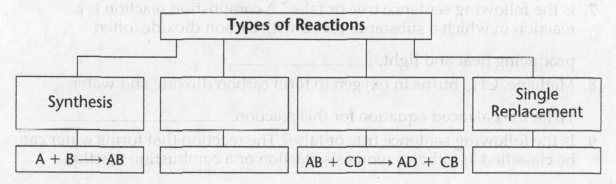

Classifying Reactions (pages 199–204)

1. Circle the letter of each equation that represents a synthesis reaction.

   a. $2Na + Cl_2 \longrightarrow 2NaCl$
   b. $2NaCl \longrightarrow 2Na + Cl_2$
   c. $2H_2 + O_2 \longrightarrow 2H_2O$

2. Is the following sentence true or false? A decomposition reaction is the opposite of a synthesis reaction. _____

3. Write the equation for the decomposition of calcium carbonate, $CaCO_3$, into calcium oxide, CaO, and carbon dioxide. _____

4. Circle the letter of the correct answer. Copper reacts with silver nitrate in a single-replacement reaction. What are the products of this reaction?

   a. copper(II) nitride and silver oxide
   b. copper(II) nitrate and silver
   c. copper, nitrogen, and silver oxide

Chapter 7   Chemical Reactions

5. What is a double-replacement reaction?

_____

6. Circle the letter of the correct answer. Calcium carbonate, $CaCO_3$, reacts with hydrochloric acid, HCl, in a double-replacement reaction. What are the products of this reaction?

a. calcium chloride, $CaCl_2$, and carbonic acid, H_2CO_3

b. calcium hydride, CaH_2, chlorine, Cl_2, and carbon dioxide, CO_2

c. calcium hydrogen carbonate, $Ca(HCO_3)_2$, and chlorine, Cl_2

7. Is the following sentence true or false? A combustion reaction is a reaction in which a substance reacts with carbon dioxide, often

producing heat and light. _____

8. Methane, CH_4, burns in oxygen to form carbon dioxide and water.

Write the balanced equation for this reaction. _____

9. Is the following sentence true or false? The reaction that forms water can be classified as either a synthesis reaction or a combustion reaction.

_____

Reactions as Electron Transfers (pages 204–205)

10. An _____ reaction is a reaction in which electrons are transferred from one reactant to another.

11. Calcium reacts with oxygen to form calcium oxide. Which reactant is

oxidized in this reaction? _____

12. Is the following sentence true or false? When calcium reacts with oxygen, each calcium atom gains two electrons and becomes a calcium

ion with a charge of 2–. _____

13. Is the following sentence true or false? Oxygen must be present in order

for an oxidation-reduction reaction to take place. _____

14. The process in which an element gains electrons during a chemical reaction is called _____. Circle the correct answer.

decomposition   oxidation   reduction

Chapter 7   Chemical Reactions

Section 7.3 Energy Changes in Reactions
(pages 206–209)

This section discusses how chemical bonds and energy relate to chemical reactions.

Reading Strategy (page 206)

Comparing and Contrasting As you read, complete the Venn diagram below to show the differences between exothermic and endothermic reactions. For more information on this Reading Strategy, see the **Reading and Study Skills** in the **Skills and Reference Handbook** at the end of your textbook.

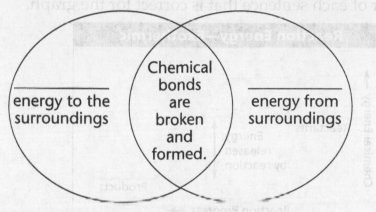

Exothermic Reaction   Endothermic Reaction

_____ energy to the surroundings

Chemical bonds are broken and formed.

_____ energy from surroundings

Chemical Bonds and Energy (pages 206–207)

1. What is chemical energy? _____

   _____

2. Chemical reactions involve the breaking of chemical bonds in the reactants and the formation of chemical bonds in the _____. Circle the correct answer.

   products   reactants   substances

3. Is the following sentence true or false? The formation of chemical bonds absorbs energy. _____

4. Is the following sentence true or false? The heat and light given off by a propane stove result from the formation of new chemical bonds.

   _____

5. The combustion of one molecule of propane (C_3H_8) results in the

   formation of 6 C=O double bonds and _____ O–H single bonds.

Chapter 7   Chemical Reactions

Exothermic and Endothermic Reactions (pages 208–209)

6. During a chemical reaction, energy is either released or _____.

7. Is the following sentence true or false? Physical and chemical changes

    can be either exothermic or endothermic changes. _____

8. What is an exothermic reaction? _____

    _____

9. Is the following sentence true or false? In exothermic reactions, the
   energy required to break the bonds in the reactants is greater than the

   energy released as the products form. _____

10. Circle the letter of each sentence that is correct for the graph.

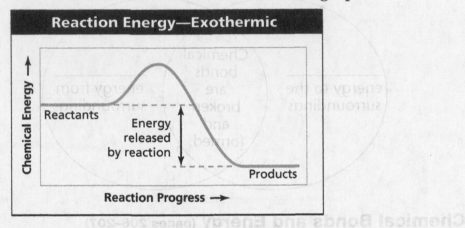

   a. The energy required to break the bonds in the reactants is greater
      than the energy released as the products form.

   b. The energy released as the products form is greater than the energy
      required to break the bonds in the reactants.

   c. The chemical energy of the reactants is greater than the chemical
      energy of the products.

Conservation of Energy (page 209)

11. In an endothermic reaction, heat from the surroundings plus the
    chemical energy of the reactants is converted into the _____
    of the products. Circle the correct answer.

    a. kinetic energy

    b. potential energy

    c. chemical energy

Chapter 7   Chemical Reactions

Section 7.4 Reaction Rates
(pages 212–215)

This section discusses the factors that affect reaction rates.

Reading Strategy (page 212)

Building Vocabulary As you read, complete the web diagram below with key terms from this section. For more information on this Reading Strategy, see the **Reading and Study Skills** in the **Skills and Reference Handbook** at the end of your textbook.

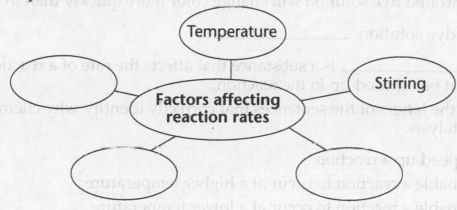

Reactions Over Time (page 212)

1. Any change that happens over time can be expressed as a(n) _____.

2. A reaction rate is the rate at which _____ change into _____ over time.

Factors Affecting Reaction Rates (pages 213–215)

3. Is the following sentence true or false? The rate of any reaction is a constant that does not change when the reaction conditions change. _____

4. Generally, an increase in temperature will _____ the reaction rate.

5. Is the following sentence true or false? Storing milk in a refrigerator stops the reactions that would cause the milk to spoil. _____

6. An increase in surface area _____ the exposure of reactants to one another. Circle the correct answer.

    increases   decreases

Chapter 7   Chemical Reactions

7. Stirring the reactants in a reaction mixture will generally _____ the reaction rate. Circle the correct answer.

   decrease   maintain   increase

8. Is the following sentence true or false? Increasing the concentration of the reactants will generally slow down a chemical reaction.

   _____

9. Is the following sentence true or false? A piece of material dipped in a concentrated dye solution will change color more quickly than in a

   dilute dye solution. _____

10. A _____ is a substance that affects the rate of a reaction without being used up in the reaction.

11. Circle the letters of the sentences that correctly identify why chemists use catalysts.

   a. to speed up a reaction

   b. to enable a reaction to occur at a higher temperature

   c. to enable a reaction to occur at a lower temperature

12. Is the following sentence true or false? Because a catalyst is quickly consumed in a reaction, it must be added to the reaction mixture

   over and over again to keep the reaction going. _____

13. Fill in the blank where the catalyst V_2O_5 should go in the formula shown and write it in the correct location.

   $$\text{\_\_\_\_} + 2SO_2 + O_2 \longrightarrow 2SO_3 + \text{\_\_\_\_}$$

14. Circle the letter of the correct answer. In the reaction represented by the

   equation $2H_2O_2 \xrightarrow{\text{Pt}} 2H_2O + O_2$, which substance acts as a catalyst?

   a. H_2O_2

   b. Pt

   c. H_2O

15. One way that a catalyst can lower the energy barrier of a reaction is by providing a surface on which the _____ can come together. Circle the correct answer.

   catalysts   reacting particles   products

Chapter 7   Chemical Reactions

Section 7.5 Equilibrium
(pages 216–219)

This section explains physical and chemical equilibria, and describes the factors that affect chemical equilibrium.

Reading Strategy (page 216)

Outlining As you read, make an outline of the most important ideas from this section. For more information on this Reading Strategy, see the **Reading and Study Skills** in the **Skills and Reference Handbook** at the end of your textbook.

I. Equilibrium
   A. Types of equilibria
      1.
      2.
   B.
      1. Temperature
      2. Pressure
      3. Concentration

Types of Equilibria (pages 216–217)

1. _____ is a state in which the forward and reverse paths of a change take place at the same rate.

2. Circle the letter of the correct answer. In the system described by the equation $H_2O(l) \rightleftharpoons H_2O(g)$, at room temperature, which of the following two physical changes are in equilibrium?

   a. sublimation and condensation

   b. evaporation and melting

   c. evaporation and condensation

3. Circle the letter of the correct answer. What does the single arrow imply about the reaction described in the following equation?

   $CH_4(g) + 2O_2(g) \longrightarrow CO_2(g) + 2H_2O(g)$

   a. The forward reaction goes to equilibrium.

   b. The reaction is in equilibrium.

   c. The reverse reaction goes to completion.

Chapter 7   Chemical Reactions

4. Circle the letter of the correct answer. In the system described by the equation $2SO_2(g) + O_2(g) \rightleftharpoons 2SO_3(g)$, what two reaction types are in equilibrium?

   a. synthesis and decomposition

   b. synthesis and double replacement

   c. synthesis and combustion

Factors Affecting Chemical Equilibrium (pages 218–219)

5. Is the following sentence true or false? A change in reaction conditions

   does not affect a chemical equilibrium. _____

6. Circle the letter of each correct answer. The synthesis of ammonia is described by the equation $N_2(g) + 3H_2(g) \rightleftharpoons 2NH_3(g) + heat$. Which reaction is favored when the temperature is lowered?

   a. the forward reaction

   b. the reaction that removes heat from the system

   c. the reaction that adds heat to the system

7. Circle the letter of each correct answer. During the synthesis of ammonia, which reaction is favored when hydrogen is added to the system?

   a. the forward reaction

   b. the reverse reaction

   c. the reaction that removes hydrogen from the system

8. Use the equation $C(s) + H_2O(g) + heat \rightleftharpoons CO(g) + H_2(g)$ to complete the table below.

An Example of Le Châtelier's Principle		
An increase in	**Shifts the equilibrium so as to**	**Favoring the**
	Remove heat	Forward reaction
Pressure	Produce fewer gas molecules	
Concentration of H_2		Reverse reaction

Chapter 7   Chemical Reactions

WordWise

Use the clues and the words below to help you write the vocabulary terms for the chapter in the blanks. Use the circled letter in each term to find the hidden vocabulary word. Then, write a definition for the hidden word.

catalyst	combustion	decomposition
coefficient	molar mass	equilibrium
exothermic	products	synthesis

Clues

Vocabulary Terms

Describes a reaction that releases energy to its surroundings

_ _ _ _ _ Ⓞ _ _ _ _ _

A state in which the forward and reverse paths of a change take place at the same rate

Ⓞ _ _ _ _ _ _ _ _ _ _

A substance that affects the reaction rate without being used up in the reaction

_ _ Ⓞ _ _ _ _ _

A reaction in which a compound breaks down into two or more simpler substances

_ _ _ _ Ⓞ _ _ _ _ _ _ _ _

A reaction in which two or more substances react to form a single substance

_ _ _ Ⓞ _ _ _ _ _

The mass of one mole of a substance

_ _ _ Ⓞ _   _ _ _ _

A number that appears before a formula in a chemical equation

_ _ _ _ _ _ _ _ _ _ Ⓞ _

A reaction in which a substance reacts rapidly with oxygen, often producing heat and light

_ _ _ _ _ _ _ Ⓞ _

The substances formed as the result of a chemical change

_ _ _ _ _ _ Ⓞ _

Hidden Term: _ _ _ _ _ _ _ _ _ _

Definition: _____

_____

Balancing Chemical Equations

Write a balanced equation for the reaction between potassium and water to produce hydrogen and potassium hydroxide, KOH.

Math Skill: Formulas and Equations

You may want to read more about this **Math Skill** in the **Skills and Reference Handbook** at the end of your textbook.

1. Read and Understand

What information are you given?

Reactants: K, H_2O
Products: H_2, KOH

2. Plan and Solve

Write a chemical equation with the reactants on the left side and the products on the right.

$$K + H_2O \longrightarrow H_2 + KOH$$

This equation is not balanced. The number of hydrogen atoms on the left does not equal the number of hydrogen atoms on the right. Change the coefficients of H_2O and KOH in order to balance the number of hydrogen atoms.

$$K + 2H_2O \longrightarrow H_2 + 2KOH$$

Change the coefficient of K in order to balance the number of potassium atoms.

$$2K + 2H_2O \longrightarrow H_2 + 2KOH$$

3. Look Back and Check

Is your answer reasonable?

The number of atoms on the left equals the number of atoms on the right.

Math Practice

On a separate sheet of paper, solve the following problems.

1. Magnesium burns in the presence of oxygen to form magnesium oxide, MgO. Write a balanced equation for this reaction.

2. Hydrogen peroxide, H_2O_2, decomposes to form water and oxygen. Write a balanced equation for this reaction.

Chapter 8 Solutions, Acids, and Bases

Summary

8.1 Formation of Solutions

- A **solute** is a substance whose particles are dissolved in a solution.
- The substance in which the solute dissolves is called the **solvent.**

☞ **Substances can dissolve in water in three ways—by dissociation, dispersion, and ionization.**

- The process in which an ionic compound separates into ions as it dissolves is called **dissociation.**
- Molecular compounds dissolve in water by **dispersion,** or breaking into small pieces that spread throughout the water.
- The process in which neutral molecules gain or lose electrons is known as **ionization.**

☞ **Three physical properties of a solution that can differ from those of its solute and solvent are conductivity, freezing point, and boiling point.**

☞ **During the formation of a solution, energy is either released or absorbed.**

- Before a solution can form, the attractions among the particles of solvent and of solute must be broken. It takes energy to break the attractions among solute particles and among solvent particles.
- As the solute dissolves, new attractions form between solute and solvent particles. The formation of these attractions releases energy.
- Rates of dissolving depend on the frequency and energy of collisions that occur between very small particles. During the formation of a solution, collisions occur between particles of the solute and solvent.

☞ **Factors that affect the rate of dissolving include surface area, stirring, and temperature.**

8.2 Solubility and Concentration

☞ **Solutions are described as saturated, unsaturated, or supersaturated, depending on the amount of solute in solution.**

- The maximum amount of a solute that dissolves in a given amount of solvent at a constant temperature is called **solubility.**
- A **saturated solution** is one that contains as much solute as the solvent can hold at a given temperature.
- A solution that has less than the maximum amount of solute that can be dissolved is called an **unsaturated solution.**
- A **supersaturated solution** is one that contains *more* solute than it can normally hold at a given temperature.

- Three factors that affect solubility of a solute are the polarity of the solvent, temperature, and pressure.
  - Solution formation is more likely to happen when the solute and the solvent are both polar or both nonpolar.
  - Usually, increasing the solvent temperature increases the solubility of solids.
  - Increasing the pressure on a gas increases its solubility in a liquid.

- Concentration can be expressed as percent by volume, percent by mass, and molarity.
  - The **concentration** of a solution is the amount of solute dissolved in a specified amount of solution.
  - **Molarity** is the number of moles of a solute dissolved per liter of solution.

8.3 Properties of Acids and Bases

- Some general properties of acids include sour taste, reactivity with metals, and ability to produce color changes in indicators.
  - An **acid** is a compound that produces hydronium ions (H_3O^+) when dissolved in water.
  - An **indicator** is any substance that changes color in the presence of an acid or base.

- Some general properties of bases include bitter taste, slippery feel, and ability to produce color changes in indicators.
  - A **base** is a compound that produces hydroxide ions (OH^-) when dissolved in water.

- The neutralization reaction between an acid and a base produces a salt and water.
  - The reaction between an acid and a base is called **neutralization**.
  - During neutralization, the negative ions in an acid combine with the positive ions in a base to produce an ionic compound called a **salt**.

- Acids can be defined as proton donors, and bases can be defined as proton acceptors.

8.4 Strength of Acids and Bases

  - The **pH** of a solution is a measure of its hydronium ion concentration. The pH can be any number from 0 to 14.
  - A pH of 7 indicates a neutral solution. Pure water has a pH of 7.
  - Acids have a pH less than 7. Bases have a pH greater than 7.

☞ **The lower the pH value, the greater the H_3O^+ ion concentration in solution is.**

☞ **The higher the pH value, the lower the H_3O^+ ion concentration is.**

☞ **When strong acids dissolve in water, they ionize almost completely.**

☞ **Strong bases dissociate almost completely in water.**

☞ **Weak acids and bases ionize or dissociate only slightly in water.**
- A **buffer** is a solution that is resistant to large changes in pH.
- Buffers can be prepared by mixing a weak acid and its salt or a weak base and its salt.

☞ **Strong acids and bases are strong electrolytes because they dissociate or ionize almost completely in water.**
- An **electrolyte** is a substance that ionizes or dissociates into ions when it dissolves in water.
- Solutions with electrolytes can conduct electricity.

Chapter 8   Solutions, Acids, and Bases

Section 8.1 Formation of Solutions
(pages 228–234)

This section explains the parts of a solution, the processes that occur when compounds dissolve, and how the properties of a solution compare with those of its solvent and solute.

Reading Strategy (page 228)

Comparing and Contrasting Contrast dissociation and ionization by listing the ways they differ in the Venn diagram below. For more information on this reading strategy, see the **Reading and Study Skills** in the **Skills and Reference Handbook** at the end of your textbook.

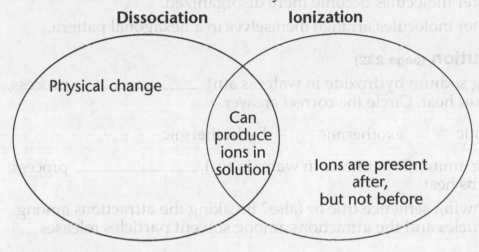

Dissolving (pages 229–230)

1. A solution is a _____ mixture of two or more substances.

2. Circle the letter that identifies a substance whose particles are dissolved in a solution.

   a. solvent

   b. solute

   c. ion

3. The process in which an ionic compound separates into ions as it dissolves is called _____. Circle the correct answer.

   dispersion   dissociation   ionization

4. The process in which particles dissolve by breaking apart and scattering is called _____. Circle the correct answer.

   dispersion   dissociation   ionization

5. Is the following sentence true or false? Dissolving by ionization is a

   physical change. _____

Chapter 8   Solutions, Acids, and Bases

Properties of Liquid Solutions (page 231)

6. Circle the letters of the physical properties of a solution that can differ from those of its solute and solvent.

    a. conductivity

    b. freezing point

    c. boiling point

7. Circle the letters that identify what happens to water as it freezes.

    a. The water molecules become more organized.

    b. The water molecules become more disorganized.

    c. The water molecules arrange themselves in a hexagonal pattern.

Heat of Solution (page 232)

8. Dissolving sodium hydroxide in water is a(n) _____ process, as it releases heat. Circle the correct answer.

    endothermic   exothermic   hydrothermic

9. Dissolving ammonium nitrate in water is a(n) _____ process, as it absorbs heat.

10. Is the following sentence true or false? Breaking the attractions among solute particles and the attractions among solvent particles releases

    energy. _____

Factors Affecting Rates of Dissolving (page 234)

11. Powdered sugar has more surface area per unit mass than granulated sugar. Which will dissolve faster in water, powdered sugar or

    granulated sugar? _____

12. Heating a solvent increases the energy of its particles and _____ the rate at which a solid solute can dissolve in the solvent.

13. Stirring or shaking a solution that contains a solid solute moves dissolved particles away from the surface of the solid. It also causes _____ collisions between the solute and solvent particles. Circle the correct answer.

    less frequent   more frequent   less forceful

Chapter 8   Solutions, Acids, and Bases

Section 8.2 Solubility and Concentration
(pages 235–239)

This section explains solubility, the factors affecting solubility, and different ways of expressing the concentration of a solution.

Reading Strategy (page 235)

Previewing Before you read the section, rewrite the topic headings as *how*, *why*, and *what* questions. As you read, write an answer to each question. For more information on this reading strategy, see the **Reading and Study Skills** in the **Skills and Reference Handbook** at the end of your textbook.

Question	Answer
What is solubility?	
	Solvent, temperature, and pressure
How can the concentration of solutions be expressed?	

Solubility (pages 235–237)

1. _____ is the maximum amount of a solute that dissolves in a given amount of solvent at a constant temperature.

2. List the following solutes in order from most soluble to least soluble in water: table salt, baking soda, table sugar.

   a. _____

   b. _____

   c. _____

3. A _____ is a solution that contains as much solute as the solvent can hold at a given temperature.

4. A solution that has less than the maximum amount of solute that can be dissolved is called a(n) _____.

5. Is the following sentence true or false? It is impossible for a solution to contain more solute than the solvent can hold at a given temperature.

   _____

Chapter 8   Solutions, Acids, and Bases

Factors Affecting Solubility (page 237)

6. Circle the letters of factors that affect the solubility of a solute.

   a. polarity of the solvent

   b. amount of solvent

   c. pressure

7. Is the following statement true or false? In general, the solubility of solids increases as the solvent temperature increases. _____

8. In general, the solubility of gases decreases as the solvent temperature _____. Circle the correct answer.

   increases   decreases   stays the same

9. In general, the solubility of a gas increases as pressure _____. Circle the correct answer.

   increases   decreases   stays the same

Concentration of Solutions (pages 238–239)

10. The _____ is the amount of a solute dissolved in a given amount of solution.

11. Circle the letters that identify ways to express the concentration of a solution.

    a. density

    b. percent by volume

    c. molarity

12. Complete the equation.

    Percent by volume = $\dfrac{\rule{3cm}{0.4pt}}{\text{Volume of solution}} \times 100\%$

13. Write the equation used to calculate percent by mass.

    Percent by mass = _____

14. Is this sentence true or false? Molarity is the number of moles of a solute per liter of solution. _____

Chapter 8   Solutions, Acids, and Bases

Section 8.3 Properties of Acids and Bases
(pages 240–245)

This section describes the general properties of acids and bases.

Reading Strategy (page 240)

Using Prior Knowledge Before you read, write your definition of each vocabulary term in the table below. After you read, write the scientific definition of each term and compare it with your original definition. For more information on this reading strategy, see the **Reading and Study Skills** in the **Skills and Reference Handbook** at the end of your textbook.

Term	Your Definition	Scientific Definition
Acid		
Base		
Salt		

Identifying Acids (pages 240–241)

1. Define an acid. _____

_____

Match these common acids to their uses.

Acids

_____ 2. acetic acid

_____ 3. hydrochloric acid

_____ 4. carbonic acid

_____ 5. nitric acid

Uses

a. fertilizer production

b. carbonated beverages

c. vinegar

d. digestive juices in stomach

6. Place the following substances in the correct column in the table: lemons, vinegar, grapefruit, sour milk, tomatoes.

Foods Containing Acetic Acid	Foods Containing Citric Acid	Foods Containing Butyric Acid

Chapter 8   Solutions, Acids, and Bases

7. The reaction between an acid and a metal can be classified as a(n)

_____ .

Identifying Bases (pages 242–243)

8. Define a base. _____

_____

9. Use the following compounds to complete the chart: aluminum hydroxide, calcium hydroxide, and magnesium hydroxide.

Common Bases		
Name	Formula	Uses
Sodium hydroxide	NaOH	Drain cleaner, soap production
	Mg(OH)$_2$	Antacid, laxative
	Ca(OH)$_2$	Concrete, plaster
	Al(OH)$_3$	Deodorant, antacid

10. Circle the letter that describes how basic solutions generally taste.

   a. sweet

   b. sour

   c. bitter

11. Is the following sentence true or false? Bases turn red litmus paper

   blue. _____

Neutralization and Salts (page 244)

12. The reaction between an acid and a base is called _____ . Circle the correct answer.

   decomposition   neutralization   oxidation

13. Complete the chemical equation describing the neutralization reaction between calcium hydroxide and hydrochloric acid.

   Ca(OH)$_2$ + 2HCl $\longrightarrow$ _____ + _____

Proton Donors and Acceptors (page 245)

14. Acids can be described as proton _____; bases can be

   described as proton _____ .

15. When hydrogen chloride ionizes in water, which reactant is the proton

   donor? _____

Chapter 8   Solutions, Acids, and Bases

Section 8.4 Strength of Acids and Bases
(pages 246–249)

This section explains how to describe acids and bases in terms of both concentration and strength.

Reading Strategy (page 246)

Comparing and Contrasting As you read, complete the diagram by comparing and contrasting acids and bases. For more information on this reading strategy, see the **Reading and Study Skills** in the **Skills and Reference Handbook** at the end of your textbook.

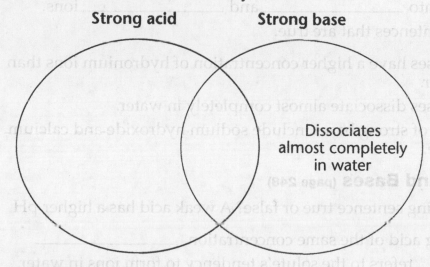

The pH Scale (page 247)

1. The pH scale ranges from _____ to _____.
2. Circle the letter that indicates the pH of a neutral solution.

    a. 0

    b. 3

    c. 7

3. Water is neutral because it contains small but equal concentrations of
    _____ and _____. Circle the correct answers.

    hydrogen   hydronium ions   hydroxide ions

4. Is the following sentence true or false? The higher the pH value of a

    solution, the greater the H_3O^+ ion concentration is. _____

5. If you add acid to pure water, the concentration of H_3O^+ _____

    and the concentration of OH^- _____.

Chapter 8   Solutions, Acids, and Bases

Strong Acids and Bases (pages 247–248)

6. Is the following sentence true or false? A strong acid always has a lower

   pH than a weak acid. _____

7. Circle the letters that identify a strong acid.

   a. HCl

   b. HNO_3

   c. H_2O

8. When dissolved in water, sodium hydroxide almost completely

   dissociates into _____ and _____ ions.

9. Circle the sentences that are true.

   a. Strong bases have a higher concentration of hydronium ions than
      pure water.

   b. Strong bases dissociate almost completely in water.

   c. Examples of strong bases include sodium hydroxide and calcium
      hydroxide.

Weak Acids and Bases (page 248)

10. Is the following sentence true or false? A weak acid has a higher pH

    than a strong acid of the same concentration. _____

11. _____ refers to the solute's tendency to form ions in water.
    Circle the correct answer.

    concentration   ionization   strength

12. Define a buffer. _____

    _____

Electrolytes (page 249)

13. An _____ is a substance that ionizes or dissociates into ions
    when it is dissolved in water.

14. Is the following sentence true or false? Strong acids and bases are
    weak electrolytes because they dissociate or ionize almost completely

    in water. _____

Chapter 8   Solutions, Acids, and Bases

WordWise

Use the clues and the words in the box below to identify some of the vocabulary terms from Chapter 8. Write the words on the line, putting one letter in each blank. When you finish, the words enclosed in the circle will reveal an important term.

acid	ionization	base	molarity
buffer	neutralization	dispersion	solvent
electrolyte	unsaturated		

Clues

1. A(n) _____ solution is one in which you can dissolve more solute.

2. A substance in which other materials dissolve is called a(n) _____.

3. A(n) _____ is a substance that forms ions when dissolved in water.

4. A(n) _____ is a solution containing either a weak acid and its salt or a weak base and its salt.

5. A(n) _____ is a compound that produces hydroxide ions when dissolved in water.

6. The process in which a substance breaks up into smaller particles as it dissolves is called _____

7. The reaction between an acid and a base is called _____.

8. A(n) _____ is a compound that produces hydronium ions when dissolved in water.

9. When neutral molecules gain or lose electrons, the process is known as _____.

10. The number of moles of solute that is dissolved in 1 liter of solution is _____.

Vocabulary Terms

1. _ _ _ _ _ _ _ _ _ _ _ _

2. _ _ _ _ _ _

3. _ _ _ _ _ _ _ _ _ _ _

4. _ _ _ _ _ _

5. _ _ _ _ _

6. _ _ _ _ _ _ _ _ _

7. _ _ _ _ _ _ _ _ _ _ _ _ _

8. _ _ _ _

9. _ _ _ _ _ _ _ _ _

10. _ _ _ _ _ _ _ _

Chapter 8   Solutions, Acids, and Bases

Calculating the Molarity of a Solution

Math Skill:
Calculating with
Significant Figures

You may want to read
more about this **Math
Skill** in the **Skills and
Reference Handbook**
at the end of your
textbook.

Suppose you dissolve 58.5 grams of sodium chloride into enough water to make exactly 1.00 liter of solution. What is the molarity of the solution?

1. Read and Understand

What information are you given?

Mass of solute = 58.5 g NaCl

Volume of solution = 1.00 L

2. Plan and Solve

What unknown are you trying to solve?

Molarity = ?

What equation can you use?

$$\text{Molarity} = \frac{\text{Moles of solute}}{\text{Liters of solution}}$$

Convert the mass of the solute into moles.

$$\text{Moles of solute} = \frac{\text{Mass of NaCl}}{\text{Molar mass of NaCl}}$$

$$= \frac{58.5 \text{ g NaCl}}{58.5 \text{ g NaCl/mol NaCl}} = 1.00 \text{ mol NaCl}$$

Solve the equation for molarity.

$$\text{Molarity} = \frac{1.00 \text{ mol NaCl}}{1.00 \text{ L}} = 1.00 \text{ M NaCl}$$

3. Look Back and Check

Is your answer reasonable?

A 1.00 M NaCl solution contains 1.00 mole of NaCl per liter of solution. The answer is reasonable.

Math Practice

On a separate sheet of paper, solve the following problems.

1. Suppose you had 4.0 moles of solute dissolved into 2.0 liters of solution. What is the molarity?

2. Table sugar has a molar mass of 342 grams. How many grams of table sugar are needed to make 2.00 liters of a 0.500 M solution?

Chapter 9 Carbon Chemistry

Summary

9.1 Carbon Compounds

- An **organic compound** contains carbon and hydrogen, often combined with a few other elements such as oxygen and nitrogen.
- Carbon has four valence electrons and can bond in several ways with other atoms.

◉ **Diamond, graphite, and fullerenes are forms of carbon.**

- In a **network solid,** all the atoms are linked by covalent bonds.
- Diamond is a network solid.
- Graphite has carbon atoms arranged in widely spaced layers that slide easily.
- In fullerenes, the carbon atoms are arranged in hollow cages.

◉ **Factors that determine the properties of a hydrocarbon are the number of carbon atoms and how the atoms are arranged.**

- A **hydrocarbon** is an organic compound that contains only the elements hydrogen and carbon.
- In a **saturated hydrocarbon,** all of the bonds are single bonds.
- Saturated hydrocarbons form straight chains, branched chains, or rings.
- A molecular formula shows the type and number of atoms in a molecule of a compound. A structural formula shows how those atoms are arranged.
- Compounds with the same molecular formula but different structural formulas are **isomers.**

◉ **There are three types of unsaturated hydrocarbons—alkenes, alkynes, and aromatic hydrocarbons.**

- A hydrocarbon that contains one or more double or triple bonds is an **unsaturated hydrocarbon.**
- Alkenes are hydrocarbons that have one or more carbon-carbon double bonds.
- Alkynes are straight- or branched-chain hydrocarbons that have one or more triple bonds.
- Hydrocarbons that contain similar ring structures are know as **aromatic hydrocarbons.**

◉ **Three types of fossil fuels are coal, natural gas, and petroleum.**

- **Fossil fuels** are mixtures of hydrocarbons that formed from the remains of plants or animals.

● **The primary products of the complete combustion of fossil fuels are carbon dioxide and water.**

- The energy released from fossil fuels through combustion is used to heat buildings, to cook food, and for transportation.

9.2 Substituted Hydrocarbons

- A hydrocarbon in which one or more hydrogen atoms have been replaced by an atom or group of atoms is a **substituted hydrocarbon.**
- The substituted atom or group of atoms is called a **functional group.**

● **The functional group in an alcohol is a hydroxyl group, –OH.**

● **The functional group in organic acids is a carboxyl group, –COOH.**

● **The functional group in an amine is an amino group, –NH$_2$.**

● **Esters form when organic acids react with alcohols.**

9.3 Polymers

● **Polymers can be classified as natural polymers or synthetic polymers.**

- A **polymer** is a large molecule that forms when many smaller molecules are linked together by covalent bonds.
- The smaller molecules that join together to form a polymer are **monomers.**

● **Rubber, nylon, and polyethylene are three examples of compounds that can be synthesized.**

● **Four types of polymers produced in plant and animal cells are starches, cellulose, nucleic acids, and proteins.**

- Simple sugars, slightly more complex sugars such as sucrose, and polymers built from sugar monomers are all classified as **carbohydrates.**
- **Nucleic acids** are large nitrogen-containing polymers found mainly in the nuclei of cells.
- There are two types of nucleic acid, deoxyribonucleic acid (DNA) and ribonucleic acid (RNA).
- An **amino acid** is a compound that contains both carboxyl and amino functional groups in the same molecule.
- Your body needs about 20 amino acids. Your cells use amino acids as the monomers for constructing protein polymers.
- A **protein** is a polymer in which at least 100 amino acid monomers are linked through bonds between an amino group and a carboxyl group.

9.4 Reactions in Cells

- Reactions that take place in cells follow the same rules as reactions that take place in a laboratory. Two important reactions in cells are photosynthesis and cellular respiration.

During photosynthesis, energy from sunlight is converted into chemical energy.

- During **photosynthesis,** plants chemically combine carbon dioxide and water into carbohydrates. The process requires light and chlorophyll, a green pigment in plants.
- The relationship between photosynthesis and cellular respiration is that each process produces the reactants for the other process.

During cellular respiration, the energy stored in the products of photosynthesis is released.

- Carbon dioxide and water are reactants in photosynthesis and are products of cellular respiration.
- Carbohydrates and oxygen are reactants in cellular respiration and are products of photosynthesis.

Enzymes and vitamins are compounds that help cells function efficiently at normal body temperature.

- **Enzymes** are proteins that act as catalysts for reactions in cells.
- **Vitamins** are organic compounds that organisms need in small amounts, but cannot produce.

Chapter 9 Carbon Chemistry

Section 9.1 Carbon Compounds
(pages 262–269)

This section describes different forms of carbon that exist in nature. It also discusses saturated and unsaturated hydrocarbons. It explains the formation of fossil fuels and describes the products of their combustion.

Reading Strategy (page 262)

Previewing Before you read, use the models in Figure 2 to describe the arrangement of carbon atoms in each form of carbon. For more information on this Reading Strategy, see the **Reading and Study Skills** in the **Skills and Reference Handbook** at the end of your textbook.

Forms of Carbon	
Diamond	
Graphite	
Buckminsterfullerene	Hollow spheres with a surface of carbon atoms arranged in alternating hexagons and pentagons

1. The two elements that all organic compounds contain are carbon and
_____. Circle the correct answer.

hydrogen   oxygen   nitrogen

2. Circle the letter of the approximate percentage of all known compounds that are organic compounds.

a. 30 percent

b. 60 percent

c. 90 percent

Forms of Carbon (page 263)

3. Circle the letter of each form of carbon.

a. soot   b. diamonds   c. fullerenes

4. A _____ is a solid in which all the atoms are linked by covalent bonds.

Saturated Hydrocarbons (pages 264–265)

5. Is the following sentence true or false? A hydrocarbon is an organic

compound that contains carbon, hydrogen, and oxygen. _____

6. The number of carbon atoms and how they are arranged determine the

   properties of a _____.

7. Circle the letter of the correct answer. What does a structural formula show that a molecular formula does not?

   a. the type of atoms in the compound

   b. the number of atoms in a molecule of the compound

   c. the arrangement of atoms in the compound

8. Define isomers. _____

   _____

Unsaturated Hydrocarbons (page 266)

9. Circle the letter of each type of unsaturated hydrocarbon.

   a. alkene   b. alkane   c. alkyne

10. Circle the letter of the most reactive type of hydrocarbon.

    a. alkanes

    b. alkynes

    c. aromatic hydrocarbons

Fossil Fuels (page 267-268)

11. Define fossil fuels. _____

    _____

12. Circle the letter of each fossil fuel.

    a. coal   b. natural gas   c. ferns

Combustion of Fossil Fuels (pages 268-269)

13. Circle the letter of each primary product of the complete combustion of fossil fuels.

    a. carbon dioxide   b. sulfur dioxide   c. water

14. When an insufficient amount of oxygen is available for complete combustion of a fossil fuel, one product of the combustion reaction is the deadly gas _____. Circle the correct answer.

    carbon dioxide   carbon monoxide   carbonic acid

Chapter 9   Carbon Chemistry

Section 9.2 Substituted Hydrocarbons
(pages 272–274)

This section discusses organic compounds that contain atoms of elements other than carbon and hydrogen. It also explains the relationship between the properties of organic compounds and functional groups.

Reading Strategy (page 272)

Monitoring Your Understanding As you read, complete the table by connecting each functional group with the type of compound that contains the functional group. For more information on this Reading Strategy, see the **Reading and Study Skills** in the **Skills and Reference Handbook** at the end of your textbook.

Connecting Functional Groups to Types of Compounds	
Functional Group	**Type of Compound**
–OH	Alcohol
–COOH	
–NH₂	

1. A _____ is a hydrocarbon in which one or more hydrogen atoms have been replaced by an atom or group of atoms.

2. Is the following sentence true or false? The functional group in a substituted hydrocarbon determines the properties of the compound.

   _____

Alcohols (page 273)

3. Methanol and ethanol are two examples of a class of organic compounds

   called _____.

4. The functional group in an alcohol is represented as –OH and is called a(n) _____ group. Circle the correct answer.

   amino   carboxyl   hydroxyl

5. Circle two ways a halocarbon can be produced.

   a. A halocarbon reacts with a base.

   b. An alkyne reacts with ether.

   c. An alkene reacts with water.

Chapter 9   Carbon Chemistry

Organic Acids and Bases (pages 273–274)

6. Circle the letters of the physical properties organic acids tend to have.

   a. sharp taste

   b. strong odor

   c. pleasant odor

7. Is the following sentence true or false? Amines are organic

   bases. _____

8. Use the terms in the box to complete the following table.

alcohol	–OH
carboxyl	–CH
chlorocarbon	–NH₂

Substituted Hydrocarbons		
Type of Compound	**Name of Functional Group**	**Formula of Functional Group**
	Hydroxyl	
Organic acid		–COOH
Organic base	Amino	

Esters (page 274)

9. Circle the types of compounds that can react and form esters.

   a. organic base

   b. organic acid

   c. alcohol

10. Circle the letter of the other product of the reaction that forms an ester.

    a. an alcohol

    b. a salt

    c. water

11. Is the following sentence true or false? Esters are used to make various

    fruit flavors in processed foods. _____

Chapter 9   Carbon Chemistry

Section 9.3 Polymers
(pages 275–280)

This section explains how polymers form. It also discusses examples of synthetic and natural polymers.

Reading Strategy (page 275)

Identifying Main Ideas As you read, complete the concept map to summarize two main ideas about polymers. For more information on this Reading Strategy, see the **Reading and Study Skills** in the **Skills and Reference Handbook** at the end of your textbook.

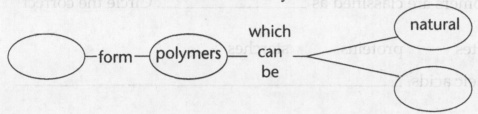

1. Define a polymer. _____

_____

2. The smaller molecules that join together to form a polymer are called

_____.

3. Is the following sentence true or false? More than one type of monomer

can be present in some polymers. _____

4. Circle the letters of the general classifications of polymers.

   a. natural

   b. organic

   c. synthetic

Synthetic Polymers (page 276)

5. Polyethylene, nylon, and rubber are _____.

6. Is the following sentence true or false? The more carbon atoms there are

in a polyethylene chain, the harder the polymer is. _____

Natural Polymers (pages 278–280)

7. Circle the letter of the molecular formula of a simple sugar.

   a. CH_2O

   b. $C_6H_{12}O_6$

   c. $C_{12}H_{22}O_{11}$

Chapter 9   Carbon Chemistry

8. Circle the letter of the simple sugar that glucose and fructose can react to form.

    a. starch

    b. cellulose

    c. sucrose

9. Plants store _____ for food and to build stems, seeds, and roots.

10. Simple sugars, slightly more complex sugars, and polymers built from sugar monomers are classified as _____. Circle the correct answer.

    carbohydrates   proteins   starches

11. Define nucleic acids. _____

    _____

12. Circle the letter for each type of nucleic acid.

    a. deoxyribonucleic acid (DNA)

    b. oxyribonucleic acid (ONA)

    c. ribonucleic acid (RNA)

13. The _____ in a strand of DNA is a code that is used to produce proteins. Circle the letter of the answer.

    a. rules for pairing amino acids

    b. order of the base pairs

    c. shape of the proteins

14. Use the terms in the box to complete the following concept map about amino acids.

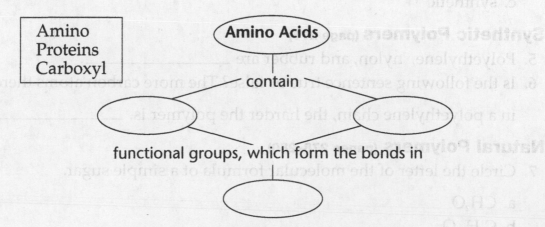

Chapter 9   Carbon Chemistry

Section 9.4 Reactions in Cells
(pages 282–284)

This section describes and compares photosynthesis and cellular respiration. It also discusses the roles of enzymes and vitamins.

Reading Strategy (page 282)

Summarizing As you read, complete the table by recording a main idea for each heading. For more information on this Reading Strategy, see the **Reading and Study Skills** in the **Skills and Reference Handbook** at the end of your textbook.

Heading	Main Idea
Photosynthesis	During photosynthesis, energy from sunlight is converted into chemical energy.
Cellular Respiration	
Enzymes and Vitamins	

Photosynthesis (page 282)

1. During photosynthesis, plants chemically combine _____ and _____ into carbohydrates. Circle the best answers.

   oxygen   carbon dioxide   water

2. During photosynthesis, energy from _____ is converted into chemical energy.

3. Circle the letter of each product of photosynthesis.

   a. carbon dioxide

   b. carbohydrates

   c. oxygen

4. Is the following sentence true or false? When all the reactions in photosynthesis are complete, energy from sunlight has been stored in the

   covalent bonds of molecules. _____

Cellular Respiration (page 283)

5. During cellular respiration, the _____ stored in the products of photosynthesis is released. Circle the correct answer.

   energy   oxygen   sugar

Chapter 9   Carbon Chemistry

6. Is the following sentence true or false? Carbohydrates produce more

   energy per gram than fats do. _____

7. Use the words in the box to complete the diagram relating
   photosynthesis to cellular respiration.

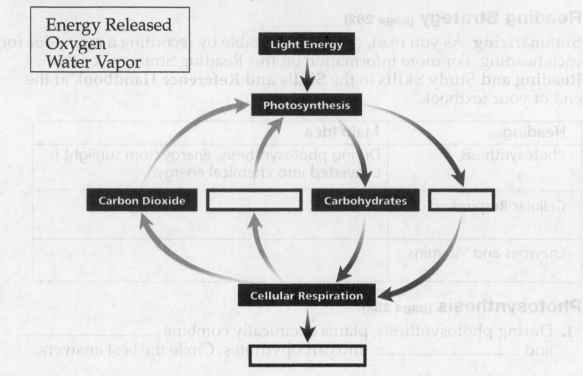

Energy Released
Oxygen
Water Vapor

Enzymes and Vitamins (page 284)

8. Define enzymes. _____

   _____

9. Is the following sentence true or false? Enzymes require high

   temperatures in order to function. _____

10. Define vitamins. _____

   _____

11. Is the following sentence true or false? All vitamins dissolve in water

   and must be replaced daily. _____

Chapter 9   Carbon Chemistry

WordWise

Complete the following crossword puzzle, using the clues and the words provided below.

amino acids	monomer	protein
hydrocarbons	nucleic	saturated
isomers	organic	vitamin

Clues across:

1. A hydrocarbon in which all of the bonds are single bonds

2. A compound containing carbon and hydrogen, often combined with other elements such as oxygen and nitrogen

3. A small molecule that joins with other small molecules to form a polymer

4. _____ acid: a large nitrogen-containing polymer found mainly in the nuclei of cells

5. Organic compounds that contain only carbon and hydrogen

Clues down:

6. An organic compound that organisms need in small amounts, but cannot produce

7. Organic compounds that contain both carboxyl and amino functional groups

8. Compounds with the same molecular formula but different structural formulas

9. A polymer in which at least 100 amino acid monomers are linked through bonds between an amino group and a carboxyl group

Balancing Equations for Organic Reactions

When methane, CH_4, combines with oxygen, the products are carbon dioxide and water. Write a balanced equation for the complete combustion of methane.

Math Skill: Ratios and Proportions

You may want to read more about this **Math Skill** in the **Skills and Reference Handbook** at the end of your textbook.

1. Read and Understand

What information are you given?

Reactants = methane (CH_4) and oxygen (O_2)

Products = carbon dioxide (CO_2) and water (H_2O)

2. Plan and Solve

What unknowns are you trying to determine?

The coefficients for the equation

What equation contains the given information?

$CH_4 + O_2 \longrightarrow CO_2 + H_2O$ (unbalanced equation)

First, balance the equation for hydrogen. Because there are 4 hydrogen atoms in CH_4 and only 2 hydrogen atoms in H_2O, you need to place the coefficient 2 in front of H_2O.

$CH_4 + O_2 \longrightarrow CO_2 + 2H_2O$

Then balance the equation for oxygen. Because there are 2 oxygen atoms in 1 molecule of CO_2 and 2 oxygen atoms in 2 molecules of H_2O for a total of 4 oxygen atoms, you need to place the coefficient 2 in front of O_2.

$CH_4 + 2O_2 \longrightarrow CO_2 + 2H_2O$

3. Look Back and Check

Is your answer reasonable?

Each side of the equation has 1 carbon atom, 4 hydrogen atoms, and 4 oxygen atoms. The equation is balanced.

Math Practice

On a separate sheet of paper, solve the following problems.

1. Balance the equation for the reaction of benzene and hydrogen to form cyclohexane.

$$C_6H_6 + \underline{\quad} H_2 \xrightarrow{\text{Pt}} C_6H_{12}$$

2. Balance the equation for the complete combustion of propane, C_3H_8.

$$C_3H_8 + \underline{\quad} O_2 \longrightarrow 3CO_2 + \underline{\quad} H_2O$$

Chapter 10 Nuclear Chemistry

Summary

10.1 Radioactivity

- **Radioactivity** is the process in which an unstable atomic nucleus emits charged particles and energy.
- Any atom containing an unstable nucleus is called a radioactive isotope, or **radioisotope** for short.

☞ **During nuclear decay, atoms of one element can change into atoms of a different element altogether.**

- When the composition of a radioisotope changes, the radioisotope is said to undergo nuclear decay.

☞ **Common types of nuclear radiation include alpha particles, beta particles, and gamma rays.**

- **Nuclear radiation** is charged particles and energy that are emitted from the nuclei of radioisotopes.
- An **alpha particle** is a positively charged particle made up of two protons and two neutrons.
- A **beta particle** is an electron emitted by an unstable nucleus.
- A **gamma ray** is a penetrating ray of energy emitted by an unstable nucleus.
- Nuclear radiation that occurs naturally in the environment is called **background radiation**.

☞ **Nuclear radiation can ionize atoms.**

- Alpha particles, beta particles, and gamma rays are all forms of ionizing radiation.

☞ **Devices that are used to detect nuclear radiation include Geiger counters and film badges.**

10.2 Rates of Nuclear Decay

☞ **Unlike chemical reaction rates, which vary with the conditions of a reaction, nuclear decay rates are constant.**

- A **half-life** is the time required for one half of a sample of a radioisotope to decay. Half-lifes can vary from fractions of a second to billions of years.
- Most materials contain at least trace amounts of radioisotopes. By looking at the rate of nuclear decay for these isotopes, scientists can estimate how old the materials are.

☞ **In radiocarbon dating, the age of an object is determined by comparing the object's carbon-14 levels with carbon-14 levels in the atmosphere.**

10.3 Artificial Transmutation

☞ **Scientists can perform artificial transmutations by bombarding atomic nuclei with high-energy particles such as protons, neutrons, or alpha particles.**

- **Transmutation** is the conversion of atoms of one element to atoms of another. It involves a nuclear change, not a chemical one.

☞ **Scientists can synthesize a transuranium element by the artificial transmutation of a lighter element.**

- Elements with atomic numbers greater than 92 (uranium) are called **transuranium elements.**
- A **quark** is a subatomic particle theorized to be among the basic units of matter.

10.4 Fission and Fusion

☞ **Over very short distances, the strong nuclear force is much greater than the electric forces among protons.**

- The **strong nuclear force** is the attractive force that binds protons and neutrons together in the nucleus. This force does not depend on charge.
- **Fission** is the splitting of an atomic nucleus into two smaller parts.

☞ **In nuclear fission, tremendous amounts of energy can be produced from very small amounts of mass.**

- In a **chain reaction,** neutrons released during the splitting of an initial nucleus trigger a series of nuclear fissions.
- A **critical mass** is the smallest possible mass of a fissionable material that can sustain a chain reaction.
- **Fusion** is a process in which the nuclei of two atoms combine to form a larger nucleus. During fusion, a small fraction of the reactant mass is converted into energy.
- **Plasma** is a state of matter in which atoms have been stripped of their electrons. Plasmas occur only at very high temperatures.

Chapter 10   Nuclear Chemistry

Section 10.1 Radioactivity
(pages 292–297)

This section discusses the different types of nuclear radiation and how they affect matter.

Reading Strategy (page 292)

Previewing Before you read the section, rewrite the topic headings in the table as *how, why,* and *what* questions. As you read, write an answer to each question. For more information on this Reading Strategy, see the **Reading and Study Skills** in the **Skills and Reference Handbook** at the end of your textbook.

Exploring Radioactivity	
Question	**Answer**
What is nuclear decay?	
	Alpha, beta, gamma
	Nuclear radiation can ionize atoms, molecules may change, and cellular function may break down.
How can nuclear radiation be detected?	

Nuclear Decay (pages 292–293)

1. Define radioactivity. _____

_____

2. A radioisotope is any atom that contains an unstable _____. Circle the correct answer.

   energy level   nucleus   orbital

Types of Nuclear Radiation (pages 293–296)

3. Circle the letters that identify each common type of nuclear radiation.

   a. X-rays
   b. gamma rays
   c. beta particles

4. Circle the letters that identify which groups of particles make up an alpha particle.

   a. two electrons   b. two protons   c. two neutrons

Chapter 10   Nuclear Chemistry

5. Circle the letters that identify each event that takes place during beta decay.

   a. A proton decomposes into a neutron and an electron.

   b. A neutron decomposes into a proton and an electron.

   c. An electron is emitted from the nucleus.

6. What is a gamma ray? _____

7. Use the terms in the box to complete the following table about nuclear radiation.

1–	4
Gamma ray	Alpha particle
Paper or clothing	0

Characteristics of Nuclear Radiation			
Radiation Type	Charge	Mass (amu)	Usually Stopped By
Alpha particle	2+		
Beta particle		$\frac{1}{1836}$	Aluminum sheet
	0		Several meters of concrete

Effects of Nuclear Radiation (pages 296–297)

8. Circle the letter of the correct answer. Why does nuclear radiation sometimes damage cells? _____

   a. It dries cells out.

   b. It strengthens chemical bonds.

   c. It ionizes atoms.

9. Is the following sentence true or false? One potential danger of radon gas is that prolonged exposure to it can lead to lung cancer.

   _____

Detecting Nuclear Radiation (page 297)

10. Geiger counters and film badges are used to detect _____.

Chapter 10   Nuclear Chemistry

Section 10.2 Rates of Nuclear Decay
(pages 298–301)

This section discusses half-lives and explains how nuclear decay can be used to estimate the age of objects.

Reading Strategy (page 298)

Identifying Details As you read, complete the concept map below to identify details about radiocarbon dating. For more information on this Reading Strategy, see the **Reading and Study Skills** in the **Skills and Reference Handbook** at the end of your textbook.

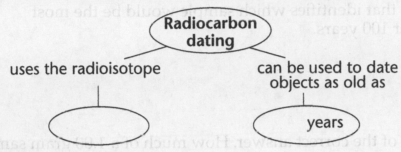

Half-life (pages 299–300)

1. Is the following sentence true or false? All radioisotopes decay at the same rate. _____

2. A half-life is the time required for one half of a sample of a _____ to decay

3. Circle the letter that describes a sample of a radioisotope after two half-lives.

    a. One eighth of the original sample is unchanged.

    b. One quarter of the original sample is unchanged.

    c. Half of the original sample is unchanged.

4. Circle the letter of the correct answer. Iodine-131 has a half-life of 8.07 days. What fraction of a sample of iodine-131 is left unchanged after 16.14 days?

    a. $\frac{1}{2}$

    b. $\frac{1}{4}$

    c. $\frac{1}{8}$

5. Is the following sentence true or false? Like chemical reaction rates, nuclear decay rates vary with the conditions of reaction. _____

Chapter 10   Nuclear Chemistry

Use the following table to answer questions 6 and 7.

Half-Lives of Selected Radioisotopes	
Isotope	**Half-life**
Radon-222	3.82 days
Iodine-131	8.07 days
Thorium-234	24.1 days
Radium-226	1620 years
Carbon-14	5730 years

6. Circle the letter that identifies which sample would be the most unchanged after 100 years.

   a. iodine-131

   b. radium-226

   c. radon-222

7. Circle the letter of the correct answer. How much of a 1.00 gram sample of radium-226 is left unchanged after 4860 years?

   a. 0.500 g

   b. 0.250 g

   c. 0.125 g

Radioactive Dating (pages 300–301)

8. Is the following sentence true or false? Plants and animals continue to absorb carbon from the atmosphere after they die. _____

9. Circle the letter of the correct answer. The age of an object can be determined in radiocarbon dating by comparing its carbon-14 levels with

   a. carbon-14 levels in the atmosphere.

   b. carbon-12 levels in the atmosphere.

   c. carbon-12 levels in the object.

10. Circle the letter of each characteristic of radiocarbon dating.

    a. Carbon-14 levels in the atmosphere can change over time.

    b. Carbon-14 levels in the atmosphere stay constant.

    c. Scientists often use objects of known age in radiocarbon dating.

11. Is the following sentence true or false? Radiocarbon dating is highly accurate in dating objects that are more than 50,000 years old.

   _____

Chapter 10   Nuclear Chemistry

Section 10.3 Artificial Transmutation
(pages 303–305)

This section discusses transmutations, transuranium elements, and particle accelerators.

Reading Strategy (page 303)

Monitoring Your Understanding Preview the Key Concepts, topic headings, vocabulary, and figures in this section. List two things you expect to learn. After reading, state what you learned about each item you listed. For more information on this Reading Strategy, see the **Reading and Study Skills** in the **Skills and Reference Handbook** at the end of your textbook.

Understanding Artificial Transmutation	
What I Expect to Learn	**What I Learned**

Nuclear Reactions in the Laboratory (page 303)

1. Define transmutation. _____

   _____

2. Bombarding atomic nuclei with high-energy particles such as protons, neutrons, or alpha particles causes _____. Circle the correct answer.

   artificial transmutations   natural transmutations   nuclear decay

3. Circle the letter that identifies the scientist who performed the first artificial transmutation.

   a. Ernest Rutherford

   b. Lise Meitner

   c. Enrico Fermi

Transuranium Elements (page 304)

4. Define a transuranium element. _____

   _____

5. Is the following sentence true or false? All transuranium elements are

   radioactive. _____

Chapter 10   Nuclear Chemistry

6. Scientists can synthesize a transuranium element by the artificial transmutation of a(n) _____ element. Circle the correct answer.

heavier   lighter   unstable

7. Circle the letter of the first transuranium element to be synthesized.

   a. plutonium
   b. americium
   c. neptunium

Particle Accelerators (page 305)

8. Is the following sentence true or false? A particle accelerator can accelerate charged particles to speeds very close to the speed of light.

   _____

9. What is a quark? _____

   _____

10. Circle the letter that identifies the number of quarks in each proton or neutron.

    a. zero
    b. two
    c. three

11. Use the terms in the box to complete the following concept map about alpha particles.

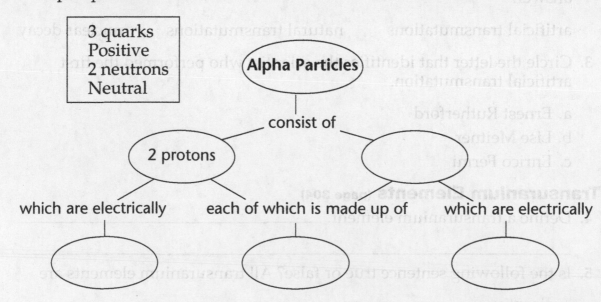

3 quarks
Positive
2 neutrons
Neutral

Chapter 10   Nuclear Chemistry

Section 10.4 Fission and Fusion
(pages 308–315)

This section discusses nuclear forces and the conversion of mass into energy. It also describes the nuclear processes of fission and fusion.

Reading Strategy (page 308)

Comparing and Contrasting As you read, contrast fission and fusion in the Venn diagram below by listing the ways they differ. For more information on this Reading Strategy, see the **Reading and Study Skills** in the **Skills and Reference Handbook** at the end of your textbook.

Contrasting Fission and Fusion

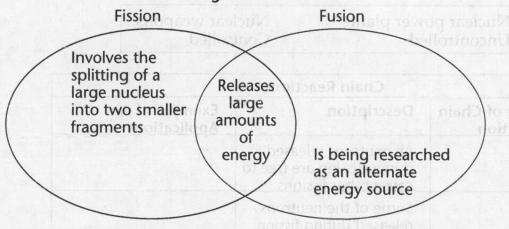

Fission — Involves the splitting of a large nucleus into two smaller fragments

Releases large amounts of energy

Fusion — Is being researched as an alternate energy source

Nuclear Forces (pages 308–309)

1. Define the strong nuclear force. _____

_____

2. Is the following sentence true or false? Over very short distances, the strong nuclear force is much greater than the electric forces among

protons. _____

3. Is the following sentence true or false? The strong nuclear force on a proton or neutron is much greater in a large nucleus than in a small

nucleus. _____

4. All nuclei with 83 or more _____ are radioactive. Circle the correct answer.

neutrons   protons   quarks

Fission (pages 309–313)

5. Define fission. _____

_____

Chapter 10   Nuclear Chemistry

6. Circle the letter that identifies what c represents in Einstein's mass-energy equation, $E = mc^2$.

   a. the charge on a proton

   b. the speed of light

   c. the charge on an electron

7. Is the following sentence true or false? During nuclear reactions mass is not conserved, but energy is conserved. _____

8. Use the terms in the box to complete the following table about chain reactions.

Nuclear power plants	Nuclear weapons
Uncontrolled	Controlled

Chain Reactions		
Type of Chain Reaction	**Description**	**Example of An Application**
	All neutrons released during fission are free to cause other fissions.	
	Some of the neutrons released during fission are absorbed by nonfissionable materials.	

9. Define a critical mass. _____

_____

Fusion (page 315)

10. The state of matter in which atoms have been stripped of their electrons is _____. Circle the correct answer.

    fusion   ion   plasma

11. Circle the letter of each main problem that scientists must face in designing a fusion reactor.

    a. Extremely high temperatures are necessary for a fusion reaction to start.

    b. The plasma that results from the reaction conditions must be contained.

    c. The hydrogen needed as a starting material is extremely scarce.

Chapter 10   Nuclear Chemistry

WordWise

Write the answer to each definition using one of the words below.

beta particle	radioactivity	fission
strong nuclear force	critical mass	nuclear radiation
gamma ray	fusion	alpha particle
radioisotope	quark	plasma

Definition   **Term**

A subatomic particle theorized to be among the basic _____
units of matter

Charged particles and energy that are emitted from the _____
nuclei of radioisotopes

A positively charged particle made up of two protons _____
and two neutrons

A state of matter in which atoms have been stripped _____
of their electrons

The process in which an unstable atomic nucleus emits _____
charged particles and energy

A penetrating ray of energy emitted by an unstable _____
nucleus

The attractive force that binds protons and neutrons _____
together in the nucleus

The splitting of an atomic nucleus into two _____
smaller parts

An electron emitted by an unstable nucleus _____

The smallest possible mass of a fissionable material _____
that can sustain a chain reaction

A process in which the nuclei of two atoms combine _____
to form a larger nucleus

Any atom containing an unstable nucleus _____

Chapter 10   Nuclear Chemistry

Nuclear Equations for Alpha Decay

Math Skill:
Formulas and
Equations

You may want to read
more about this **Math
Skill** in the **Skills and
Reference Handbook**
at the end of your
textbook.

Write a balanced nuclear equation for the alpha decay of
polonium-218.

1. Read and Understand

What information are you given?

Reactant isotope = polonium-218

Radiation emitted = $_2^4$He (alpha particle)

Use the periodic table to obtain the atomic number of polonium.

Reactant isotope = $_{84}^{218}$Po

2. Plan and Solve

What unknowns are you trying to calculate?

Atomic number of product isotope, Z = ?

Mass number of product isotope, A = ?

Chemical symbol of product isotope, X = ?

What equation contains the given information?

$$_{84}^{218}\text{Po} \longrightarrow {}_Z^A\text{X} + {}_2^4\text{He}$$

Write and solve equations for atomic mass and atomic number.

$218 = A + 4$	$84 = Z + 2$
$218 - 4 = A$	$84 - 2 = Z$
$214 = A$	$82 = Z$

On the periodic table, lead, Pb, has an atomic number of 82.
So, X is Pb. The balanced nuclear equation is shown below.

$$_{84}^{218}\text{Po} \longrightarrow {}_{82}^{214}\text{Pb} + {}_2^4\text{He}$$

3. Look Back and Check

Is your answer reasonable?

The mass number on the left equals the sum of the mass numbers on
the right. The atomic number on the left equals the sum of the atomic
numbers on the right. The equation is balanced.

Math Practice

On a separate sheet of paper, solve the following problem.

1. Write a balanced nuclear equation for the alpha decay of uranium-238.

Chapter 11 Motion

Summary

11.1 Distance and Displacement

To describe motion accurately and completely, a frame of reference is necessary.

- A **frame of reference** is a system of objects that are not moving with respect to one another.
- **Relative motion** is movement in relation to a frame of reference.

Distance is the length of the path between two points. Displacement is the direction from the starting point and the length of a straight line from the starting point to the ending point.

- Displacement gives information both about how far away an object is from a given point and in what direction the object is from that point. Displacement is a vector.

Add displacements using vector addition.

- A **vector** is a quantity that has magnitude and direction. The magnitude can be size, length, or amount.
- When two vectors have the same direction, you can add their magnitudes. When two vectors are in opposite directions, subtract one magnitude from the other.
- When two or more vectors have different directions, combine them by graphing.
- The **resultant vector** is the vector sum of two or more vectors.

11.2 Speed and Velocity

Average speed is computed for the entire duration of a trip, and instantaneous speed is measured at a particular instant.

- **Speed** is the ratio of the distance an object moves to the amount of time the object moves.
- **Average speed** is the total distance traveled divided by the time it takes to travel that distance. The formula for average speed is $\bar{v} = \dfrac{d}{t}$.
- **Instantaneous speed** is the rate at which an object is moving at a given moment in time.

The slope of a line on a distance-time graph is speed.

Velocity is a description of both speed and direction of motion. Velocity is a vector.

- Together, the speed and direction in which an object is moving are called **velocity**. A change in velocity can be the result of a change in speed, a change in direction, or both.

Two or more velocities add by vector addition.

11.3 Acceleration

◉ **Acceleration can be described as changes in speed, changes in direction, or changes in both. Acceleration is a vector.**

- The rate at which velocity changes is called **acceleration.**
- **Free fall** is the movement of an object toward Earth solely because of gravity.
- **Constant acceleration** is a steady change in velocity.

◉ **You calculate acceleration for straight-line motion by dividing the change in velocity by the total time.**

◉ **The slope of a speed-time graph is acceleration.**

- In a **linear graph**, the displayed data form straight-line parts.
- In a **nonlinear graph,** a curve connects the data points that are plotted.

◉ **Instantaneous acceleration is how fast a velocity is changing at a specific instant.**

Chapter 11 Motion

Section 11.1 Distance and Displacement
(pages 328–331)

This section defines distance and displacement. It presents methods of describing motion and introduces vector addition and subtraction.

Reading Strategy (page 328)

Predicting Write a definition for *frame of reference* in your own words in the left column of the table. After you read the section, compare your definition to the scientific definition and write a correct definition. For more information on this Reading Strategy, see the **Reading and Study Skills** in the **Skills and Reference Handbook** at the end of your textbook.

Frame of Reference	
Frame of reference probably means	Frame of reference actually means

Choosing a Frame of Reference (pages 328–329)

1. Is the following sentence true or false? A frame of reference is not

   necessary to describe motion accurately and completely. _____

2. Movement in relation to a frame of reference is called _____. Circle the correct answer.

   distance   motion   relative motion

3. Imagine that you are a passenger in a car. Circle the letter of the best frame of reference you could use to determine how fast the car is moving relative to the ground.

   a. the people sitting next to you in the backseat

   b. a van traveling in the lane next to your car

   c. a signpost on the side of the road

Measuring Distance (page 329)

4. Define distance. _____.

5. Circle the letter of the SI unit best suited for measuring the length of a room in your home.

   a. kilometers

   b. meters

   c. centimeters

Chapter 11   Motion

Measuring Displacements (page 330)

6. Is the following sentence true or false? Five blocks south is an example

of a displacement. _____

7. What would your total displacement be if you walked from your front
door, around the block, and then stopped when you reached your
front door again? Circle the letter of the correct answer.

    a. one block

    b. zero

    c. the entire distance of your trip

Combining Displacements (pages 330–331)

8. A vector is a quantity that has both _____ and _____.
Circle the best answer(s).

    direction   speed   magnitude

9. Circle the letter of each answer that could describe the magnitude of a
vector.

    a. length

    b. direction

    c. amount

For questions 10 and 11, refer to the figure below.

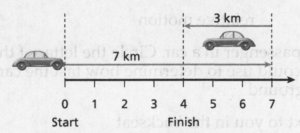

10. The magnitudes of the two displacement vectors are

_____ and _____.

11. Because the two displacements are in opposite directions, the

magnitude of the total displacement is _____.

12. The vector sum of two or more other vectors is called the
_____. Circle the correct answer.

    added vector   displacement vector   resultant vector

Chapter 11   Motion

Section 11.2 Speed and Velocity
(pages 332–337)

This section defines and compares speed and velocity. It also describes how to calculate average speed.

Reading Strategy (page 332)

Monitoring Your Understanding After you read this section, identify several things you have learned that are relevant to your life. Explain why they are relevant to you. For more information on this Reading Strategy, see the **Reading and Study Skills** in the **Skills and Reference Handbook** at the end of your textbook.

Facts About Speed and Velocity	
What Is Important	**Why It Is Important**

Speed (pages 332–334)

1. Define speed. _____

_____

2. Circle the letter of each sentence that is true for either instantaneous speed or average speed, but not both.

   a. It is measured in meters per second.

   b. It is measured at a particular instance.

   c. It is computed for an entire trip.

3. Is the following sentence true or false? You can determine how fast you were going at the midpoint of a trip by calculating average speed for the

   entire trip. _____

4. A student walked 2 km in .5 hour. Circle the letter of his average speed on the way to school.

   a. 0.5 km/h

   b. 1.5 km/h

   c. 4.0 km/h

Chapter 11   Motion

Graphing Motion (page 334)

For questions 5 through 8, refer to the graph below.

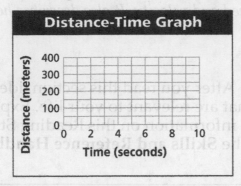

Distance-Time Graph

5. Draw a point on the graph that represents 200 m traveled in 4 seconds. Draw a line connecting this point with the origin (0,0). Label this as line A.

6. Draw a point on the graph that represents 100 m traveled in 10 seconds. Draw a line connecting this point with the origin (0,0). Label this as line B.

7. Circle the letter of the average speed (slope) of line A.

    a. 10 m/s   b. 20 m/s   c. 50 m/s

8. Circle the letter of the average speed (slope) of line B.

    a. 10 m/s   b. 20 m/s   c. 50 m/s

Velocity (page 336)

9. Circle the letter of each sentence that describes a change in velocity.

    a. A moving object gains speed.
    b. A moving object changes direction.
    c. A moving object moves in a straight line at a constant speed.

10. Is the following sentence true or false? If a car travels around a gentle curve on a highway at 60 km/h, the velocity does not change.

    _____

Combining Velocities (page 337)

11. How do velocities combine? Circle the correct answer.

    a. by vector addition
    b. by vector subtraction
    c. by vector graphing

Chapter 11   Motion

Section 11.3 Acceleration
(pages 342–348)

This section describes the relationships among speed, velocity, and acceleration. It discusses examples of these concepts. It also shows sample calculations of acceleration and graphs representing accelerated motion.

Reading Strategy (page 342)

Summarizing Read the section on acceleration. Then complete the concept map to organize what you know about acceleration. For more information on this Reading Strategy, see the **Reading and Study Skills** in the **Skills and Reference Handbook** at the end of your textbook.

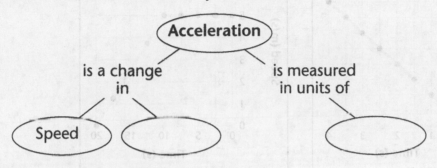

What Is Acceleration? (pages 342–345)

1. The rate at which velocity changes is called _____.

2. Circle the letter for each way an object can accelerate.

    a. change in speed

    b. change in velocity

    c. change in direction

3. Circle the letter of the correct answer. A horse on a carousel that is moving at a constant speed is accelerating because _____.

    a. its direction constantly changes

    b. its speed constantly changes

    c. its height constantly changes

Calculating Acceleration (pages 345–346)

4. Circle the letter of the equation used to calculate the acceleration of an object.

    a. acceleration = change in velocity

    b. acceleration = change in velocity/total time

    c. acceleration = total time/change in velocity

Chapter 11   Motion

5. Is the following sentence true or false? When the final velocity is less than the initial velocity of an object, the acceleration is negative. _____

Graphs of Accelerated Motion (pages 346–348)

For questions 6 through 9, refer to the graphs below.

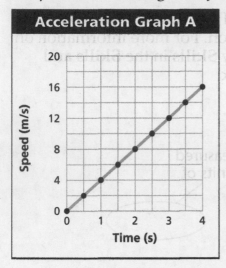

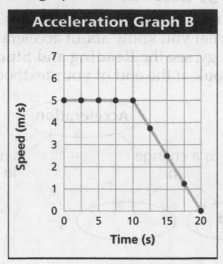

6. Graph A represents the motion of a downhill skier. How fast was the

   skier moving after traveling down the hill for 2.5 seconds? _____

7. In which graph does an object move at constant speed during the first

   4 seconds? _____

8. Is the following sentence true or false? If Graph B represents the motion of a mountain biker, then the biker's speed at times of 10 s is 5 m/s.

   _____

9. Graph B represents the motion of a mountain biker. Determine the biker's acceleration during the 10 second to 20 second time period.

   Show your work. _____

   _____

Instantaneous Acceleration (page 348)

10. The measure of how fast a velocity is changing at a specific instant is known as _____. Circle the correct answer.

    a. average acceleration

    b. constant acceleration

    c. instantaneous acceleration

Chapter 11   Motion

WordWise

Complete the sentences by using one of the vocabulary words below.

speed	acceleration	linear
vector	relative motion	nonlinear
free fall	frame of reference	velocity
distance	average speed	resultant vector

An expression for _____ is $(v_f - v_i)/t$.

A quantity that has both magnitude and direction is called
a(n)_____.

The total distance traveled divided by the total time is _____.

A speed-time graph in which data points form a straight line is an example
of a(n) _____ graph.

Common units for _____ include meters per second (m/s).

In order to accurately and completely describe the motion of an object, a(n)
_____ is necessary.

You can determine _____ by measuring the length of the actual
path between two points in space.

Two or more vectors combine to form a(n) _____.

Objects in _____ accelerate at 9.8 m/s^2.

A curve often connects data points on a(n) _____ graph.

Together, the speed and direction in which an object is moving are called
_____.

Movement in relation to a frame of reference is _____.

Interpreting a Distance-Time Graph

The distance-time graph below illustrates the motion of a car whose speed varied with time during a trip. Calculate the average speed of the car during the first 8 seconds of the trip.

Math Skill:
Line Graphs and Conversion Factors

You may want to read more about this **Math Skill** in the **Skills and Reference Handbook** at the end of your textbook.

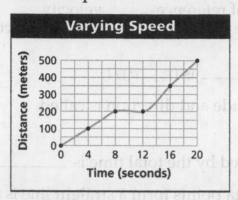

1. Read and Understand

What information are you given?

A graph of distance versus time.

2. Plan and Solve

How will you determine speed for the time interval referenced in the question?

1. To determine the distance traveled in 8 s, move your finger up from the 8 s mark on the time axis to the plotted line.

2. Now move your finger horizontally to the left to the distance axis. Read the value from the axis. (200 m)

3. Calculate the average speed using the formula

Speed = Distance/Time = 200 m/8 s = 25 m/s

3. Look Back and Check

Is your answer reasonable?

A quick calculation from the interval of constant speed shows that the car traveled 100 meters in 4 seconds—an average speed of 25 m/s.

Math Practice

On a separate sheet of paper, solve the following problems.

1. How long did it take the car to travel a distance of 350 m? _____

2. Determine the speed of the car during the interval 0 s to 12 s.

Chapter 12 Forces and Motion

Summary

12.1 Forces

☞ **A force can cause a resting object to move, or it can accelerate a moving object by changing the object's speed or direction.**

- A **force** is a push or a pull that acts on an object. One **newton** is the force that causes a 1-kilogram mass to accelerate at a rate of 1 meter per second each second.
- The **net force** is the overall force acting on an object after all the forces are combined.

☞ **When the forces on an object are balanced, the net force is zero and there is no change in the object's motion.**

☞ **When an unbalanced force acts on an object, the object accelerates.**

☞ **There are four main types of friction: static friction, sliding friction, rolling friction, and fluid friction.**

- **Friction** is a force that opposes the motion of objects that touch as they move past each other.
- **Static friction** is the friction force that acts on objects that are not moving.
- **Sliding friction** is a force that opposes an object's direction of motion as it slides over a surface.
- **Rolling friction** is the friction force that acts on rolling objects.
- The force of **fluid friction** opposes an object's motion through a fluid. **Air resistance** is fluid friction that acts on an object moving through the air.

☞ **Earth's gravity acts downward toward the center of Earth.**

- **Gravity** is a force that acts between any two masses. It is an attractive force.

☞ **Gravity causes objects to accelerate downward, whereas air resistance acts in the direction opposite to the motion and reduces acceleration.**

- **Terminal velocity** is the constant velocity of a falling object when the force of air resistance equals the force of gravity.

☞ **The combination of an initial forward velocity and the downward vertical force of gravity causes the ball to follow a curved path.**

- **Projectile motion** is a falling object's motion after it is given a forward velocity.

12.2 Newton's First and Second Laws of Motion

☞ According to Newton's first law of motion, the state of motion of an object does not change as long as the net force acting on the object is zero.

- **Inertia** is the tendency of an object to resist a change in its motion.

☞ According to Newton's second law of motion, the acceleration of an object is equal to the net force acting on it divided by the object's mass.

☞ Mass is a measure of the inertia of an object; weight is a measure of the force of gravity acting on an object.

- **Mass** depends on the amount of matter the object contains.

12.3 Newton's Third Law of Motion and Momentum

☞ According to Newton's third law of motion, whenever one object exerts a force on a second object, the second object exerts an equal and opposite force on the first object.

☞ An object has a large momentum if the product of its mass and velocity is large.

- **Momentum** is the product of an object's mass and its velocity.
- According to the **law of conservation of momentum**, if no net force acts on a system, then the total momentum of the system does not change.

☞ In a closed system, the loss of momentum of one object equals the gain in momentum of another object—momentum is conserved.

12.4 Universal Forces

☞ Electric force and magnetic force are the only forces that can both attract and repel.

- **Electromagnetic force** is associated with charged particles.

☞ Two forces, the strong nuclear force and the weak nuclear force, act within the nucleus to hold it together.

- The **strong nuclear force** is a powerful force of attraction that acts only on the neutrons and protons in the nucleus, holding them together.
- The **weak nuclear force** is an attractive force that acts only over a short range.
- **Gravitational force** is an attractive force that acts between any two masses.

☞ Newton's law of universal gravitation states that every object in the universe attracts every other object.

- A **centripetal force** is a center-directed force that continuously changes an object's direction to make it move in a circle.

Chapter 12   Forces and Motion

Section 12.1 Forces
(pages 356–362)

This section describes what forces are and explains how forces affect the motion of various objects.

Reading Strategy (page 356)

Relating Text and Visuals As you read about forces, look carefully at Figures 2, 3, and 5 in your textbook. Then complete the table by describing the forces and motion shown in each figure. For more information on this Reading Strategy, see the **Reading and Study Skills** in the **Skills and Reference Handbook** at the end of your textbook.

Forces and Motion		
Figure	**Is Net Force 0?**	**Effect on Motion**
2A	Yes	None
2B		
3		
5A		
5B		

What Is a Force? (pages 356–357)

1. A force is defined as a(n) _____ or a(n) _____ that acts on an object.

2. Is the following sentence true or false? A force can act to cause an object at rest to move or it can accelerate an object that is already moving. _____

3. Circle the letter of the best answer. What force causes a 1-kg mass to accelerate at a rate of 1 meter per second each second?

   a. $1 \text{ kg/m} \cdot \text{s}^2$ b. 1 kg/s   c. 1 newton

Combining Forces (pages 357–358)

4. The combination of all the forces acting on an object is the

   _____.

5. Circle the letter of the correct answer. How do unbalanced forces affect the motion of an object?

   a. no change because the net force is zero

   b. no change because the net force is negative

   c. acceleration because the net force is not zero

Chapter 12   Forces and Motion

Friction (pages 359–360)

6. Is the following sentence true or false? Friction is a force that helps objects that are touching move past each other more easily.

_____

7. Circle the letters that identify types of friction.

    a. rolling
    b. gravity
    c. sliding

8. The friction force that acts on objects that are at rest is _____.

9. Use the terms in the box to complete the table below about friction forces.

> In-line skates
> Sliding
> Walking

Types of Friction Forces	
Friction Force	**Example**
Static	
	Pushing a book along your desk
Rolling	

10. Is the following sentence true or false? Fluid friction is a force that opposes the motion of an object through a fluid such as water.

_____

Gravity (page 361)

11. Gravity is a(n) _____ force that pulls objects together.

12. Is the following sentence true or false? Earth's gravity acts downward toward the center of Earth. _____

13. Is the following sentence true or false? Terminal velocity is the constant velocity of a falling object when the force of air resistance equals the force of gravity. _____

Projectile Motion (page 362)

14. The curved path caused by the combination of an initial forward velocity and the downward force of gravity is known as

_____ motion.

Chapter 12   Forces and Motion

Section 12.2 Newton's First and Second Laws of Motion
(pages 363–369)

This section discusses how force and mass affect acceleration. It also defines acceleration due to gravity and compares mass and weight.

Reading Strategy (page 363)

Building Vocabulary As you read this section, write a definition in the table for each vocabulary word you encounter. Use your own words in the definitions. For more information on this Reading Strategy, see the **Reading and Study Skills** in the **Skills and Reference Handbook** at the end of your textbook.

Matter and Motion	
Vocabulary	**Definition**
Inertia	
Mass	
Weight	

Aristotle, Galileo, and Newton (pages 363–364)

Match each scientist with his accomplishment.

Accomplishment

_____ **1.** Italian scientist who experimented with force and motion

_____ **2.** Scientist who introduced laws describing force and motion

_____ **3.** An ancient Greek philosopher who made many scientific discoveries through observation and logical reasoning

Scientist

a. Aristotle

b. Galileo

c. Newton

Newton's First Law of Motion (pages 364–365)

4. Is the following sentence true or false? According to Newton's first law of motion, an object's state of motion does not change as long as the net force acting on it is zero. _____

5. What is inertia? _____

_____

Newton's Second Law of Motion (pages 365–368)

6. According to Newton's second law of motion, acceleration of an object depends upon the _____ of the object and the _____ acting on it. Circle the best answers.

   inertia   mass   net force

Match each term with its description.

Description	Term
_____ 7. A measure of the inertia of an object	a. mass
_____ 8. Net force/Mass	b. net force
_____ 9. Causes an object's velocity to change	c. acceleration

10. Is the following sentence true or false? The acceleration of an object is always in the same direction as the net force acting on the

    object._____

11. Is the following sentence true or false? If the same force acts upon two objects with different masses, the acceleration will be greater for the

    object with greater mass. _____

Weight and Mass (pages 368–369)

12. What is weight? _____

    _____

13. Circle the letter of the formula used to calculate the weight of an object.

    a. weight = mass × velocity of an object
    b. weight = mass × acceleration of an object
    c. weight = mass × acceleration due to gravity

14. Is the following sentence true or false? Because the weight formula shows that mass and weight are proportional, doubling the mass of an

    object will not affect its weight. _____

15. On the moon, the acceleration due to gravity is only about one sixth that on Earth. Will an object weigh more or less on the moon than it

    weighs on Earth? _____

Chapter 12   Forces and Motion

Section 12.3 Newton's Third Law of Motion and Momentum
(pages 372–377)

This section describes action-reaction forces and how the momentum of objects is determined.

Reading Strategy (page 372)

Summarizing As you read about momentum in this section, complete the concept map to organize what you learn. For more information on this Reading Strategy, see the **Reading and Study Skills** in the **Skills and Reference Handbook** at the end of your textbook.

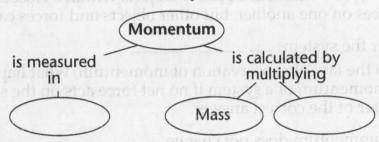

Newton's Third Law (page 373)

1. According to Newton's third law of motion, whenever one object exerts a force on a second object, the second object exerts _____ on the first object. Circle the best answer.

   a. an equal force

   b. an opposite force

   c. an equal and opposite force

2. Circle the letters that identify each sentence that is true about action-reaction forces.

   a. All action-reaction forces produce motion.

   b. Forces always exist in pairs.

   c. Action-reaction forces never cancel.

Momentum (pages 374–375)

3. Circle the letter of each factor that affects the momentum of a moving object.

   a. mass

   b. volume

   c. velocity

4. Is the following sentence true or false? An object with a small mass can have a large momentum if the object is traveling at a high speed.

_____

5. Circle the letter of the object that has the greatest momentum.

a. a 700-gram bird flying at a velocity of 2.5 m/s

b. a 40-kilogram shopping cart rolling along at 0.5 m/s

c. a 300-kilogram roller coaster car traveling at 25 m/s

Conservation of Momentum (pages 376–377)

6. Is the following sentence true or false? Objects within a closed system can exert forces on one another, but other objects and forces cannot leave or enter the system. _____

7. According to the law of conservation of momentum, what happens to the total momentum of a system if no net force acts on the system? Circle the letter of the correct answer.

a. The total momentum does not change.

b. The total momentum decreases.

c. The total momentum increases.

8. Is the following sentence true or false? In a closed system with two objects, the loss of momentum of one object equals the gain in momentum of the other object. _____

For questions 9 and 10, refer to the graph below.

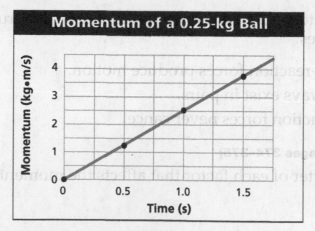

9. The momentum of the ball at 1 second is _____.

10. What is the speed of the ball at 0.5 seconds? Show your calculation. Use the momentum formula, momentum = mass × velocity.

Chapter 12   Forces and Motion

Section 12.4 Universal Forces
(pages 378–382)

This section defines four forces that exist throughout the universe. It describes each force and discusses its significance.

Reading Strategy (page 378)

Comparing and Contrasting As you read this section, compare two universal forces by completing the table. For more information on this Reading Strategy, see the **Reading and Study Skills** in the **Skills and Reference Handbook** at the end of your textbook.

Universal Nuclear Forces			
Force	Acts on Which Particles?	Acts Over What Distance?	Relative Strength
Strong nuclear		Very short	
Weak nuclear			Weaker than the strong force

Electromagnetic Forces (pages 378–379)

1. Is the following sentence true or false? Electromagnetic force is

   associated with charged particles. _____

2. Circle the two forces that can both attract and repel.

   electric force   gravitational force   magnetic force

3. Complete the sentence using the words *attract* and *repel*. Objects with like

   charges _____ one another, and objects with opposite

   charges _____ one another.

4. Circle the letters of the sentences that correctly describe magnets or magnetic forces.

   a. Magnetic forces act on certain metals.

   b. Magnets have two poles, north and south.

   c. Two poles that are alike attract each other.

Nuclear Forces (pages 379–380)

5. The force that holds particles in the nucleus together is the

   _____.

Chapter 12   Forces and Motion

6. Nuclear forces are strong enough to overcome the electric force of repulsion that acts among the positively charged _____ in the nucleus. Circle the correct answer.

   neutrons   particles   protons

7. Circle the letter of the best answer. Over extremely short distances, approximately how many times stronger is the strong nuclear force than the electric force of repulsion?

   a. 10

   b. 100

   c. 1000

Gravitational Force (pages 380–382)

8. Newton's law of universal gravitation states that every object in

   the universe _____ every other object.

9. Circle the letter of each sentence that is true about gravitational force.

   a. The farther apart two objects are, the weaker the gravitational force.

   b. The greater the mass of an object, the stronger its gravitational force.

   c. Earth's gravitational force is stronger than the gravitational force of the sun.

10. The gravitational force of attraction between two objects depends on _____ and _____. Circle the best answers.

    mass   velocity   distance

11. Is the following sentence true or false? Gravity is the weakest universal force, but it is the most effective force over long distances.

    _____

12. The sun's mass is much greater than the mass of Earth, so the sun's

    gravitational force is much _____ than that of Earth.

13. Is the following sentence true or false? The gravitational pull of the

    moon is the primary cause of Earth's ocean tides. _____

14. Is the following sentence true or false? An artificial satellite in a high orbit will slow down and lose altitude due to the pull of Earth's

    gravity. _____

Name _____ Class _____ Date _____

WordWise

Complete the sentences using one of the words below.

friction	momentum	weight
mass	gravity	newtons
net force	acceleration	inertia
fluid friction	weak nuclear	

A measure of an object's inertia is its _____.

The _____ force affects all particles in a nucleus and acts only over a short range.

A sky diver experiences _____, which opposes the force of gravity.

A change in an object's speed or direction of motion is called _____.

The product of an object's mass and its velocity is _____.

A measure of the force of gravity acting on an object is its _____.

Mass is the measure of the _____ of an object.

A force that opposes the motion of objects that touch as they move past each other is called _____.

The universal force that causes every object to attract every other object is _____.

A person's weight on Mars, measured in _____, is 0.38 times the weight on Earth.

Acceleration equals _____ divided by mass.

Chapter 12   Forces and Motion

Calculating Acceleration

A car with a mass of 1300 kg accelerates as it leaves a parking lot. If the net force on the car is 3900 newtons, what is the car's *acceleration*?

Math Skill: Formulas and Equations

You may want to read more about this **Math Skill** in the **Skills and Reference Handbook** at the end of your textbook.

1. Read and Understand

What information are you given?

Mass , m = 1300 kg

Force, F = 3900 N (in the forward direction)

2. Plan and Solve

What unknown are you trying to calculate?

Acceleration, a = ?

What formula contains the given quantities and the unknown?

$$a = \frac{F}{m}$$

Replace each variable with its known value and solve.

$$a = \frac{3900 \text{ N}}{1300 \text{ kg}} = 3 \ \frac{\text{N}}{\text{kg}} = 3 \ \frac{\text{kg} \cdot \text{m/s}^2}{\text{kg}} = 3 \text{ m/s}^2$$

a = 3 m/s² in the forward direction

3. Look Back and Check

Is your answer reasonable?

Powerful sports cars can accelerate at 6 m/s², so a smaller acceleration of 3 m/s² seems reasonable.

Math Practice

On a separate sheet of paper, solve the following problems.

1. A construction worker pushes a wheelbarrow with a total mass of 50.0 kg. What is the acceleration of the wheelbarrow if the net force on it is 75 N?

2. A van with a mass of 1500 kg accelerates at a rate of 3.5 m/s² in the forward direction. What is the net force acting on the van? (*Hint:* Solve the acceleration formula for force.)

Chapter 13 Forces in Fluids

Summary

13.1 Fluid Pressure

👄 To calculate pressure, divide the force by the area over which the force acts.

- The force is measured in newtons (N), and the area in square meters (m^2).
- The SI unit of pressure is a **pascal**. It is equal to newtons per square meter.
- **Pressure** is the result of a force distributed over an area.

👄 Water pressure increases as depth increases. The pressure in a fluid at any given depth is constant, and it is exerted equally in all directions.

- A **fluid** is a substance that takes the shape of its container.
- Both liquids and gases are fluids.
- A fluid exerts pressure. The shape of a fluid's container and the area of its bottom do not affect fluid pressure.

👄 Air pressure decreases as altitude increases.

- The atmosphere is exerting more than 1000 newtons of force on the top of your head.
- The inside of your body also exerts pressure, and that pressure balances the air pressure outside.

13.2 Forces and Pressure in Fluids

👄 According to Pascal's principle, a change in pressure at any point in a fluid is transmitted equally and unchanged in all directions throughout the fluid.

- A **hydraulic system** is a device that uses pressurized fluid acting on pistons of different sizes to change a force.
- In a hydraulic system, an input force is applied to a small piston, which pushes against the fluid sealed in the hydraulic system. The pressure produced by the small piston is transmitted through the fluid to the large piston.

👄 In a hydraulic lift system, an increased output force is produced because a constant fluid pressure is exerted on the larger area of the output piston.

👄 According to Bernoulli's principle, as the speed of a fluid increases, the pressure within the fluid decreases.

- The air traveling over the top of an airplane wing moves faster than the air passing underneath. This creates a low-pressure area above the wing.
- The pressure difference between the top and the bottom of the wing creates an upward force known as **lift**.

13.3 Buoyancy

💬 **Buoyancy results in the apparent loss of weight of an object in a fluid.**

- **Buoyancy** is the ability of a fluid to exert an upward force on an object placed in it.
- The upward force that acts in the opposite direction of gravity is called **buoyant force.**
- According to **Archimedes' principle,** the buoyant force on an object is equal to the weight of the fluid displaced by the object.
- Density and buoyancy are closely related. They both involve the ratio of an object's mass to its volume.

💬 **If an object is less dense than the fluid it is in, it will float. If the object is more dense than the fluid it is in, it will sink.**

💬 **When the buoyant force is equal to the weight, an object floats or is suspended. When the buoyant force is less than the weight, the object sinks.**

Chapter 13   Forces in Fluids

Section 13.1 Fluid Pressure
(pages 390–393)

This section defines pressure and describes factors that determine fluid pressure. The atmosphere as a fluid is discussed, including how air pressure changes with altitude.

Reading Strategy (page 390)

Using Prior Knowledge Before reading the section, write a common definition of the word *pressure*. After you have read the section, write the scientific definition of *pressure* and contrast it to your original definition. For more information on this Reading Strategy, see the **Reading and Study Skills** in the **Skills and Reference Handbook** at the end of your textbook.

Meanings of *Pressure*	
Common definition	
Scientific definition	

Pressure (pages 390–391)

1. Pressure is the result of a(n) _____ distributed over

    a(n) _____ .

2. The same force is exerted by each of the following. Which exerts the most pressure?

    a. a foot

    b. a large book

    c. the tip of a ballpoint pen

3. Circle the letter of the equation that shows how to calculate pressure.

    a. pressure = area/force

    b. pressure = force/area

    c. pressure = N/m²

Pressure in Fluids (pages 391–392)

4. A substance that assumes the shape of its container is called a(n)

    _____ .

5. List three examples of fluids.

    a. _____

    b. _____

    c. _____

6. Circle the letter of each sentence that is true about fluid pressure.

   a. Fluid pressure is exerted only at the base of the container holding the fluid.

   b. The pressure in a fluid at any given depth is constant, and it is exerted equally in all directions.

   c. The two factors that determine the pressure a fluid exerts are the type of fluid and its depth.

7. Is the following sentence true or false? The pressure at a depth of 2 feet in a large lake is greater than the pressure at the same depth in a swimming pool. _____

Air Pressure and the Atmosphere (pages 392–393)

For questions 8 through 10, refer to the air pressure table below.

Changes in Air Pressure With Altitude		
Altitude Above Sea Level (m)	Air Pressure (bars)	Air Pressure (kPa)
0	1.000	
200	0.9971	
400		96.68
600		94.42
800	0.9103	92.21
1000	0.8888	
1200	0.8677	87.89

8. Complete the air pressure columns in the table by converting between units of air pressure. *Hint:* 1 bar = 101.3 kPa.

9. Does air pressure increase or decrease as a function of altitude?

   _____

10. Suppose a hiker is on a mountain ridge 1200 meters above sea level. Approximately what air pressure will she experience?

    _____

11. Is the following sentence true or false? Air exerts a force of more than 1000 N on top of your head. _____

Chapter 13   Forces in Fluids

Section 13.2 Forces and Pressure in Fluids
(pages 394–397)

This section presents Pascal's and Bernoulli's principles. It also discusses examples of each principle from nature and industry.

Reading Strategy (page 394)

Predicting Imagine two small foam balls hanging from strings at the same height with about 3 centimeters of space between them. Before you read the section, write a prediction about what will happen to the balls when you blow air through the space between them. Identify your reasons. After you have read the section, check the accuracy of your prediction. For more information on this Reading Strategy, see the **Reading and Study Skills** in the **Skills and Reference Handbook** at the end of your textbook.

Predicting Forces and Pressure in Fluids	
Prediction	
Reason for Prediction	

Transmitting Pressure in a Fluid (pages 394–395)

1. In a fluid-filled container, the pressure is greater _____ of the container. Circle the correct answer.

   at the top   in the middle   at the bottom

2. Is the following sentence true or false? If you squeeze a container filled with fluid, the pressure within the fluid increases equally throughout

   the fluid. _____

3. In a hydraulic lift system, an increased output force is produced because

   constant _____ is exerted on the larger area of the output piston.

4. Is the following sentence true or false? In a hydraulic system, the output force is greater than the input force because the pressure acting on the output piston is greater than the pressure acting on the input piston.

   _____

Bernoulli's Principle (pages 396–397)

5. Circle the letter of the sentence that correctly states Bernoulli's principle.

   a. As the speed of a fluid decreases, the pressure within the fluid decreases.

   b. As the speed of a fluid increases, the pressure within the fluid increases.

   c. As the speed of a fluid increases, the pressure within the fluid decreases.

6. Because the air traveling over the top of an airplane wing moves faster than the air passing underneath the wing, the pressure above the wings is _____ than the pressure below the wing.

For questions 7 through 10, refer to the figure below. Place the correct letter after each phrase.

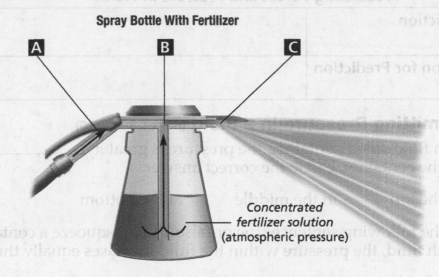

Spray Bottle With Fertilizer

Concentrated fertilizer solution (atmospheric pressure)

7. Location where the water and fertilizer solution mix. _____

8. Location where water enters the sprayer at high speed. _____

9. Location where the water-fertilizer mixture exits the sprayer. _____

10. Circle the principle that explains why the fertilizer solution moves up the tube.

    a. Archimedes' principle

    b. Bernoulli's principle

    c. Pascal's principle

Chapter 13   Forces in Fluids

Section 13.3 Buoyancy
(pages 400–404)

This section discusses buoyancy and Archimedes' principle of factors that determine whether an object will sink or float in a fluid.

Reading Strategy (page 400)

Summarizing As you read about buoyancy, write a brief summary of the text following each green heading. Your summary should include only the most important information. For more information on this Reading Strategy, see the **Reading and Study Skills** in the **Skills and Reference Handbook** at the end of your textbook.

Buoyant Force	Buoyant force is the apparent loss of weight of an object submerged in a fluid.

Buoyant Force (page 400)

1. What is buoyancy? _____

_____

2. Circle the letter of the correct answer. In which direction does a buoyant force act?

    a. in the direction of gravity
    b. perpendicular to gravity
    c. in the direction opposite of gravity

3. Is the following sentence true or false? The greater a fluid's density,

    the greater its buoyant force. _____

4. Circle the letter of each sentence that is true about buoyancy.

    a. Forces pushing up on a submerged object are greater than the forces pushing down on it.

    b. Forces acting on the sides of a submerged object cancel each other out.

    c. Gravitational forces work together with buoyant forces.

Chapter 13   Forces in Fluids

Archimedes' Principle (page 401)

5. According to Archimedes' principle, the weight of fluid displaced by a floating object is equal to the _____ acting on that object. Circle the correct answer.

   buoyant force   fluid pressure   gravity

6. Is the following sentence true or false? When an object floats partially submerged in a fluid, it displaces a volume of fluid equal to its own volume. _____

Density and Buoyancy (pages 401–404)

Match each description with the correct property. Properties may be used more than once.

Description	Property
_____ 7. This property is the ratio of an object's mass to its volume, often expressed in g/cm³.	a. weight
	b. buoyant force
_____ 8. This force is equal to the force of gravity that acts on a floating object.	c. density
_____ 9. When this property is greater for an object than for the fluid it is in, the object sinks.	
_____ 10. These two forces act on every object in a fluid.	

11. Use what you know about density and buoyancy to predict whether each of the substances listed in the table will float or sink in water. The density of water is 1.0 g/cm³.

Will It Float or Sink?		
Substance	Density (g/cm³)	Float or Sink?
Gold	19.3	
Balsa Wood	0.15	Float
Ice	0.92	
Brick	1.84	Sink
Milk	1.03	
Gasoline	0.70	

Chapter 13   Forces in Fluids

WordWise

Use the clues and the words in the list to help you write the vocabulary terms from the chapter in the blanks. Then find and circle the terms in the puzzle. The terms may occur vertically, horizontally, or diagonally.

```
h  y  d  r  a  u  l  i  c  s  y  s  t  e  m
v  a  h  u  s  p  i  a  c  f  r  h  y  e  b
s  r  q  a  z  f  f  r  e  r  f  v  d  c  q
p  c  i  u  y  t  t  p  r  e  s  s  u  r  e
t  h  d  f  r  g  s  f  l  u  t  m  a  o  e
k  i  u  b  p  l  o  e  k  j  h  t  u  f  z
k  m  t  y  u  i  r  f  l  u  i  d  l  t  d
v  e  k  p  o  o  p  f  v  b  n  m  i  n  m
o  d  k  a  r  p  y  o  i  m  q  c  c  a  f
p  e  g  s  y  h  z  a  v  b  n  h  s  y  b
p  s  e  c  u  h  n  j  n  m  l  o  m  o  q
l  r  i  a  j  u  e  r  t  c  v  f  d  u  a
p  o  i  l  m  j  g  b  h  f  y  u  j  b  o
```

Archimedes
buoyancy
buoyant force
fluid
hydraulic system
lift
pascal
pressure

Clues   Hidden Words

Mathematician who discovered that the buoyant   _____
force on an object equals the weight of the fluid
displaced by the object

The result of a force distributed over an area   _____

Type of substance that assumes the shape of   _____
its container

Ability of a fluid to exert an upward force   _____
on an object within it

SI unit of measure used to express pressure   _____

Upward force that keeps an aircraft aloft   _____

Device that uses pressurized fluids acting on   _____
pistons of different sizes to change a force

Force that opposes the weight of an object   _____
floating in a fluid

Chapter 13 Forces in Fluids

Calculating Pressure

Each tile on the bottom of a swimming pool has an area of 0.50 m². The water above each tile exerts a force of 11,000 N on each tile. How much pressure does the water exert on each tile?

Math Skill:
Formulas and
Equations

You may want to read more about this **Math Skill** in the **Skills and Reference Handbook** at the end of your textbook.

1. Read and Understand

What information are you given?

   Force = 11,000 N

   Area = 0.50 m²

2. Plan and Solve

What formula contains the given quantities and the unknown?

$$\text{Pressure} = \frac{\text{Force}}{\text{Area}}$$

Replace each variable with its known value and solve.

$$\text{Pressure} = \frac{11,000 \text{ N}}{0.50 \text{ m}^2} = 22,000 \text{ N/m}^2 = 22,000 \text{ Pa} = 22 \text{ kPa}$$

3. Look Back and Check

Is your answer reasonable?

Because the area of each tile is a half square meter and pressure is defined as force per square meter, the pressure exerted will be double the magnitude of the force. Thus, an 11,000 N force will produce 22,000 Pa of pressure on the tiles. The calculation verifies this result.

Math Practice

On a separate sheet of paper, answer the following questions.

1. The weight of the gasoline in a 55-gallon drum creates a force of 1456 newtons. The area of the bottom of the drum is 0.80 m². How much pressure does the gasoline exert on the bottom of the drum?

2. The weight of a gallon of milk is about 38 N. If you pour 3.0 gallons of milk into a container whose bottom has an area of 0.60 m², how much pressure will the milk exert on the bottom of the container?

Chapter 14 Work, Power, and Machines

Summary

14.1 Work and Power

🞂 **For a force to do work on an object, some of the force must act in the same direction as the object moves. If there is no movement, no work is done.**

- **Work** is the product of force and distance.
- Work is done when a force moves an object over a distance.

🞂 **Any part of a force that does not act in the direction of motion does no work on an object.**

- The **joule** (J) is the SI unit of work.
- When a force of 1 newton moves an object 1 meter in the direction of the force, 1 joule of work is done.

🞂 **Doing work at a faster rate requires more power. To increase power, you can increase the amount of work done in a given time, or you can do a given amount of work in less time.**

- **Power** is the rate of doing work.
- The SI unit of power is the **watt** (W), which is equal to one joule per second.
- One **horsepower** (hp) is equal to about 746 watts.

14.2 Work and Machines

🞂 **Machines make work easier to do. They change the size of a force needed, the direction of a force, or the distance over which a force acts.**

- A **machine** is a device that changes a force.

🞂 **Because of friction, the work done by a machine is always less than the work done on the machine.**

- The force you exert on a machine is the **input force.**
- The distance the input force acts through is the **input distance.**
- The work done by the input force acting through the input distance is the **work input.**
- The work input equals the input force times the input distance. You can increase the work input by increasing the input force, the input distance, or both.
- The force that is exerted by a machine is the **output force.**
- The distance the output force is exerted through is the **output distance.**
- The **work output** of a machine is the output force multiplied by the output distance.
- The work output equals the output force times the output distance. The only way to increase the work output is to increase the work input.

14.3 Mechanical Advantage and Efficiency

- The **mechanical advantage** of a machine is the number of times that the machine increases an input force.
- The **actual mechanical advantage** equals the ratio of the output force to the input force.
- The **ideal mechanical advantage** of a machine is the mechanical advantage in the absence of friction.

☞ **Because friction is always present, the actual mechanical advantage of a machine is always less than the ideal mechanical advantage.**

☞ **Because there is always some friction, the efficiency of any machine is always less than 100 percent.**

- The percentage of the work input that becomes work output is the **efficiency** of a machine.

14.4 Simple Machines

☞ **The six types of simple machines are the lever, the wheel and axle, the inclined plane, the wedge, the screw, and the pulley.**

- A **lever** is a rigid bar that is free to move around a fixed point.
- The fixed point the bar rotates around is the **fulcrum**.

☞ **To calculate the ideal mechanical advantage of any lever, divide the input arm by the output arm.**

- The **input arm** of a lever is the distance between the input force and the fulcrum. The **output arm** is the distance between the output force and the fulcrum.
- Levers are classified into three categories.
- First-class levers have the fulcrum between the input force and output force.
- Second-class levers have the output force between the input force and the fulcrum.
- Third-class levers have the input force between the fulcrum and the output force.
- A **wheel and axle** is a simple machine that consists of two disks or cylinders, each one with a different radius.

⬭ **To calculate the ideal mechanical advantage of the wheel and axle, divide the radius (or diameter) where the input force is exerted by the radius (or diameter) where the output force is exerted.**

⬭ **The ideal mechanical advantage of an inclined plane is the distance along the inclined plane divided by its change in height.**

- An **inclined plane** is a slanted surface along which a force moves an object to a different elevation.

⬭ **A thin wedge of a given length has a greater ideal mechanical advantage than a thick wedge of the same length.**

- A **wedge** is a V-shaped object whose sides are two inclined planes sloped toward each other.

⬭ **Screws with threads that are closer together have a greater ideal mechanical advantage.**

- A **screw** is an inclined plane wrapped around a cylinder.

⬭ **The ideal mechanical advantage of a pulley or pulley system is equal to the number of rope sections supporting the load being lifted.**

- A **pulley** is a simple machine that consists of a rope that fits into a groove in a wheel.
- A pulley may be fixed or movable.
- A fixed pulley has the wheel attached in a fixed location. It changes the direction, but not the size, of the input force.
- A movable pulley is attached to the object being moved. A movable pulley changes both the direction and the size of the input force.
- A **compound machine** is a combination of two or more simple machines that operate together.

Chapter 14   Work, Power, and Machines

Section 14.1 Work and Power
(pages 412–416)

This section defines work and power, describes how they are related, and explains how to calculate their values.

Reading Strategy (page 412)

Relating Text and Visuals As you read, look carefully at Figures 1 and 2 and read their captions. Complete the table by describing the work shown in each figure. For more information on this Reading Strategy, see the **Reading and Study Skills** in the **Skills and Reference Handbook** at the end of your textbook.

Figure	Direction of Force	Direction of Motion	Is Work Done?
1			
2A	Horizontal	Horizontal	Yes
2B			
2C			

What Is Work? (pages 412–413)

1. In science, work is done when a(n) _____ acts on an object in the direction the object moves.

2. Circle the letter of the best answer. Is work being done on a barbell when a weight lifter is holding the barbell over his head?

   a. No, because the weight lifter isn't moving.

   b. Yes, because the weight lifter is exerting force.

   c. No, because the barbell isn't moving.

3. Is the following sentence true or false? A vertical force does work on an object that is moving in a horizontal direction. _____

Calculating Work (pages 413–414)

4. In science, work that is done on an object can be described as the force acting on the object multiplied by the _____ the object moves.

5. Circle the letter of the correct form of the work equation to use when determining the distance an object moves as a result of a force applied to it.

   a. Distance = Force × Work

   b. Distance = $\dfrac{\text{Force}}{\text{Work}}$

   c. Distance = $\dfrac{\text{Work}}{\text{Force}}$

6. The SI unit of work is the _____.

7. Circle the letter of the amount of work done when a 1 newton force moves an object 1 meter.

   a. 1 newton per second

   b. 1 joule

   c. 1 watt

What Is Power? (page 414)

8. Is the following sentence true or false? Power is the rate of doing work.

   _____

9. Circle the letter of each sentence that is true about power.

   a. You can increase power by doing a given amount of work in a shorter period of time.

   b. When you decrease the force acting on an object, the power increases.

   c. When you do less work in a given time period, the power decreases.

Calculating Power (page 415)

10. Circle the letter of the word equation that describes how to calculate power.

    a. Power equals work divided by time.

    b. Power is a relationship between work and time.

    c. Power equals the rate of work.

11. The SI unit of power is the _____.

12. Circle the letter of the expression that is equivalent to one watt.

    a. one joule per meter

    b. one newton per second

    c. one joule per second

James Watt and Horsepower (page 416)

13. Circle the letter of the quantity that is approximately equal to one horsepower.

    a. 746 J

    b. 746 W

    c. 7460 N/m

Chapter 14   Work, Power, and Machines

Section 14.2 Work and Machines
(pages 417–420)

This section describes how machines change forces to make work easier to do. It identifies input forces exerted on and output forces exerted by machines and discusses input work and output work.

Reading Strategy (page 417)

Summarizing As you read, complete the table for each machine. After you read, write a sentence summarizing the idea that your table illustrates. For more information on this Reading Strategy, see the **Reading and Study Skills** in the **Skills and Reference Handbook** at the end of your textbook.

Machine	Increases or Decreases Input Force	Increases or Decreases Input Distance
Tire jack	Decreases	Increases
Lug wrench		
Rowing oar		
Summary: As input force decreases, the input distance increases.		

Machines Do Work (pages 417–418)

1. Is the following sentence true or false? A machine can make work easier to do by changing the size of the force needed, the direction of a force, or

   the distance over which a force acts. _____

2. Consider the equation Work = Force × Distance. If a machine increases the distance over which a force is exerted, the force required to do a

   given amount of work _____.

3. You make several trips to unload a few heavy items from a car instead of moving them all at once. Does the total distance over which you exert

   yourself increase or decrease? _____

Work Input and Work Output (pages 419–420)

4. The work done by a machine is always less than the work done on a machine because of _____. Circle the correct answer.

   attraction   friction   gravity

Chapter 14   Work, Power, and Machines

5. Circle the letter of the definition for input force.

   a. the amount of force exerted by a machine

   b. the amount of work done by a machine

   c. the amount of force exerted on a machine

6. Is the following sentence true or false? Every machine uses some of its

   work input to overcome friction. _____

7. Circle the letter of the expression that equals the work output
   of a machine.

   a. $\dfrac{\text{Input distance}}{\text{Output distance}}$

   b. Output distance × Input distance

   c. Output distance × Output force

8. Is the following sentence true or false? Output work always is less than

   input work. _____

For questions 9 through 11, refer to the figure below.

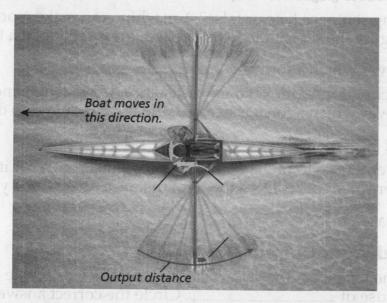

Boat moves in this direction.

Output distance

9. Which arrow represents the input force? Label it on the figure.

10. Which arrow represents the input distance? Label it on the figure.

11. Which arrow represents the output force? Label it on the figure.

Chapter 14   Work, Power, and Machines

Section 14.3 Mechanical Advantage and Efficiency
(pages 421–426)

This section describes mechanical advantage and efficiency and how to calculate these values. It also discusses ways to maximize mechanical advantage and efficiency.

Reading Strategy (page 421)

Building Vocabulary As you read the section, write a definition in the table for each vocabulary term in your own words. For more information on this Reading Strategy, see the **Reading and Study Skills** in the **Skills and Reference Handbook** at the end of your textbook.

Mechanical Advantage	
Vocabulary	**Definition**
Mechanical advantage	The number of times a machine increases force

Mechanical Advantage (pages 421–423)

1. The number of times that a machine increases an input force is the

    _____ of the machine.

2. Circle the letter of the correct answer. For a given input force, what affects the output force that a nutcracker can exert on a nut?

    a. the location of the hand holding the nutcracker

    b. the angle of the legs of the nutcracker

    c. the position of the nut

3. Mechanical advantage describes the relationship between input force

    and _____ force.

4. Is the following sentence true or false? A loading ramp with a rough surface has a greater mechanical advantage than one with a smooth

    surface. _____

Chapter 14   Work, Power, and Machines

5. Because friction is always present, the actual mechanical advantage
   of a machine is never _____ than its ideal mechanical
   advantage (IMA).

6. A machine's _____ is the mechanical advantage
   in the absence of friction.

Calculating Mechanical Advantage (pages 424–425)

7. Is the following sentence true or false? To calculate ideal mechanical
   advantage, divide input distance by output distance, and then divide
   the result by the force of friction. _____

8. Is the following sentence true or false? An inclined plane is an example
   of a machine. _____

9. Calculate the IMA of a ramp for the distances given in the table.

Ideal Mechanical Advantages of Ramps		
Horizontal Distance	Vertical Rise	IMA
1.5 meters	0.5 meters	3
12 meters	1.5 meters	
3.6 meters	0.3 meters	

Efficiency (pages 425–426)

10. Choose the letter of each statement that tells why the efficiency of a
    machine is always less than 100 percent.

    a. Machines get hot and need fans.

    b. Friction must be overcome.

    c. Gravity prevents machine parts from moving easily.

11. Is the following sentence true or false? To calculate the efficiency of a
    machine, divide the work output by work input, and then multiply
    by 100. _____

12. Calculate the efficiency of a machine with a work output of 120 J and
    a work input of 500 J. _____

13. Circle the letter of the work input for a machine with a work output of
    240 J and an efficiency of 80 percent.

    a. 300 J   b. 200 J   c. 320 J

14. Reducing friction _____ the efficiency of a machine.

Chapter 14   Work, Power, and Machines

Section 14.4 Simple Machines
(pages 427–435)

This section presents the six types of simple machines. It discusses how each type works and how to determine its mechanical advantage. It also describes common uses of simple machines.

Reading Strategy (page 427)

Summarizing After reading the section on levers, complete the concept map to organize what you know about first-class levers. On a separate sheet of paper, construct and complete similar concept maps for second- and third-class levers. For more information on this Reading Strategy, see the **Reading and Study Skills** in the **Skills and Reference Handbook** at the end of your textbook.

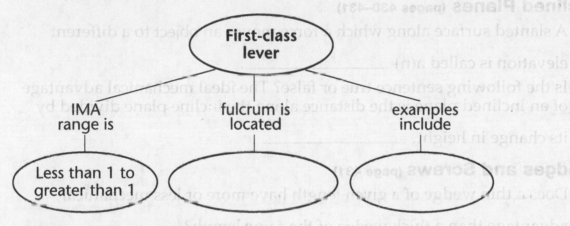

Levers (pages 428–429)

1. A screwdriver used to pry the lid off a paint can is an example of a(n) _____.

2. The fixed point that a lever rotates around is called the _____.

3. To calculate the ideal mechanical advantage of any lever, divide the input

   arm by the _____.

4. Circle the letter of the characteristic(s) that distinguishes levers as first-class, second-class, or third-class.

   a. relative positions of input force and output force

   b. position of fulcrum

   c. relative position of fulcrum, input force, and output force

5. Is the following sentence true or false? First-class levers always have a

   mechanical advantage that is greater than one. _____

6. Is the following sentence true or false? All second-class levers have a mechanical advantage greater than one because the input arm is longer than the output arm. _____

Wheel and Axle (page 430)

7. Circle the letter of the sentence that describes how to calculate the IMA of a wheel and axle.

   a. Multiply the area of the wheel by the area of the axle.
   b. Divide the diameter where input force is exerted by the diameter where output force is exerted.
   c. Divide the radius of the wheel by the force exerted on it.

Inclined Planes (pages 430–431)

8. A slanted surface along which a force moves an object to a different elevation is called a(n) _____.

9. Is the following sentence true or false? The ideal mechanical advantage of an inclined plane is the distance along the incline plane divided by its change in height. _____

Wedges and Screws (page 431)

10. Does a thin wedge of a given length have more or less mechanical advantage than a thick wedge of the same length? _____

Pulleys (pages 432–433)

11. A simple machine consisting of a rope fitted into a groove in a wheel is a(n) _____.

12. Circle the letter of the correct answer. What determines the ideal mechanical advantage of a pulley or pulley system?

   a. the number of rope sections that support the load
   b. the number of ropes threaded over the pulley
   c. the number of rope sections that support the pulley

Compound Machines (page 435)

13. Is the following sentence true or false? A compound machine is a combination of two or more simple machines that operate together. _____

Chapter 14   Work, Power, and Machines

WordWise

Use the clues and the words below to help you write the vocabulary terms from the chapter in the blanks. Use the circled letter(s) in each term to find the hidden vocabulary word. Then, write a definition for the hidden word.

compound machine	input arm	joule
inclined plane	machine	output distance
efficiency	horsepower	wedge

Clues

Vocabulary Terms

One way to determine this is to divide output work by output force.

_ _ _ _ _ _ _ _Ⓞ_ _ _ _ _

The IMA of this machine is the is the distance along its surface divided by the change in height.

_ _ _ _ _ _ Ⓞ _ _ Ⓞ _ _ _ _

This is the SI unit of work.

_ _Ⓞ_ _

On a lever, it is the distance between the fulcrum and the input force.

_ _ _ _Ⓞ _ _ _

$\dfrac{\text{Work output}}{\text{Work input}} \times 100\%$

_ _Ⓞ_ _ _ _ _ _ _

A mechanical watch is an example of this.

_ _ _ _ _Ⓞ_ _ _ _ _ _ _ _

This unit equals about 746 joules.

_ _Ⓞ_ _ _ _ _ _ _

A device that can change the size of the force required to do work.

_ _Ⓞ_ _ _ _ _

The IMA of this machine increases as its thickness decreases relative to its length.

_Ⓞ_ _ _

Hidden words: _ _ _ _ _ _ _ _ _ _

Definition: _____

_____

Chapter 14   Work, Power, and Machines

Calculating Work and Power

Calculate the power of a machine that exerts a force of 800.0 N over a distance of 6.0 m in 2.0 s.

Math Skill:
Formulas and
Equations

You may want to read more about this **Math Skill** in the **Skills and Reference Handbook** at the end of your textbook.

1. Read and Understand

What information are you given?

Force = 800.0 N

Distance = 6.0 m

Time = 2.0 s

2. Plan and Solve

What variable are you trying to determine?

Power =?

What formula contains the given quantities and the unknown?

$$\text{Power} = \frac{\text{Work}}{\text{Time}} = \frac{\text{Force} \times \text{Distance}}{\text{Time}}$$

$$\text{Power} = \frac{800.0 \text{ N} \times 6.0 \text{ m}}{2.0 \text{ s}}$$

$$\text{Power} = \frac{4800 \text{ J}}{2.0 \text{ s}} = 2400 \text{ J/s} = 2400 \text{ W}$$

3. Look Back and Check

Is your answer reasonable?

Work = (2400 J/s) × 2.0 s = 4800 J

This is a reasonable answer. Substituting power and time back into the power equation yields the original value for work.

Math Practice

On a separate sheet of paper, solve the following problems.

1. Suppose 900.0 J of work is done by a light bulb in 15.0 s. What is the power of the light bulb?

2. The power of a machine is 6.0×10^3 J/s. This machine is scheduled for design improvements. What would its power be if the same work could be done in 0.5 s?

Chapter 15 Energy

Summary

15.1 Energy and Its Forms

○ Work is a transfer of energy.

- **Energy** is the ability to do work.

○ The kinetic energy of any moving object depends upon its mass and speed.

- The energy of motion is called **kinetic energy**.
- To calculate the kinetic energy of an object, multiply half the object's mass (m) by its speed (v) squared: Kinetic energy = $\frac{1}{2}mv^2$.
- **Potential energy** is energy that is stored as a result of position or shape.
- The potential energy of an object that is stretched or compressed is known as **elastic potential energy**.

○ An object's gravitational potential energy depends on its mass, its height, and the acceleration due to gravity.

- Potential energy that depends upon an object's height is called **gravitational potential energy**.
- Gravitational potential energy = mgh, where m is mass, g is acceleration due to gravity, and h is the object's height.

○ The major forms of energy are mechanical energy, thermal energy, chemical energy, electrical energy, electromagnetic energy, and nuclear energy.

- The energy associated with the motion and position of everyday objects is **mechanical energy**.
- The total potential and kinetic energy of all the microscopic particles in an object make up its **thermal energy**.
- **Chemical energy** is the energy stored in chemical bonds.
- **Electrical energy** is the energy associated with electric charges.
- **Electromagnetic energy** is a form of energy that travels through space in the form of waves.
- The energy stored in atomic nuclei is known as **nuclear energy**.

15.2 Energy Conversion and Conservation

☜ **Energy can be converted from one form to another.**

- The process of changing energy from one form to another is **energy conversion.**

☜ **The law of conservation of energy states that energy cannot be created or destroyed.**

- When energy changes from one form to another, the total amount of energy stays the same.

☜ **The gravitational potential energy of an object is converted to the kinetic energy of motion as the object falls.**

☜ **Einstein's equation, $E = mc^2$, says that energy and mass are equivalent and can be converted into each other.**

15.3 Energy Resources

☜ **Nonrenewable energy resources include oil, natural gas, coal, and uranium.**

- **Nonrenewable energy resources** exist in limited quantities and, once used, cannot be replaced except over the course of millions of years.
- Oil, natural gas, and coal are known as **fossil fuels.** They formed underground from the remains of once-living organisms.

☜ **Renewable energy resources include hydroelectric, solar, geothermal, wind, biomass, and, possibly in the future, nuclear fusion.**

- **Renewable energy sources** are resources that can be replaced in a relatively short period of time.
- Energy obtained from flowing water is known as **hydroelectric energy.**
- Sunlight that is converted into usable energy is called **solar energy.**
- **Geothermal energy** is thermal energy beneath Earth's surface.
- The chemical energy stored in living things is called **biomass energy.**
- A **hydrogen fuel cell** generates electricity by reacting hydrogen with oxygen.

☜ **Energy resources can be conserved by reducing energy needs and by increasing the efficiency of energy use.**

- Finding ways to use less energy or to use energy more efficiently is known as **energy conservation.**

Chapter 15 Energy

Section 15.1 Energy and Its Forms
(pages 446–452)

This section describes how energy and work are related. It defines kinetic energy and potential energy, and gives examples for calculating these forms of energy. It also discusses examples of various types of energy.

Reading Strategy (page 446)

Building Vocabulary As you read, complete the concept map with vocabulary terms and definitions from this section. For more information on this Reading Strategy, see the **Reading and Study Skills** in the **Skills and Reference Handbook** at the end of your textbook.

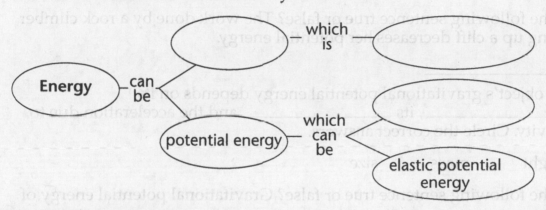

Energy and Work (page 447)

1. What is energy? _____

2. When work is done on an object, _____ is transferred to that object. Circle the correct answer.

   energy   heat   height

3. Circle the letter of each sentence that is true about work and energy.

   a. Energy in food is converted into muscle movement.

   b. Both work and energy are usually measured in joules.

   c. One joule equals one meter per newton.

Kinetic Energy (pages 447–448)

4. The energy of motion is called _____.

5. Is the following sentence true or false? You can determine the kinetic energy of an object if you know its mass and its volume. _____

6. Circle the letter of the formula used to calculate an object's kinetic energy.

   a. Kinetic energy = $\frac{1}{2} mv^2$

   b. Kinetic energy = mv^2

   c. Kinetic energy = $\frac{v^2}{m}$

Potential Energy (pages 448–450)

7. What is potential energy? _____

_____

8. Is the following sentence true or false? The work done by a rock climber going up a cliff decreases her potential energy.

_____

9. An object's gravitational potential energy depends on its _____, its _____, and the acceleration due to gravity. Circle the correct answers.

   height   mass   size

10. Is the following sentence true or false? Gravitational potential energy of an object increases as its height increases. _____

11. The potential energy of an object that is stretched or compressed is known as _____.

Forms of Energy (pages 450–452)

For numbers 12 through 17, write the letter of the form of energy that best matches the description.

Descriptions	Forms of Energy
_____ **12.** Energy stored in gasoline, coal, and wood	a. mechanical energy
_____ **13.** The sum of an object's potential energy and kinetic energy, excluding atomic-scale movements	b. chemical energy
	c. electrical energy
_____ **14.** Produces the sun's heat and light	d. thermal energy
_____ **15.** Travels through space in the form of waves	e. nuclear energy
	f. electromagnetic energy
_____ **16.** Produces lightning bolts	
_____ **17.** Increases as atoms within an object move faster	

Chapter 15   Energy

Section 15.2 Energy Conversion and Conservation
(pages 453–459)

This section describes how energy is converted from one form to another and presents the law of conservation of energy.

Reading Strategy (page 453)

Relating Cause and Effect As you read, complete the flowchart to explain an energy conversion used by some gulls to obtain food. For more information on this Reading Strategy, see the **Reading and Study Skills** in the **Skills and Reference Handbook** at the end of your textbook.

How Gulls Use Energy Conversions

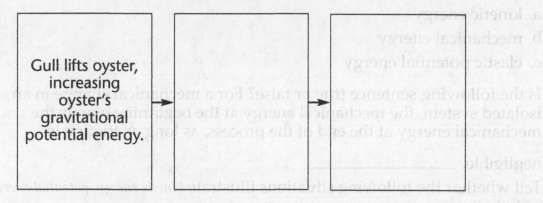

Gull lifts oyster, increasing oyster's gravitational potential energy.

Energy Conversion (page 454)

1. Is the following sentence true or false? Energy can be converted from one form to another. _____

2. When a wind-up toy is set in motion, elastic potential energy that was stored in a compressed spring is converted into the _____ of the toy's moving parts.

Conservation of Energy (page 455)

3. What does the law of conservation of energy state? _____
_____

4. A moving object slows down because friction causes a continual conversion of kinetic energy into _____. Circle the correct answer.

    mechanical   potential   thermal
    energy   energy   energy

Chapter 15 Energy

Energy Conversions (pages 456–458)

5. As an object falls, the gravitational potential energy of the object is

converted into _____.

6. At what point during a pole-vaulter's jump is his gravitational potential energy the greatest? Circle the letter of the correct answer.

    a. when he leaves the ground

    b. at his greatest height

    c. when he hits the ground

7. Circle the letter of the type of energy that increases as the pole bends before it propels a pole-vaulter up into the air.

    a. kinetic energy

    b. mechanical energy

    c. elastic potential energy

8. Is the following sentence true or false? For a mechanical change in an isolated system, the mechanical energy at the beginning equals the mechanical energy at the end of the process, as long as friction is

negligible. _____

9. Tell whether the following situations illustrate *kinetic energy*, *potential energy*, or *both*.

What Type of Energy Is It?	
Situation	**Form of Energy**
A stationary wind-up toy with a compressed spring	
A descending roller coaster car	
A skier poised to take off at the top of a hill	
A car driving on a flat road	
A vibrating guitar string	

Energy and Mass (page 459)

10. Circle the letters of each correct sentence. What does Einstein's equation imply about mass and energy?

    a. Mass and energy are equivalent.

    b. Mass and energy are never created.

    c. Mass and energy can be converted to each other.

Chapter 15   Energy

Section 15.3 Energy Resources
(pages 462–466)

This section describes types of energy resources and ways to conserve them.

Reading Strategy (page 462)

Identifying Main Ideas As you read the section, write the main idea for each heading in the table. For more information on this Reading Strategy, see the **Reading and Study Skills** in the **Skills and Reference Handbook** at the end of your textbook.

Heading	Main Idea
Nonrenewable energy resources	Nonrenewable energy resources include oil, natural gas, and coal. They exist in limited quantities.
Renewable energy resources	
Conserving energy resources	

Nonrenewable Energy Resources (page 462)

1. What are nonrenewable energy resources? _____

_____

2. List three examples of nonrenewable energy resources.

   a. _____

   b. _____

   c. _____

3. Circle the letter of each resource that is considered to be a fossil fuel.

   a. tree

   b. oil

   c. coal

4. Is the following sentence true or false? Although fossil fuels are evenly distributed throughout Earth, they only represent ten percent of total

   energy consumed. _____

Renewable Energy Resources (pages 463–464)

5. An energy resource that can be replaced in a reasonably short period of

   time is called a(n) _____ resource.

6. Circle the letter of each sentence that is true about renewable energy resources.

    a. Wind and solar energy are both renewable energy resources.

    b. Renewable energy resources are always more efficient than nonrenewable resources.

    c. Renewable energy resources can be used to generate electricity and to heat homes.

7. Is the following sentence true or false? One disadvantage of hydroelectric power is that it is among the most expensive energy

    sources. _____

For numbers 8 through 13, match the letter of each renewable energy source to its description.

Description	Renewable Energy Sources
_____ **8.** Water pumped below ground is converted to steam.	**a.** hydroelectric
_____ **9.** The most likely raw material is hydrogen.	**b.** solar
_____ **10.** Mirrors concentrate sunlight to produce electricity.	**c.** geothermal
_____ **11.** Kinetic energy of moving air is converted into rotational energy of a turbine.	**d.** wind
_____ **12.** Energy is obtained from flowing water.	**e.** biomass
_____ **13.** Chemical energy stored in wood, peat, and agricultural waste can be converted into thermal energy.	**f.** nuclear fusion

14. Is the following sentence true or false? Hydrogen fuel cells generate

electricity by combining hydrogen with oxygen. _____

Conserving Energy Resources (page 466)

15. Name two practical ways in which people can conserve energy. _____

_____

_____

Chapter 15   Energy

WordWise

Complete the sentences by using one of the vocabulary words below.

biomass energy	energy conservation	fossil fuels
solar energy	potential energy	energy
thermal energy	gravitational	kinetic energy
chemical energy	nuclear energy	

When an object is raised to a higher level, its _____ potential energy increases.

The motion of microscopic particles in matter partly determines the amount of _____ within it.

As a pole-vaulter springs higher into the air, her kinetic energy decreases as her gravitational potential energy increases. This is an example of

_____.

Atomic fission and fusion produce _____.

When your muscles move, _____ from the cereal you ate for breakfast is converted into _____.

The _____ of a 100-kg boulder perched high on a cliff is greater than that of a 50-kg boulder at the same height.

You can recognize _____ by the changes it causes, such as motion and sound.

Formed from the remains of once-living organisms, _____ are nonrenewable energy resources.

Photovoltaic cells convert _____ into electrical energy.

When you sit around a campfire, you are enjoying energy stored in wood—a type of _____.

Chapter 15 Energy

Calculating Potential Energy

A 60.0-kg swimmer is standing on the edge of a pier that is 2.5 m above the surface of a lake. The swimmer steps onto a diving board. This raises the swimmer's gravitational potential energy by 10 percent. What is the swimmer's new gravitational potential energy?

Math Skill: Percents and Decimals

You may want to read more about this **Math Skill** in the **Skills and Reference Handbook** at the end of your textbook.

1. Read and Understand

What information are you given?

Mass of person = m = 60.0 kg

Height above lake level = h = 2.5 m

Acceleration due to gravity = g = 9.8 m/s²

2. Plan and Solve

What variable are you trying to determine?

Gravitational potential energy = ?

What formula contains the given variables?

Gravitational potential energy (PE) = mgh

Initial PE = (60.0 kg)(9.8 m/s²)(2.5 m) = 1500 J

Determine the 10-percent increase of PE.

(1500 J)(0.10) = 150 J

Final PE = 1500 J + 150 J = 1650 J

3. Look Back and Check

Is your answer reasonable?

This is a reasonable answer because 1650 J is more than 1500 J. When the height of a person or object increases, its gravitational potential energy should increase.

Math Practice

On a separate sheet of paper, solve the following problems.

1. A .3-kg toy car and a .5-kg toy car are sitting on a shelf that is 2 meters higher than the floor. What is the PE of the two cars?

2. An 80-kg rock climber is standing on a cliff 10 m high, so that his gravitational PE = 7840 J. His partner gives him 15 kg of rope and other gear to carry on his way down. What is the climber's gravitational PE now?

Chapter 16 Thermal Energy and Heat

Summary

16.1 Thermal Energy and Matter

☞ **Heat flows spontaneously from hot objects to cold objects.**

- **Heat** is the transfer of thermal energy from one object to another because of a temperature difference.

☞ **Temperature is related to the average kinetic energy of the particles in an object due to their random motions through space.**

- **Temperature** is a measure of how hot or cold an object is compared to a reference point.
- On the Celsius scale, the reference points are the freezing and boiling points of water. On the Kelvin scale, another reference point is **absolute zero,** which is defined as a temperature of 0 kelvins.

☞ **Thermal energy depends on the mass, temperature, and phase (solid, liquid, or gas) of an object.**

☞ **Thermal expansion occurs when particles of matter move farther apart as temperature increases.**

- **Thermal expansion** is an increase in the volume of a material due to a temperature increase.

☞ **The lower a material's specific heat, the more its temperature rises when a given amount of energy is absorbed by a given mass.**

- **Specific heat** is the amount of heat needed to raise the temperature of one gram of a material by one degree Celsius.
- The amount of heat absorbed by a material (Q) is the product of the mass of the material (m), the specific heat of the material (c), and the change in temperature (ΔT): $Q = m \times c \times \Delta T$.

☞ **A calorimeter uses the principle that heat flows from a hotter object to a colder object until both reach the same temperature.**

- A **calorimeter** is an instrument used to measure changes in thermal energy.

16.2 Heat and Thermodynamics

⬤ Conduction in gases is slower than in liquids and solids because the particles in a gas collide less often.

- **Conduction** is the transfer of thermal energy with no overall transfer of matter. Conduction occurs within a material or between materials that are touching.
- A **thermal conductor** is a material that conducts thermal energy well.
- A material that conducts thermal energy poorly is a **thermal insulator**.

⬤ Convection currents are important in many natural cycles, such as ocean currents, weather systems, and movements of hot rock in Earth's interior.

- **Convection** is the transfer of thermal energy when particles of a fluid move from one place to another. The moving particles transfer thermal energy from hot areas to cold areas.
- A **convection current** occurs when a fluid circulates in a loop as it alternately heats up and cools down. In a heated room, a convection current helps keep the temperature about the same throughout the room.

⬤ All objects radiate energy. As an object's temperature increases, the rate at which it radiates energy increases.

- **Radiation** is the transfer of energy by waves moving through space.
- The study of conversions between thermal energy and other forms of energy is called **thermodynamics**.

⬤ The first law of thermodynamics states that energy is conserved.

⬤ The second law of thermodynamics states that thermal energy can flow from colder objects to hotter objects only if work is done on the system.

- A **heat engine** is any device that converts heat (thermal energy) into work.
- Thermal energy that is not converted into work is called **waste heat**.

⬤ The third law of thermodynamics states that absolute zero cannot be reached.

16.3 Using Heat

➣ **The two main types of heat engines are the external combustion engine and the internal combustion engine.**

- An **external combustion engine** is an engine that burns fuel outside the engine.
- An **internal combustion engine** is a heat engine in which the fuel burns inside the engine.

➣ **Most heating systems use convection to distribute thermal energy.**

- A **central heating system** heats many rooms from one central location.
- There are several types of heating systems, including hot-water heating, steam heating, electric baseboard heating, and forced-air heating systems.

➣ **Heat pumps must do work on a refrigerant in order to reverse the normal flow of thermal energy.**

- A **heat pump** is a device that reverses the normal flow of thermal energy. A heat pump causes thermal energy to move from a cold area to a hot area.
- A **refrigerant** is a fluid that vaporizes and condenses inside the tubing of a heat pump.
- Refrigerators and air conditioners are cooling systems that use heat pumps.

Section 16.1 Thermal Energy and Matter
(pages 474–478)

This section defines heat and describes how work, temperature, and thermal energy are related to heat. It also discusses thermal expansion and contraction of materials, and explains uses of a calorimeter.

Reading Strategy (page 474)

Previewing Before you read, preview the figures in this section and add two more questions to the table. As you read, write answers to your questions. For more information on this Reading Strategy, see the **Reading and Study Skills** in the **Skills and Reference Handbook** at the end of your textbook.

Thermal Energy and Matter	
Questions About Thermal Energy and Matter	**Answers**
Which has more thermal energy, a cup of tea or a pitcher of juice?	
	The brass was hot enough to make water boil only during drilling, so the heat must be related to the motion of the drill.

Work and Heat (page 474)

1. Heat is the transfer of thermal energy from one object to another as the result of a difference in _____. Circle the correct answer.

   density   potential energy   temperature

2. Circle the letter of each sentence that is true about heat.
   a. Heat is a fluid that flows between particles of matter.
   b. Heat flows spontaneously from hot objects to cold objects.
   c. Friction produces heat.

Temperature (page 475)

3. What is temperature? _____

   _____

Chapter 16   Thermal Energy and Heat

4. Circle the letter of each sentence that explains what happens when an object heats up.

   a. Its particles move faster, on average.

   b. The average kinetic energy of its particles decreases.

   c. Its temperature increases.

Thermal Energy (page 475)

5. Thermal energy is the total potential and _____ energy of all the particles in an object.

6. Is the following sentence true or false? Two substances can be the same temperature and have different thermal energies. _____

Thermal Contraction and Expansion (page 476)

7. Is the following sentence true or false? Thermal contraction occurs when matter is heated, because particles of matter tend to move closer together as temperature increases. _____

8. Use the terms in the box below to describe thermal expansion and contraction by completing the table.

Increases	Thermal expansion
Decreases	Thermal contraction

Thermal Expansion and Contraction			
Condition	Temperature	Space Between Particles	Volume
	Increases		
			Decreases

Specific Heat (pages 476–477)

9. The amount of heat needed to raise the temperature of one gram of material by one degree Celsius is called _____.

Measuring Heat Changes (page 478)

10. What is a calorimeter? _____

_____

11. Is the following sentence true or false? A calorimeter uses the principle that heat flows from a hotter object to a colder object until both reach the same temperature. _____

Chapter 16   Thermal Energy and Heat

Section 16.2 Heat and Thermodynamics
(pages 479–483)

This section discusses three kinds of thermal energy transfer and introduces the first, second, and third laws of thermodynamics.

Reading Strategy (page 479)

Building Vocabulary As you read this section, add definitions and examples to complete the table. For more information on this Reading Strategy, see the **Reading and Study Skills** in the **Skills and Reference Handbook** at the end of your textbook.

Transfer of Thermal Energy	
Definitions	**Examples**
Conduction: transfer of thermal energy with no net transfer of matter	Frying pan handle heats up
Convection:	
Radiation: transfer of energy by waves moving through space	

Conduction (pages 479–480)

1. The transfer of thermal energy with no overall transfer of matter is called _____.

2. Is the following sentence true or false? Conduction is faster in metals than in other solids because metals have free electrons that transfer thermal energy. _____

3. Circle the letter of each sentence that is true about conduction.

   a. Thermal energy is transferred without transfer of matter.

   b. Conduction can occur between materials that are not touching.

   c. In most solids, conduction takes place as particles vibrate in place.

4. Complete the table about conduction.

Conduction		
Type of Material	**Quality of Conduction**	**Two Examples**
	Conducts thermal energy well	Copper;
Thermal insulator		Wood;

Chapter 16   Thermal Energy and Heat

Convection (pages 480–481)

5. The transfer of thermal energy when particles of a fluid move from one

   place to another is called _____.

6. When a fluid circulates in a loop as it alternately heats up and cools
   down, a(n) _____ occurs. Circle the correct answer.

   air current   convection current   heat circulation

Radiation (page 481)

7. The transfer of energy by waves moving through space is called

   _____.

8. Circle the letter of each sentence that is true about radiation.

   a. Energy is transferred by waves.

   b. All objects radiate energy.

   c. The amount of energy radiated from an object decreases as its
   temperature increases.

Thermodynamics (pages 482–483)

9. Thermodynamics is the study of conversions between _____
   and other forms of energy.

10. Is the following sentence true or false? Energy cannot be created or

    destroyed, but it can be converted into different forms. _____

11. Circle the letter of the correct answer. According to the second law of
    thermodynamics, when can thermal energy flow from a colder object to
    a hotter object?

    a. only when you use a heat pump

    b. only when you do work on the system

    c. whenever two objects touch each other

12. Define waste heat. _____

    _____

13. Is the following sentence true or false? Scientists have created a heat
    engine with 100 percent efficiency by reducing the temperature of the

    outside environment to absolute zero. _____

14. Is the following sentence true or false? Matter can be cooled to absolute

    zero. _____

Chapter 16   Thermal Energy and Heat

Section 16.3 Using Heat
(pages 486–492)

This section describes ways in which humans benefit from heat engines, heating systems, and cooling systems. It also discusses how each of these systems works.

Reading Strategy (page 486)

Sequencing As you read, complete the cycle diagram to show the sequence of events in a gasoline engine. For more information on this Reading Strategy, see the **Reading and Study Skills** in the **Skills and Reference Handbook** at the end of your textbook.

Sequence of Events in a Gasoline Engine

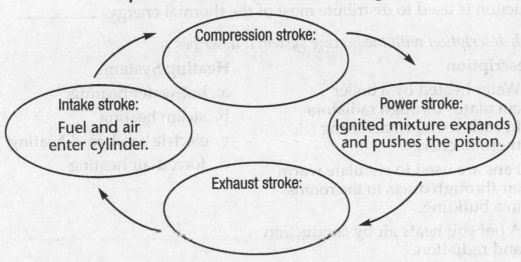

Heat Engines (pages 486–487)

1. Circle the two main types of heat engines.

    external combustion   heat pump   internal combustion
        engine   engine

2. A steam engine is an external combustion engine because it burns fuel

    _____ the engine.

3. Who developed the first practical steam engine?

    a. James Prescott Joule
    b. Thomas Newcomen
    c. Benjamin Thompson

4. A heat engine used by most cars in which fuel burns inside the engine is

    called a(n) _____.

Chapter 16   Thermal Energy and Heat

5. Is the following sentence true or false? In a typical car, the crankshaft produces a linear motion that turns the wheels. _____

6. Is the following sentence true or false? Gasoline engines operate very efficiently in converting fuel energy to work. _____

Heating Systems (pages 489–490)

7. What is a central heating system? _____

_____

8. Is the following sentence true or false? In most heating systems, conduction is used to distribute most of the thermal energy. _____

Match each description with the heating system it describes.

Description	Heating System
____ 9. Water heated by a boiler circulates through radiators in each room, transferring thermal energy.	a. hot-water heating
	b. steam heating
____ 10. Fans are used to circulate warm air through ducts to the rooms in a building.	c. electric baseboard heating
	d. forced-air heating
____ 11. A hot coil heats air by conduction and radiation.	
____ 12. This system is often used in older buildings or to heat many buildings from a single location.	

Cooling Systems (pages 490–492)

13. Is the following sentence true or false? Most cooling systems, such as air conditioners and refrigerators, are heat pumps. _____

14. Define refrigerant. _____

_____

15. Circle each sentence that describes how a heat pump affects the flow of thermal energy.

a. It uses a refrigerant.

b. It reverses the normal flow of energy.

c. It increases thermal energy.

Name _____ Class _____ Date _____

Chapter 16   Thermal Energy and Heat

WordWise

Use the clues and the words below to help you write the vocabulary terms from the chapter in the blanks. Use the circled letter(s) in each term to find the hidden vocabulary word. Then, write a definition for the hidden word.

energy	heat	convection
radiation	refrigerant	temperature
calorimeter	heat engine	specific heat

Clues   **Vocabulary Terms**

This flows spontaneously from
hot objects to cold objects.   _ _ _ Ⓞ

Any device that converts heat
into work   Ⓞ Ⓞ _ _ _ _ _ _ _ _

A heat pump does work on this so
you can keep your veggies cold.   _ _ _ _ Ⓞ _ _ _ _ _

The Kelvin scale is used to
measure this.   _ _ Ⓞ _ _ _ _ _ _ _ _

A device used to determine
the specific heat of a material   _ Ⓞ Ⓞ _ _ _ _ _ _ _

The transfer of thermal energy
when particles of a fluid move
from place to place   _ _ _ _ _ Ⓞ _ _ _ Ⓞ _

The amount of heat needed to raise
the temperature of one gram of a
material by one degree Celsius   _ _ _ _ Ⓞ _ _ _ _ _ _ _

The transfer of energy by waves
moving through space   Ⓞ _ _ _ _ _ _ _ _

According to the first law of
thermodynamics, this is
conserved.   _ _ _ Ⓞ Ⓞ _

Hidden words: _ _ _ _ _ _ _ _ _ _ _ _ _ _ _ _ _ _

Definition: _____

_____

Copyright © Savvas Learning Company LLC. All Rights Reserved.

Physical Science Reading and Study Workbook Level B • Chapter 16 **191**

Chapter 16   Thermal Energy and Heat

Calculating With Specific Heat

How much heat is required to raise the temperature of a gold earring from 25.0°C to 30.0°C? The earring weighs 25 grams, and the specific heat of gold is 0.128 J/g•°C.

Math Skill:
Formulas and
Equations

You may want to read more about this **Math Skill** in the Skills and **Reference Handbook** at the end of your textbook.

1. Read and Understand

What information are you given?

Specific heat = c = 0.128 J/g•°C

Mass = m = 25.0 grams

Change in temperature = ΔT = (30.0°C − 25.0°C) = 5.0°C

2. Plan and Solve

What unknown are you trying to calculate?

Amount of heat needed = Q = ?

What formula contains the given quantities and the unknown?

Q = Mass × Specific heat × Change in temperature

$Q = m \times c \times \Delta T$

Replace each variable with its known value.

Q = 25.0 g × 0.128 J/g•°C × 5.0°C = 16 J

3. Look Back and Check

Is your answer reasonable?

$$\frac{\text{Heat absorbed}}{(m \times c)} = 16 \text{ J}/(25.0 \text{ g} \times 0.128 \text{ J/g•°C}) = 5.0°C$$

This is a reasonable answer for the heat required to raise the temperature of the earring.

Math Practice

On a separate sheet of paper, solve the following problems.

1. How much heat is required to raise the temperature of 25 grams of water from 25.0°C to 30.0°C? The specific heat of water is 4.18 J/g•°C.

2. Determine the mass of a sample of silver if 705 J of heat are required to raise its temperature from 25°C to 35°C. The specific heat of silver is 0.235 J/g•°C.

Chapter 17 Mechanical Waves and Sound

Summary

17.1 Mechanical Waves

👄 **A mechanical wave is created when a source of energy causes a vibration to travel through a medium.**

- A **mechanical wave** is a disturbance in matter that carries energy from one place to another.
- The material through which a wave travels is called a **medium.**

👄 **The three main types of mechanical waves are transverse waves, longitudinal waves, and surface waves.**

- A **transverse wave** causes the medium to vibrate at right angles to the direction in which the wave travels.
- The highest point above the rest position is the **crest** of a transverse wave.
- The lowest point below the rest position is the **trough.**
- A **longitudinal wave** causes the medium to vibrate parallel to the direction the wave travels.
- In a longitudinal wave, an area where the particles in a medium are spaced close together is called a **compression.**
- An area where the particles in a medium are spread out is called a **rarefaction.**
- A **surface wave** is a wave that travels along a surface separating two media.
- In a surface wave, particles of the medium move up and down, and back and forth. When these two motions are combined, the particles move in circles.

17.2 Properties of Mechanical Waves

👄 **A wave's frequency equals the frequency of the vibrating source producing the wave.**

- Any motion that repeats at regular time intervals is called **periodic motion.**
- The time required for one cycle, a complete motion that returns to its starting point, is called the **period.**
- Any periodic motion has a **frequency,** which is the number of complete cycles in a given time.
- Frequency is measured in cycles per second, or **hertz** (Hz).

👄 **Increasing the frequency of a wave decreases its wavelength.**

- **Wavelength** is the distance between a point on one wave and the same point on the next cycle of the wave.

- The wavelength of a transverse wave is the distance from one crest or trough to the next. The wavelength of a longitudinal wave is the distance from one compression or rarefaction to the next.

☞ **If you assume that waves are traveling at a constant speed, then wavelength is inversely proportional to frequency.**

☞ **The more energy a wave has, the greater is its amplitude.**

- The **amplitude** of a wave is the maximum displacement of the medium from its rest position.

17.3 Behavior of Waves

☞ **Reflection does not change the speed or frequency of a wave, but the wave can be flipped upside down.**

- **Reflection** occurs when a wave bounces off a surface that it cannot pass through.

☞ **When a wave enters a medium at an angle, refraction occurs because one side of the wave moves more slowly than the other side.**

- **Refraction** is the bending of a wave as it enters a new medium at an angle.

☞ **A wave diffracts more if its wavelength is large compared to the size of an opening or obstacle.**

- **Diffraction** is the bending of a wave as it moves around an obstacle or passes through a narrow opening.

☞ **Two types of interference are constructive interference and destructive interference.**

- **Interference** occurs when two or more waves overlap and combine together.
- **Constructive interference** occurs when two or more waves combine to produce a wave with a larger displacement.
- **Destructive interference** occurs when two or more waves combine to produce a wave with a smaller displacement.

☞ **A standing wave forms only if half a wavelength or a multiple of half a wavelength fits exactly into the length of a vibrating cord.**

- A **standing wave** is a wave that appears to stay in one place—it does not seem to move through the medium.
- A **node** is a point on a standing wave that has no displacement from the rest position.
- An **antinode** is a point where a crest of trough occurs midway between two nodes.

17.4 Sound and Hearing

☺ **Many behaviors of sound can be explained using a few properties—speed, intensity and loudness, and frequency and pitch.**

- **Sound waves** are longitudinal waves—compressions and rarefactions that travel through a medium.
- Sound is carried by longitudinal waves.
- Speed is how fast sound travels. Sound waves travel fastest in solids, slower in liquids, and slowest in gases.
- **Intensity** is the rate at which a wave's energy flows through a given area. It depends on the wave's amplitude and the distance from the sound source.
- Sound intensity levels are measured in decibels. The **decibel** (dB) is a unit that compares the intensity of different sounds.
- **Loudness** is a physical response to the intensity of sound, modified by physical factors.
- The frequency of a sound wave depends on how fast the source of the sound is vibrating.
- **Pitch** is how high or low a sound seems to a listener.

☺ **Ultrasound is used in a variety of applications including sonar and ultrasound imaging.**

- **Sonar** is a technique for determining the distance to an object under water.
- The **Doppler effect** is a change in sound frequency caused by motion of the sound source, motion of the listener, or both.

☺ **As a source of sound approaches, an observer hears a higher frequency. When the sound source moves away, the observer hears a lower frequency.**

☺ **The outer ear gathers and focuses sound into the middle ear, which receives and amplifies the vibrations. The inner ear uses nerve endings to sense vibrations and send signals to the brain.**

- The ear is the organ that responds to sound.
- The ear has three main regions: the outer ear, the middle ear, and the inner ear.

☺ **Sound is recorded by converting sound waves into electronic signals that can be processed and stored. Sound is reproduced by converting electronic signals back into sound waves.**

☺ **Most musical instruments vary pitch by changing the frequency of standing waves.**

- Musical instruments often use resonance to amplify sound.
- **Resonance** is the response of a standing wave to another wave of the same frequency. Resonance can dramatically amplify sound.

Chapter 17   Mechanical Waves and Sound

Section 17.1 Mechanical Waves
(pages 500–503)

This section explains what mechanical waves are, how they form, and how they travel. It discusses three main types of mechanical waves—transverse, longitudinal, and surface waves—and gives examples for each type.

Reading Strategy (page 500)

Previewing As you read this section, use Figure 2 on page 501 to complete the web diagram. Then use Figures 3 and 4 to make similar diagrams for longitudinal waves and surface waves on a separate sheet of paper. For more information on this Reading Strategy, see the **Reading and Study Skills** in the **Skills and Reference Handbook** at the end of your textbook.

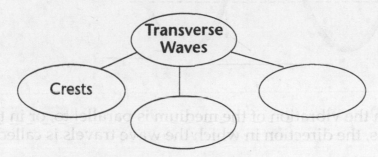

What Are Mechanical Waves? (page 500)

1. A disturbance in matter that carries energy from one place to another is called a(n) _____.

2. Is the following sentence true or false? Mechanical waves can travel through empty space. _____

3. The material through which a wave travels is called a(n)

   _____.

4. Is the following sentence true or false? Solids, liquids, and gases all can act as mediums for waves. _____

5. A mechanical wave is created when an energy source causes a

   _____ to travel through a medium.

Types of Mechanical Waves (pages 501–503)

6. Circle the letter of the characteristic used to classify a mechanical wave.

   a. the height of its crest

   b. the way it travels through a medium

   c. the type of medium through which it travels

Chapter 17 Mechanical Waves and Sound

7. What is a transverse wave? _____

_____

8. Look at the figure below. Use the words in the box to label the missing aspects of the wave in the rope.

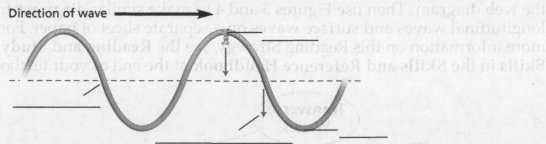

Crest	Rest position
Trough	Direction of vibration

Direction of wave ⟶

9. A wave in which the vibration of the medium is parallel to, or in the same direction as, the direction in which the wave travels is called a(n)

_____.

10. When a longitudinal wave carries energy through a spring, the area where the coils of a spring are closer together than they would be in the rest position is called a(n) _____. Circle the correct answer.

compression   frequency   rarefaction

11. Is the following sentence true or false? A rarefaction is a region in a longitudinal wave where particles of a medium spread out.

_____

Match the type of wave to each description below. The type of wave may be used more than once.

Description

_____ **12.** P wave

_____ **13.** Direction of travel is perpendicular to vibration direction

_____ **14.** Rarefactions with particles that are spread out

_____ **15.** A wave that travels along a boundary separating two mediums

_____ **16.** An ocean wave

Type of Wave

a. transverse wave

b. longitudinal wave

c. surface wave

Chapter 17   Mechanical Waves and Sound

Section 17.2 Properties of Mechanical Waves
(pages 504–507)

This section introduces measurable properties used to describe mechanical waves, including frequency, period, wavelength, speed, and amplitude.

Reading Strategy (page 504)

Building Vocabulary As you read, write a definition in your own words for each term in the table below. For more information on this Reading Strategy, see the **Reading and Study Skills** in the **Skills and Reference Handbook** at the end of your textbook.

Properties of Waves	
Vocabulary Term	**Definition**
Period	The time required for one cycle
Frequency	
Wavelength	
Amplitude	

Frequency and Period (page 504)

1. Is the following sentence true or false? A periodic motion repeats at regular time intervals. _____

2. The time required for one cycle, a complete motion that returns to its starting point, is called the _____. Circle the correct answer.

    frequency   period   wavelength

3. The number of complete cycles in a given period of time is the

    _____ of a periodic motion.

Wavelength (page 505)

4. The distance between a point on one wave and the same point on the next cycle of the wave is called _____. Circle the correct answer.

    frequency   period   wavelength

Chapter 17   Mechanical Waves and Sound

5. Circle the letter of the correct answer. How is wavelength determined for a longitudinal wave?

   a. Measure the distance between adjacent rarefactions.

   b. Measure the distance between adjacent crests.

   c. Measure the distance between adjacent troughs.

Wave Speed (pages 505–506)

6. Write a formula you can use to determine the speed of a wave. _____

7. Is the following sentence true or false? The speed of a wave equals

   its wavelength divided by its period. _____

8. Circle the letter of the sentence that tells how wavelength is related to frequency for a wave traveling at a constant speed.

   a. Wavelength is directly proportional to frequency.

   b. Wavelength is inversely proportional to frequency.

   c. A wave with a higher frequency will have a longer wavelength.

Amplitude (page 507)

9. What is the amplitude of a wave? _____

   _____

Questions 10–13 refer to the figure below.

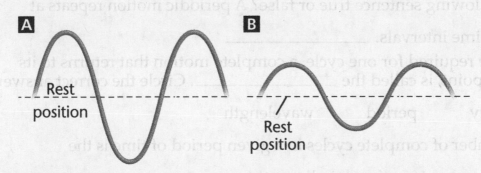

10. The type of waves shown are _____.

11. Add arrows to the figure to indicate the amplitude of each wave. Which wave has the greater amplitude? _____

12. Which wave shown has more energy? _____

13. Add an arrow to indicate one wavelength on wave B.

Chapter 17   Mechanical Waves and Sound

Section 17.3 Behavior of Waves
(pages 508–512)

This section describes different interactions that can occur when a mechanical wave encounters an obstacle, a change in medium, or another wave. These interactions include reflection, refraction, diffraction, and interference.

Reading Strategy (page 508)

Identifying Main Ideas Complete the table below. As you read, write the main idea of each topic. For more information on this Reading Strategy, see the **Reading and Study Skills** in the **Skills and Reference Handbook** at the end of your textbook.

Wave Interactions	
Topic	**Main Idea**
Reflection	A wave reflected at a fixed boundary will be flipped upside down.
Refraction	
Diffraction	
Interference	The types of interference are constructive and destructive interference.
Standing waves	

Reflection (page 508)

1. Is the following sentence true or false? Reflection occurs when a wave bounces off a surface that it cannot pass through.

_____

2. Circle the letter of the results that occur when a wave reflects off a fixed boundary.

   a. The reflected wave will be turned upside down.

   b. The speed of the wave will decrease.

   c. The frequency of the wave will decrease.

Refraction (page 509)

3. Is the following sentence true or false? Refraction always involves a

change in the speed and direction of a wave. _____

Diffraction (page 510)

4. Circle the letter of each correct sentence. What is required in order for diffraction to occur?

   a. Waves move into a larger space.

   b. Waves encounter an obstacle.

   c. Waves pass through a narrow opening.

5. Is the following sentence true or false? A wave diffracts more if its wavelength is small compared to the size of an opening or obstacle.

   _____

Interference (pages 510–511)

6. Complete the table about interference.

Interference		
Type	**Alignment**	**Displacement Change**
Constructive	Crests align with crests; troughs align with troughs.	
		Displacements combine to produce a reduced amplitude.

7. Is the following sentence true or false? Destructive interference can result in wave displacements that are above the rest position.

   _____

Standing Waves (page 512)

8. At certain frequencies, interference between a wave and its reflection

   can produce a(n) _____.

9. Circle the letter of the sentence that is true about standing waves.

   a. A node is a point that has no displacement from the rest position.

   b. Standing waves appear to move through a medium, such as a string.

   c. Complete destructive interference occurs at antinodes.

10. Is the following sentence true or false? If a standing wave occurs in a medium at a given frequency, another standing wave will occur if this

    frequency is doubled. _____

11. Give an example of a common standing wave. _____

    _____

Chapter 17   Mechanical Waves and Sound

Section 17.4 Sound and Hearing
(pages 514–521)

This section discusses properties of sound waves, how they are produced, and how the ear perceives sound. It also descibes how music is produced and recorded.

Reading Strategy (page 514)

Using Prior Knowledge Before you read, add properties you already know about sound waves to the diagram below. Then add details about each property as you read the section. For more information on this Reading Strategy, see the **Reading and Study Skills** in the **Skills and Reference Handbook** at the end of your textbook.

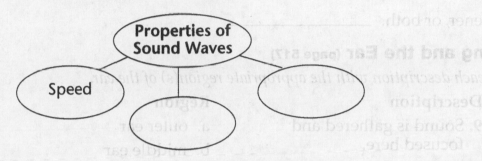

Properties of Sound Waves (pages 514–515)

1. Circle the letter of each sentence that is true about sound.

   a. Many behaviors of sound can be explained using a few properties.

   b. Sound waves are compressions and rarefactions that travel through a medium.

   c. Sound waves usually travel more slowly in solids than in gases.

Match each description with one or more sound properties.

Description	Property
_____ 2. This property is measured in units called decibels.	a. loudness
_____ 3. These properties are affected by the length of tubing in a musical instrument.	b. pitch
	c. intensity
_____ 4. This property is the frequency of a sound as your ears perceive it.	d. frequency
_____ 5. This property is a physical response to the intensity of sound.	

Chapter 17 Mechanical Waves and Sound

Ultrasound (page 516)

6. Is the following sentence true or false? Ultrasound has frequencies that are lower than most people are capable of hearing. _____

7. Describe one application of ultrasound. _____

_____

The Doppler Effect (page 516)

8. Is the following sentence true or false? The Doppler effect is a change in sound frequency caused by motion of the sound source, motion of the

listener, or both. _____

Hearing and the Ear (page 517)

Match each description with the appropriate region(s) of the ear.

	Description	Region
_____	9. Sound is gathered and focused here.	a. outer ear
_____	10. Nerve endings send signals to the brain.	b. middle ear
_____	11. Hammer, anvil, and stirrup are located here.	c. inner ear
_____	12. Sound vibrations are amplified.	

How Sound Is Reproduced (pages 518–519)

13. In recording sound, _____ are converted to electronic signals that are processed and stored. Circle the correct answer.

   electronic waves   sound waves   ultrasound waves

14. Sound is reproduced by converting _____ back into sound waves.

Music (page 521)

15. Is the following sentence true or false? Many musical instruments vary

pitch by changing the frequency of standing waves. _____

16. The response of a standing wave to another wave of the same frequency is called _____. Circle the correct answer.

   amplification   interference   resonance

Chapter 17 Mechanical Waves and Sound

WordWise

Test your knowledge of vocabulary terms from Chapter 17 by completing this crossword puzzle. Use the clues and the words in the list below.

interference	diffraction	Doppler effect
decibel	transverse	trough
node	rarefaction	wavelength

Clues across:

1. An apparent change in frequency of a sound source that moves relative to an observer

3. A point of no displacement in a standing wave

7. Area where particles in a medium are spread out as a longitudinal wave travels through it

8. Distance from one point to the next identical point on a wave

Clues down:

1. Occurs when a wave encounters an object or opening that is close in size to its wavelength

2. Type of mechanical wave whose direction of vibration is perpendicular to its direction of travel

4. A unit used to compare sound intensity levels

5. Occurs when waves overlap

6. Lowest point of a wave below the rest position

Chapter 17   Mechanical Waves and Sound

Calculating Wave Properties

**Math Skill:
Formulas and
Equations**

You may want to read
more about this **Math
Skill** in the **Skills and
Reference Handbook**
at the end of your
textbook.

A transverse wave in a rope is traveling at a speed of
3.0 m/s. The period of this mechanical wave is 0.25 s.
What is the wavelength?

1. Read and Understand

What information are you given?

Speed = 3.0 m/s

Period = 0.25 s

2. Plan and Solve

What unknown are you trying to calculate?

Wavelength = ?

What formula contains the given quantities and the unknown?

$$\text{Speed} = \text{Wavelength} \times \text{Frequency} = \frac{\text{Wavelength}}{\text{Period}}$$

Wavelength = Period × Speed

Replace each variable with its known value.

Speed = 3.0 m/s

Period = 0.25 s

Wavelength = 0.25 s × 3.0 m/s = 0.75 m

3. Look Back and Check

Is your answer reasonable?

$$\text{Speed} = \text{Wavelength} \times \text{Frequency} = \text{Wavelength} \times \frac{1}{\text{Period}}$$

$$\text{Speed} = 0.75 \text{ m} \times \frac{1}{0.25 \text{ s}} = 3.0 \text{ m/s}$$

Substituting the calculated wavelength into the equation yields the
original speed of 3.0 m/s.

Math Practice

On a separate sheet of paper, solve the following problems.

1. If a wave on a cord has a wavelength of 4 m and a period of 0.5 s, what is
its speed, in m/s?

2. Calculate the frequency, in Hz, of a wave in a string traveling
1.25 m/s, with a wavelength of 0.50 m.

Chapter 18 The Electromagnetic Spectrum and Light

Summary

18.1 Electromagnetic Waves

☞ **Electromagnetic waves are produced when an electric charge vibrates or accelerates.**

- **Electromagnetic waves** are transverse waves consisting of changing electric fields and changing magnetic fields.
- An **electric field** in a region of space exerts electric forces on charged particles.
- A **magnetic field** in a region of space produces magnetic forces.

☞ **Electromagnetic waves can travel through a vacuum, or empty space, as well as through matter.**

- The transfer of energy by electromagnetic waves traveling through matter or across space is called **electromagnetic radiation.**

☞ **The speed of light in a vacuum, *c*, is 3.00×10^8 meters per second.**

☞ **Electromagnetic waves vary in wavelength and frequency.**

☞ **Electromagnetic radiation behaves sometimes like a wave and sometimes like a stream of particles.**

- The **photoelectric effect** is the emission of electrons from a metal caused by light striking the metal.
- **Photons** are packets of electromagnetic energy. Each photon's energy is proportional to the frequency of the light.

☞ **The intensity of light decreases as photons travel farther from the source.**

- **Intensity** is the rate at which a wave's energy flows through a given unit of area.

18.2 The Electromagnetic Spectrum

☞ **The electromagnetic spectrum includes radio waves, infrared rays, visible light, ultraviolet rays, X-rays, and gamma rays.**

- The full range of frequencies of electromagnetic radiation is called the **electromagnetic spectrum.**

● **Radio waves are used in radio and television technologies, as well as in microwave ovens and radar.**

- In **amplitude modulation,** the amplitude of the wave varies. The frequency remains the same.
- In **frequency modulation,** the frequency of the wave varies. The amplitude remains the same.

● **Infrared rays are used as a source of heat and to discover areas of heat differences.**

- **Thermograms** are color-coded pictures that show variations in temperature.

● **People use visible light to see, to help keep them safe, and to communicate with one another.**

● **Ultraviolet rays have applications in health and medicine, and in agriculture.**

● **X-rays are used in medicine, industry, and transportation to make pictures of the inside of solid objects.**

● **Gamma rays are used in the medical field to kill cancer cells and make pictures of the brain, and in industrial situations as an inspection tool.**

18.3 Behavior of Light

● **Materials can be transparent, translucent, or opaque.**

- A **transparent** material transmits light, which means it allows most of the light that strikes it to pass through it. Clear glass is transparent.
- A **translucent** material scatters light. Frosted glass is translucent.
- An **opaque** material either absorbs or reflects all of the light that strikes it. Wood is opaque.

● **When light strikes a new medium, the light can be reflected, absorbed, or transmitted. When light is transmitted, it can be refracted, polarized, or scattered.**

- An **image** is a copy of an object formed by reflected (or refracted) waves of light.
- **Regular reflection** occurs when parallel light waves strike a surface and reflect all in the same direction. A regular image is sharp.
- **Diffuse reflection** occurs when parallel light waves strike a rough, uneven surface, and reflect in many different directions. A diffuse image is blurry.

- A light wave can refract, or bend, when it passes at an angle from one medium into another.
- Refraction sometimes causes mirages. A **mirage** is a false or distorted image.
- Light with waves that vibrate in only one plane is **polarized light.**
- **Scattering** means that light is redirected as it passes through a medium.

18.4 Color

As white light passes through a prism, shorter wavelengths refract more than longer wavelengths, and the colors separate.

- The process in which white light separates into colors is called **dispersion.**
- A rainbow forms when droplets of water in the air act like prisms. The droplets separate sunlight into the spectrum.

The color of any object depends on what the object is made of and on the color of light that strikes the object.

The primary colors of light are red, green, and blue.

- **Primary colors** are three specific colors that can be combined in varying amounts to create all possible colors.
- The secondary colors of light are cyan, yellow, and magenta. Each **secondary color** of light is a combination of two primary colors.
- Any two colors of light that combine to form white light are **complementary colors of light.**

The primary colors of pigments are cyan, yellow, and magenta.

- A **pigment** is a material that absorbs some colors of light and reflects other colors.
- Any two colors of pigments that combine to make black pigment are **complementary colors of pigments.**

18.5 Sources of Light

Common light sources include incandescent, fluorescent, laser, neon, tungsten-halogen, and sodium-vapor bulbs.

- Objects that give off their own light are **luminous.**

When electrons flow through the filament of an incandescent bulb, the filament gets hot and emits light.

- The light produced when an object gets hot enough to glow is **incandescent.**

◎ **Fluorescent light bulbs emit light by causing a phosphor to steadily emit photons.**

- In a process called **fluorescence,** a material absorbs light at one wavelength and then emits light at a longer wavelength.
- A **phosphor** is a solid material that can emit light by fluorescence.

◎ **Laser light is emitted when excited atoms of a solid, liquid, or gas emit photons.**

- A **laser** is a device that generates a beam of coherent light.
- Light in which waves have the same wavelength, and the crests and troughs are lined up, is **coherent light.**

◎ **Neon lights emit light when electrons move through a gas or a mixture of gases inside glass tubing.**

◎ **As electric current passes through a sodium-vapor bulb, it ionizes the gas mixture. The mixture warms up and the heat causes the sodium to change from a solid into a gas.**

◎ **Inside a tungsten-halogen bulb, electrons flow through a tungsten filament. The filament gets hot and emits light.**

Chapter 18   The Electromagnetic Spectrum and Light

Section 18.1 Electromagnetic Waves
(pages 532–538)

This section describes the characteristics of electromagnetic waves.

Reading Strategy (page 532)

Comparing and Contrasting As you read about electromagnetic waves, fill in the table below. If the characteristic listed in the table describes electromagnetic waves, write E in column 2. Write M for mechanical waves and B for both. For more information on this Reading Strategy, see the **Reading and Study Skills** in the **Skills and Reference Handbook** at the end of your textbook.

Electromagnetic and Mechanical Waves	
Travels through vacuum	E
Travels through medium	
Fits wave model	B
Fits particle model	
Transverse wave	
Longitudinal wave	M

What Are Electromagnetic Waves? (page 533)

1. What are electromagnetic waves? _____

_____

2. Electric fields are produced by electrically charged particles and by

changing _____.

3. Circle the letter of each sentence that is true about electric and magnetic fields.

   a. An electromagnetic wave occurs when electric and magnetic fields vibrate at right angles to each other.

   b. A magnetic field is surrounded by an electric current.

   c. Changing electric and magnetic fields regenerate each other.

4. Is the following sentence true or false? Electromagnetic waves need a

medium to travel through. _____

5. The transfer of energy by electromagnetic waves traveling through

matter or across space is called _____.

Chapter 18   The Electromagnetic Spectrum and Light

The Speed of Electromagnetic Waves (page 534)

6. Is the following sentence true or false? All electromagnetic waves travel
at the same speed through a vacuum. _____

7. Circle the letter that gives the correct speed of light in a vacuum.

   a. 3.00×10^8 kilometers per second
   b. 3.00×10^8 meters per hour
   c. 3.00×10^8 meters per second

Wavelength and Frequency (page 535)

8. Circle the letter of each sentence that is true about electromagnetic
   waves.

   a. Different electromagnetic waves can have different frequencies.
   b. Electromagnetic waves always travel at the speed of light.
   c. All electromagnetic waves travel at the same speed in
      a vacuum.

9. As the wavelengths of electromagnetic waves increase, the frequencies

   _____, for waves moving in a vacuum.

Wave or Particle? (pages 536–537)

10. Use the words in the box to fill in the blanks.

ion	particles
wave	water

    Electromagnetic radiation behaves sometimes like a(n)

    _____ and sometimes like a stream of _____.

11. The emission of electrons from a metal caused by light striking the

    metal is called the _____ effect.

12. Blue light has a higher frequency than red light. Do photons of blue

    light have more or less energy than photons of red light? _____

Intensity (page 538)

13. The closer you get to a source of light, the _____ the light
    appears.

14. Intensity is the _____ at which a wave's energy flows
    through a given unit of area.

Chapter 18   The Electromagnetic Spectrum and Light

Section 18.2 The Electromagnetic Spectrum
(pages 539–545)

This section identifies the waves in the electromagnetic spectrum and describes their uses.

Reading Strategy (page 539)

Summarizing Complete the table for the electromagnetic spectrum. List at least two uses for each kind of wave. For more information on this Reading Strategy, see the **Reading and Study Skills** in the **Skills and Reference Handbook** at the end of your textbook.

The Electromagnetic Spectrum		
Type of Waves	**Uses**	
Radio waves	Communications	
Infrared rays		Keeping food warm
Visible light		
Ultraviolet rays		
X-rays		
Gamma rays		

The Waves of the Spectrum (pages 539–540)

1. The electromagnetic spectrum includes visible light, gamma rays, ultraviolet rays, X-rays, infrared rays, and radio waves. List the types of waves in order from the longest to shortest wavelength.

   a. _____   b. _____

   c. _____   d. _____

   e. _____   f. _____

Chapter 18   The Electromagnetic Spectrum and Light

Radio Waves (pages 540–542)

2. Circle the letter of each way that radio waves might be used.

   a. X-ray machines

   b. microwave ovens

   c. radio technology

Infrared Rays (page 543)

3. Circle the letter of each way infrared rays are used.

   a. source of light

   b. to discover areas of heat differences

   c. source of heat

4. Thermograms show variations in _____ and are used to find places where a building loses heat to the environment. Circle the correct answer.

   light   temperature   X-rays

Visible Light (page 543)

5. Is the following sentence true or false? One use for visible light is to

   help people communicate with one another. _____

Ultraviolet Rays (page 544)

6. Circle the letter for each application for ultraviolet radiation.

   a. agriculture

   b. health and medicine

   c. transportation

X-Rays (page 544)

7. Is the following sentence true or false? X-rays have higher frequencies

   than ultraviolet rays. _____

Gamma Rays (page 545)

8. Circle the letter of each way gamma radiation is used in medicine.

   a. to kill cancer cells

   b. to make brain scans

   c. to take pictures of bones

Chapter 18 The Electromagnetic Spectrum and Light

Section 18.3 Behavior of Light
(pages 546–549)

This section discusses the behavior of light when it strikes different types of materials.

Reading Strategy (page 546)

Monitoring Your Understanding As you read, complete the flowchart to show how different materials affect light. For more information on this Reading Strategy, see the **Reading and Study Skills** in the **Skills and Reference Handbook** at the end of your textbook.

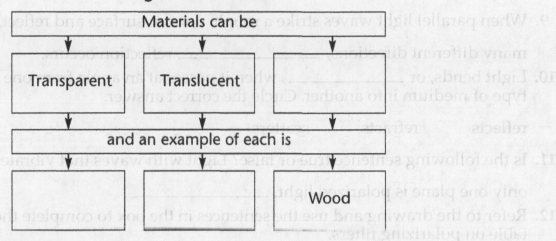

Light and Materials

Materials can be

Transparent | Translucent |

and an example of each is

| | | Wood |

Light and Materials (pages 546–547)

1. Is the following sentence true or false? Without light, nothing is

   visible. _____

Match each term to its definition.

Term	Definition
_____ 2. transparent	a. Material that absorbs or reflects all of the light that strikes it
_____ 3. opaque	b. Material that transmits light
_____ 4. translucent	c. Material that scatters light

Interactions of Light (pages 547–549)

5. Is the following sentence true or false? Just as light can affect matter,

   matter can affect light. _____

Chapter 18   The Electromagnetic Spectrum and Light

6. When light is transmitted, it can be refracted, polarized, or

_____.

7. A copy of an object formed by reflected or refracted light waves is
known as a(n) _____. Circle the best answer.

image   mirage   photograph

8. When parallel light waves strike a smooth surface and reflect off it in
the same direction, _____ reflection occurs. Circle the correct
answer.

diffuse   irregular   regular

9. When parallel light waves strike a rough, uneven surface and reflect in

many different directions, _____ reflection occurs.

10. Light bends, or _____, when it passes at an angle from one
type of medium into another. Circle the correct answer.

reflects   refracts   scatters

11. Is the following sentence true or false? Light with waves that vibrate in

only one plane is polarized light. _____

12. Refer to the drawing and use the sentences in the box to complete the
table on polarizing filters.

Light is blocked.	Light passes through.

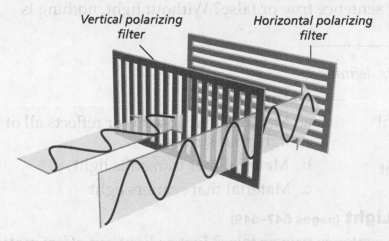

Vertical polarizing filter   Horizontal polarizing filter

Polarizing Filters		
Direction of Light Vibration	**Filter Type**	**Action**
Horizontal wave	Vertical polarizing filter	
Vertical wave	Vertical polarizing filter	

Chapter 18   The Electromagnetic Spectrum and Light

Section 18.4 Color
(pages 550–553)

This section explains how a prism separates white light. It also discusses factors that influence the various properties of color.

Reading Strategy (page 550)

Venn Diagram As you read, label the Venn diagram for mixing primary colors of light. For more information on this Reading Strategy, see the **Reading and Study Skills** in the **Skills and Reference Handbook** at the end of your textbook.

Mixing Colors of Light

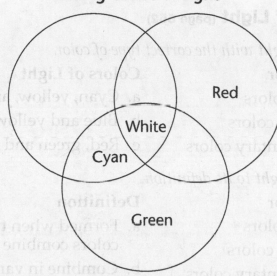

Separating White Light Into Colors (page 551)

1. Use the words in the box to fill in the blanks.

reflect	separate
refract	intensify

When white light passes through a prism, shorter wavelengths

_____ more than longer wavelengths, and the colors _____.

2. Circle the letter of the process in which white light is separated into the colors of the rainbow.

   a. reflection

   b. dispersion

   c. absorption

3. When a rainbow forms, what acts as the prism and what is the light

   source? _____

Chapter 18   The Electromagnetic Spectrum and Light

The Colors of Objects (pages 551–552)

4. Circle the letter of the factors that determine the color of an object seen by reflected light.

    a. what the object is made of

    b. the color of light that strikes the object

    c. the way the eye works

5. Is the following sentence true or false? I see a red car in sunlight because the color of light reaching my eyes is mostly red light.

_____

Mixing Colors of Light (page 552)

Match the colors of light with the correct type of color.

Type of Color		Colors of Light
_____ **6.** primary colors		a. Cyan, yellow, and magenta
_____ **7.** secondary colors		b. Blue and yellow
_____ **8.** complementary colors		c. Red, green and blue

Match each color of light to its definition.

Type of Color		Definition
_____ **9.** primary colors		a. Formed when two primary colors combine
_____ **10.** secondary colors		b. Combine in varying amounts to form all possible colors
_____ **11.** complementary colors		c. Combine to form white light

Mixing Pigments (page 553)

12. What is a pigment? _____

_____

Match the primary colors of pigment to the color they produce when combined.

Primary Colors		Color Produced
_____ **13.** Cyan and magenta		a. green
_____ **14.** Cyan and yellow		b. red
_____ **15.** Yellow and magenta		c. blue

Chapter 18   The Electromagnetic Spectrum and Light

Section 18.5 Sources of Light
(pages 558–562)

This section discusses the major sources of light and their uses.

Reading Strategy (page 558)

Sequencing Complete the incandescent-bulb flowchart. For more information on this Reading Strategy, see the **Reading and Study Skills** in the **Skills and Reference Handbook** at the end of your textbook.

Incandescent Bulb

Electrons flow through filament.

↓   ↓   ↓

↓   ↓   ↓

Filament radiates light.

1. Objects that give off their own light are _____. Circle the correct answer.

   colored   luminous   reflective

Incandescent Light (page 558)

2. Use the words in the box to fill in the blanks.

filament	fluorescent
phosphor	incandescent

   As electrons flow through a(n) _____ light bulb, the

   _____ heats up and glows.

3. Most of the energy given off by incandescent bulbs is in the form of _____. Circle the correct answer.

   heat   photons   waves

Fluorescent Light (page 559)

4. Fluorescent bulbs emit most of their energy in the form of _____. Circle the correct answer.

   heat   photons   waves

5. Is the following sentence true or false? Incandescent bulbs are more

   energy efficient than fluorescent bulbs. _____

Chapter 18   The Electromagnetic Spectrum and Light

Laser Light (page 560)

6. A laser is a device that generates _____.

7. What is coherent light? _____

_____

8. Circle the letter of the correct answer. Why does coherent light have a relatively constant intensity?

   a. It isn't easily absorbed.

   b. It diffuses almost instantly.

   c. It doesn't spread out much.

Neon Light (page 561)

9. Neon light is emitted when _____ move through a gas or a mixture of gases inside glass tubing. Circle the correct answer.

   beta particles   electrons   photons

Match the gases used to produce neon light with the color each produces.

   Gas   **Color**
   _____ **10.** helium   a. pale violet
   _____ **11.** neon   b. pink
   _____ **12.** krypton   c. red

13. Circle the letter of each factor that affects the color of neon light.

   a. reactivity of gas

   b. energy of photons

   c. color of glass tube

Sodium-Vapor Light (page 562)

14. Number the events from 1 to 3 to show what happens when a sodium-vapor bulb lights up.

   _____ Sodium changes from solid to gas.

   _____ The gas mixture heats up.

   _____ Electric current ionizes a gas mixture.

Tungsten-Halogen Light (page 562)

15. The gas in a tungsten-halogen light bulb is _____

   and the filament is _____.

Chapter 18   The Electromagnetic Spectrum and Light

WordWise

Complete the sentences using one of the words below.

electrons	fields	frequency
reflects	refraction	radio
filament	photons	coherent
mercury	translucent	

Electromagnetic waves consist of changing electric and changing magnetic

_____.

If you know the wavelength of an electromagnetic wave in a vacuum, you

can calculate its _____.

Although light behaves as a wave, the photoelectric effect shows that light

also consists of bundles of energy called _____.

Antennas use _____ waves to send signals to television

receivers.

If you can look through a material but what you see is not clear or distinct,

then the material is said to be _____.

When a beam of light enters a new medium at an angle, it changes

direction, and _____ occurs.

A truck appears red in the sunlight because its paint _____

mainly red light.

An incandescent bulb produces light by using an electric current to heat

a(n) _____.

Inside a fluorescent bulb, an electric current passes through _____

vapor and produces ultraviolet light.

Light that consists of a single wavelength of light with its crests and troughs

lined up is called _____ light.

Neon lights emit light when _____ flow through gas in a tube.

Chapter 18   The Electromagnetic Spectrum and Light

Calculating Wavelength and Frequency

Math Skill:
Multiplication
and Division
of Exponents

You may want to read
more about this **Math
Skill** in the **Skills and
Reference Handbook**
at the end of your
textbook.

A particular AM radio station broadcasts at a frequency of 1030 MHz. What is the wavelength of the transmitted radio wave assuming it travels in a vacuum?

1. Read and Understand

What information are you given?

Speed = c = 3.00×10^8 m/s

Frequency = 1030 kHz =1030 $\times 10^3$ Hz

2. Plan and Solve

What unknown are you trying to calculate?

Wavelength = ?

What formula contains the given quantities and the unknown?

Speed = Wavelength $\times$ Frequency

Wavelength = $\dfrac{\text{Speed}}{\text{Frequency}}$

Replace each variable with its known value.

Wavelength = $\dfrac{3.00 \times 10^8 \text{ m/s}}{1030 \text{ Hz} \times 10^8 \text{Hz}}$

$= \dfrac{3.00 \times 10^8 \text{ m/s}}{1.030 \times 10^6 \text{ 1/s}} = 291$ m

3. Look Back and Check

Is your answer reasonable?

Radio waves have frequencies greater that 1 mm, so 291 m is a reasonable wavelength for a radio wave.

Math Practice

On a separate sheet of paper, solve the following problems.

1. In a vacuum, the wavelength of light from a laser is 630 nm (630×10^{-9} m). What is the frequency of the light?

2. If a radio wave vibrates at 80.0 MHz, what is its wavelength?

Chapter 19 Optics

Summary

19.1 Mirrors

🔹 **The law of reflection states that the angle of reflection is equal to the angle of incidence.**

- A **ray diagram** shows how rays change direction when they strike mirrors and pass through lenses.
- The **angle of incidence** is the angle the incident ray makes with a line drawn perpendicular to the surface of the mirror. The **angle of reflection** is the angle the reflected ray makes with the perpendicular line.

🔹 **A plane mirror always produces a virtual image.**

- A mirror with a flat surface is a **plane mirror**. A **virtual image** is a copy of an object formed at the location from which the light rays appear to come.
- A **real image** is a copy of an object formed at the point where light rays meet.

🔹 **Concave mirrors can form either real or virtual images.**

- The surface of a **concave mirror** is shaped like the inside of a bowl. The light rays from a concave mirror meet at the **focal point.**

🔹 **Convex mirrors always cause light rays to spread out and can only form virtual images.**

- The surface of a **convex mirror** is shaped like the outside of a bowl.

19.2 Lenses

🔹 **When light enters a new medium at an angle, the change in speed causes the light to bend, or refract.**

- The **index of refraction** for a material is the ratio of the speed of light in a vacuum to the speed of the light in the material.

🔹 **Concave lenses always cause light rays to spread out and can only form virtual images.**

- A **lens** is made of transparent material that has one or two curved surfaces that can refract light.
- A **concave lens** is curved inward at the center and is thickest at the outside edges.

🔹 **Convex lenses form either real or virtual images.**

- A **convex lens** is curved outward at the center and is thinnest at the outer edges.

☛ **Materials that have small critical angles are likely to cause most of the light entering them to be totally internally reflected.**

- The **critical angle** is the angle of incidence that causes light to reflect along the boundary between glass and air. **Total internal reflection** is the complete reflection of a light ray back into its original medium.

19.3 Optical Instruments

- A **telescope** is an instrument that uses lenses or mirrors to collect and focus light from distant objects.

☛ **There are two main types of telescopes, reflecting telescopes and refracting telescopes.**

- The **reflecting telescope** uses mirrors and convex lenses to collect and focus light.
- The **refracting telescope** uses convex lenses to collect and focus light.

☛ **Light rays enter a camera through an opening, are focused by the opening or lens, and form an image that is recorded on film or by a sensor.**

- A **camera** is an optical instrument that records an image of an object.

☛ **The compound microscope uses two convex lenses to magnify small objects.**

- A **microscope** is an optical instrument that uses lenses to provide enlarged images of very small, near objects.

19.4 The Eye and Vision

☛ **The main parts of the eye are the cornea, the pupil and iris, the lens, and the retina.**

- Light rays enter your eyes through the transparent coating of the eye, the **cornea.**
- The **pupil** is the opening that allows light rays to enter your eye. The colored part of your eye, the **iris,** contracts and expands to control the amount of light that enters your eye.
- The **retina** is the inner surface of the eye. Its surface is covered by light-sensitive nerve endings called **rods** and **cones.**

☛ **Several common vision problems are nearsightedness, farsightedness, and astigmatism.**

- **Nearsightedness** causes distant objects to appear blurry.
- **Farsightedness** is a condition that causes nearby objects to appear blurry.
- **Astigmatism** is a condition in which objects at any distance appear blurry because the cornea or lens is misshapen.

Chapter 19   Optics

Section 19.1 Mirrors
(pages 570–573)

This section describes the law of reflection and explains how images are formed by plane, concave, and convex mirrors. It also describes uses of mirrors.

Reading Strategy (page 570)

Comparing and Contrasting After reading this section, compare mirror types by completing the table. For more information on this Reading Strategy, see the **Reading and Study Skills** in the **Skills and Reference Handbook** at the end of your textbook.

Mirror Types		
Mirror	**Shape of Surface**	**Image (virtual, real, or both)**
Plane	Flat	Virtual
Concave		
Convex	Outside curved surface	

The Law of Reflection (pages 570–571)

1. A ray diagram shows how rays _____ when they strike mirrors and pass through lenses.

2. Circle the letter of the sentence that best answers the following question. What does a ray diagram and the law of reflection show?

   a. The angle of incidence is greater than the angle of reflection.
   b. The angle of reflection is greater than the angle of incidence.
   c. The angle of incidence is equal to the angle of reflection.

Plane Mirrors (page 571)

3. A mirror with a flat surface is known as a(n) _____.

4. Circle the letter of each sentence that is true about plane mirrors.

   a. Plane mirrors always produce virtual images.
   b. Plane mirrors produce right-left reversed images of objects.
   c. Light rays reflect from a mirror at an angle that is twice as large as the angle of incidence.

5. Circle the letter of the correct answer. What type of image is a copy of an object formed at the location from which the light rays appear to come?

   a. reversed image

   b. virtual image

   c. real image

Concave and Convex Mirrors (pages 572–573)

6. What is the focal point? _____

_____

7. Is the following sentence true or false? A real image is a copy of an object formed at the point where light rays actually meet.

   _____

For questions 8 through 10, refer to the diagrams below.

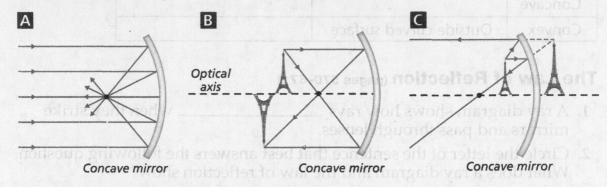

8. Label the focal point on each diagram.

9. In B and C, label the object and image locations and identify the image as real or virtual. (*Hint:* The object is always right-side up and in front of the reflecting surface of the mirror.)

10. Circle the letter of the correct answer. What determines whether a concave mirror produces a real image or a virtual image?

   a. the size of the object

   b. the shape of the object

   c. the position of the object relative to the focal point

11. A curved mirror whose outside surface is the reflecting surface is called

   a(n) _____ mirror.

12. Is the following sentence true or false? The image formed by a convex

   lens is always upright and smaller than the object. _____

Chapter 19   Optics

Section 19.2 Lenses
(pages 574–578)

This section defines index of refraction and discusses how it is related to the way light behaves upon entering different materials. It also presents image formation in concave and convex lenses.

Reading Strategy (page 574)

Building Vocabulary As you read the section, define in your own words each vocabulary word listed in the table. For more information on this Reading Strategy, see the **Reading and Study Skills** in the **Skills and Reference Handbook** at the end of your textbook.

Refraction and Reflection	
Vocabulary Term	**Definition**
Index of refraction	Ratio of the speed of light in a vacuum to the speed of light in the material
Critical angle	
Total internal reflection	

Index of Refraction of Light (pages 574–575)

1. Circle the letter of each sentence that is true about the speed of light through media.

   a. Once light passes from a vacuum into any medium, it speeds up.

   b. Compared to other media, air slows the speed of light only slightly.

   c. The speed of light is greater in water than in air.

2. The ratio of the speed of light in a vacuum to the speed of light in a

   particular material is known as the _____ of that material.

Concave and Convex Lenses (pages 576–577)

3. An object made of transparent material that has one or two curved

   surfaces that can refract light is called a(n) _____.

4. Circle the properties of a lens that affect the way it refracts light.

   curvature   focal point   thickness

5. A lens that is curved inward at the center and is thickest at the outside edges is called a(n) _____ lens. Circle the correct answer.

   concave   convex   plane

Chapter 19   Optics

6. Circle the letter of each sentence that is true about convex lenses.

    a. Convex lenses are diverging lenses.

    b. Convex lenses can form either real or virtual images.

    c. Convex lenses are shaped like the inside of a bowl.

For questions 7 and 8, refer to the diagrams below.

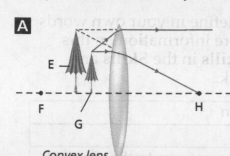

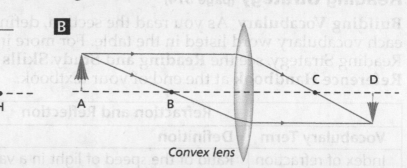

Convex lens   Convex lens

7. In each diagram, identify the labeled items as the object, focal point, or image. Also, identify the image as virtual or real.

    A. _____   B. _____

    C. _____   D. _____

    E. _____   F. _____

    G. _____   H. _____

8. Which diagram shows the formation of a virtual image?

    _____

Total Internal Reflection (page 578)

9. Circle the letter of each sentence that is true about the critical angle.

    a. At the critical angle, light refracts along the surface between two media.

    b. Only concave lenses have critical angles.

    c. All the light is reflected back into the second, denser medium when the critical angle is exceeded.

10. Is the following sentence true or false? Materials that have small critical angles, such as the glass used in fiber optics, cause most of the light

    entering them to be totally internally reflected. _____

Chapter 19 Optics

Section 19.3 Optical Instruments
(pages 580–585)

This section describes optical instruments, including telescopes, cameras, and microscopes. It explains how these instruments form images.

Reading Strategy (page 580)

Using Prior Knowledge Add the names and descriptions of other optical instruments you know to the diagram. Revise the diagram after you read the section. For more information on this Reading Strategy, see the **Reading and Study Skills** in the **Skills and Reference Handbook** at the end of your textbook.

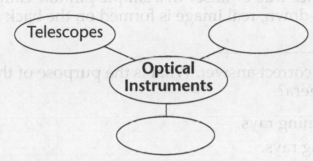

Telescopes (pages 580–581)

1. Circle the letter that best describes the amount of time it takes light from the most distant stars to reach Earth.

   a. seconds

   b. hours

   c. billions of years

2. An instrument that uses lenses or mirrors to collect and focus light from

   distant objects is called a(n) _____.

3. Complete the table about telescopes.

Telescopes		
Type	**Parts That Collect and Focus Light**	**Type of Image Formed**
Reflecting telescope		
	Convex lenses	Real image inside the telescope; an upside-down virtual image of the real image

Chapter 19   Optics

Cameras (pages 582–584)

4. What is a camera? _____

_____

5. Circle the letter of each sentence that describes how cameras form or record images.

    a. An image is recorded on film or by a sensor.

    b. Light rays enter through an opening.

    c. Light rays are focused by the opening or lens.

6. Is the following sentence true or false? In a simple pinhole camera made from a box, an upside-down, real image is formed on the back

    wall of the box. _____

7. Circle the letter of the correct answer. What is the purpose of the lens elements in a film camera?

    a. They disperse incoming rays.

    b. They focus incoming rays.

    c. They record images.

Microscopes (page 584)

8. An optical instrument that uses two convex lenses to magnify small

    objects is called a(n) _____.

9. Circle the letter that describes the path light rays follow through a compound microscope.

    a. Light rays from above pass up through the object and then pass through the objective lens.

    b. Light rays from below pass up through the object, the objective lens, and the eyepiece lens.

    c. Light rays from below pass up through the object, the concave lens, and the objective lens.

10. Is the following sentence true or false? When you look through the eyepiece of a compound microscope you see an enlarged, virtual image

    of the object. _____

Chapter 19   Optics

Section 19.4 The Eye and Vision
(pages 588–592)

This section describes the eye as an optical instrument and defines parts of the eye and their functions. It also describes vision problems and how they can be corrected.

Reading Strategy (page 588)

Outlining As you read, make an outline of the important ideas in this section. Use the green headings as the main topics and the blue headings as subtopics. For more information on this Reading Strategy, see the **Reading and Study Skills** in the **Skills and Reference Handbook** at the end of your textbook.

<table>
<tr><td align="center">Section 19.4 Outline</td></tr>
</table>

I. The Eye and Vision

  A. Structure of the Eye

    1. _____

    2. _____

    3. _____

    4. _____

    5. _____

  B. _____

    1. Nearsightedness

    2. _____

    3. _____

Structure of the Eye (pages 588–590)

Write the letter of the part of the eye that best matches each description.

Description	Part of Eye
_____ **1.** Its curved surface helps to focus light entering the eye.	a. pupil
_____ **2.** It focuses light onto sensor cells at the back of the eye.	b. retina
_____ **3.** This opening allows light to pass through the eye.	c. cornea
_____ **4.** This expands and contracts to control the amount of light entering the eye.	d. iris
_____ **5.** This is the transparent outer coating of the eye.	e. lens
_____ **6.** Its surface has rods and cones.	

Correcting Vision Problems (pages 590–592)

For questions 7 and 8, refer to the figures below.

Problem: Nearsightedness (Eyeball is too long.)

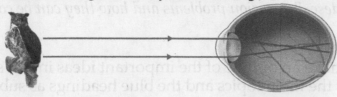

Correction:

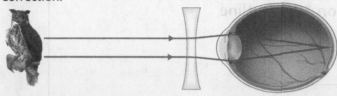

7. Circle the letter of the location where the image forms when nearsightedness occurs.

   a. on the retina

   b. behind the retina

   c. before it reaches the retina

8. Nearsightedness can be corrected by placing a(n) _____ lens in front of the eye. Circle the correct answer.

   converging concave   diverging concave   diverging convex

Match each type of vision problem to its definition.

Vision Problem	Definition
_____ 9. astigmatism	a. A condition that causes distant objects to appear blurry because the cornea is too curved or the eyeball is too long
_____ 10. farsightedness	b. A condition that causes objects at any distance to appear blurry because the cornea or lens is misshapen
_____ 11. nearsightedness	c. A condition that causes nearby objects to appear blurry because the cornea is not curved enough or the eyeball is too short

Chapter 19   Optics

WordWise

Use the clues and the words in the box below to write the vocabulary terms from the chapter in the blanks. The term enclosed in the diagonal is a term that is important in the study of optics.

astigmatism	plane mirror	camera
concave lens	ray diagram	cornea
lens	telescope	iris

Clues

1. Shows how the paths of light rays change when they strike mirrors

2. Transparent material with one or two curved surfaces that can refract light

3. A mirror with a flat surface

4. An instrument that uses mirrors to collect and focus light

5. Expands and contracts to control the amount of light entering the eye

6. An optical instrument that records an image of an object

7. Transparent outer layer of the eye

8. When the cornea is misshapen, this vision problem can result.

9. Type of lens that causes light rays to diverge

1. _ _ _ _ _ _ _ _ _ _

2. _ _ _ _ _ _

3. _ _ _ _ _ _ _ _ _ _ _

4. _ _ _ _ _ _ _ _ _

5. _ _ _ _

6. _ _ _ _ _ _

7. _ _ _ _ _ _

8. _ _ _ _ _ _ _ _ _ _ _

9. _ _ _ _ _ _ _ _ _ _ _ _ _

Chapter 19   Optics

Calculating Index of Refraction

The speed of light in the mineral halite, NaCl, is
approximately 1.95×10^8 m/s. Calculate the index of
refraction for halite. (Recall that the speed of light in a
vacuum is 3.00×10^8 m/s.)

1. Read and Understand

What information are you given?

Speed of light in halite = 1.95×10^8 m/s

Speed of light in vacuum = 3.00×10^8 m/s

2. Plan and Solve

What variable are you trying to determine?

Index of refraction = ?

What formulas contain the given variables?

$$\text{Index of refraction} = \frac{\text{Speed of light }_{vacuum}}{\text{Speed of light }_{material}}$$

Replace each variable with its known value.

$$\text{Index of refraction} = \frac{(3.00 \times 10^8 \text{ m/s})}{(1.95 \times 10^8 \text{ m/s})} = 1.54$$

3. Look Back and Check

Is your answer reasonable?

Speed of light in vacuum = $(1.95 \times 10^8$ m/s$)(1.54) = 3.00 \times 10^8$ m/s

Yes, the answer is reasonable. Substituting the calculated index of
refraction for halite back into the equation yields the value of the
speed of light in a vacuum.

Math Practice

On a separate sheet of paper, solve the following problems.

1. The mineral uvarovite has an index of refraction of 1.86. Calculate the
speed of light in this sample of uvarovite.

2. What is the index of refraction of a sample of opal, if the speed of light
passing through it is 2.05×10^8 m/s?

Chapter 20 Electricity

Summary

20.1 Electric Charge and Static Electricity

☞ **An excess or shortage of electrons produces a net electric charge.**

- **Electric charge** is a property that causes subatomic particles such as protons and electrons to attract or repel each other.

☞ **Like charges repel, and opposite charges attract.**

- **Electric force** is the pushing or pulling between electrically charged objects.

☞ **The strength of an electric field depends on the amount of charge that produces the field and on the distance from the charge.**

- The effect an electric charge has on other charges in the space around it is the charge's **electric field**.

☞ **Charge can be transferred by friction, by contact, and by induction.**

- **Static electricity** is the study of the behavior of electric charges, including the transfer of charges.
- The **law of conservation of charge** states that the total charge in an isolated system is constant.
- **Induction** is the transfer of charge without contact between materials.

☞ **Static discharge occurs when a pathway through which charges can move forms suddenly.**

20.2 Electric Current and Ohm's Law

- **Electric current** is a flow of electric charges.

☞ **The two types of current are direct current and alternating current.**

- **Direct current** (DC) always flows in one direction. **Alternating current** (AC) is a flow of electric charge that regularly reverses its direction.

☞ **Metals such as copper and silver are good electrical conductors. Wood, plastic, rubber, and air are good electrical insulators.**

- An **electrical conductor** is a material through which charge can flow easily.
- An **electrical insulator** is a material through which charge cannot flow easily.

☞ **A material's thickness, length, and temperature affect its resistance.**

- **Resistance** is opposition to the flow of charges in a material.
- A **superconductor** is a material that has almost zero resistance at low temperatures.

In order for charge to flow in a conducting wire, the wire must be connected in a complete loop that includes a source of electrical energy.

- **Potential difference** is the difference in electrical potential energy between two places in an electric field. Potential difference is also called **voltage**, because it is measured in volts.
- A **battery** is a device that converts chemical energy to electrical energy.

Increasing the voltage increases the current. Keeping the same voltage and increasing the resistance decreases the current.

- According to **Ohm's law**, the voltage in a circuit equals the product of the current and the resistance. The equation for this relationship is $V = I \times R$.

20.3 Electric Circuits

- An **electric circuit** is a complete path through which charge can flow.

Circuit diagrams use symbols to represent parts of a circuit, including a source of electrical energy and devices that are run by the electrical energy.

If one element stops functioning in a series circuit, none of the elements can operate.

- In a **series circuit**, charge has only one path through which it can flow.

If one element stops functioning in a parallel circuit, the rest of the elements still can operate.

- A **parallel circuit** is an electric circuit with two or more paths through which charges can flow.

Electric power can be calculated by multiplying voltage by current.

- The rate at which electrical energy is converted to another form of energy is **electric power**.

Correct wiring, fuses, circuit breakers, insulation, and grounded plugs help make electrical energy safe to use.

- A **fuse** prevents overload in a circuit.
- A **circuit breaker** is a switch that opens when current in a circuit is too high.
- The transfer of excess charge through a conductor to Earth is called **grounding**.

20.4 Electronic Devices

⊙ **Electronics conveys information with electrical patterns called analog and digital signals.**

- The science of using electric current to process or transmit information is **electronics.**
- An **electric signal** is information sent as patterns in the controlled flow of electrons through a circuit.
- An **analog signal** is a smoothly varying signal produced by continuously changing the voltage or current in a circuit.
- A **digital signal** encodes information as a string of ones and zeros.

⊙ **Vacuum tubes can change alternating current into direct current, increase the strength of a signal, or turn a current on or off.**

⊙ **In n-type semiconductors, the current is a flow of electrons. In p-type semiconductors, it appears as though positive charge flows.**

- A **semiconductor** is a crystalline solid that conducts current only under certain conditions.

⊙ **Most modern electronic devices are controlled by solid-state components.**

- A **diode** is a solid-state component that combines an n-type and a p-type semiconductor. Current flows in only one direction, so diodes can change AC to DC.
- A **transistor** is a solid-state component with three layers of semiconductors. It can be used as a switch or an amplifier.
- An **integrated circuit** is a thin slice of silicon that contains many solid-state components.

⊙ **Communication devices use microchips to make them more portable, reliable, and affordable.**

- A **computer** is a programmable device that can store and process information. It usually has many microchips.

Chapter 20   Electricity

Section 20.1 Electric Charge and Static Electricity
(pages 600–603)

This section explains how electric charge is created and how positive and negative charges affect each other. It also discusses the different ways that electric charge can be transferred.

Reading Strategy (page 600)

Identifying Main Ideas Copy the table on a separate sheet of paper. As you read, write the main ideas. For more information on this Reading Strategy, see the **Reading and Study Skills** in the **Skills and Reference Handbook** at the end of your textbook.

Characteristics of Electric Charge	
Topic	**Main Idea**
Electric charge	An excess or shortage of electrons produces a net electric charge.
Electric forces	
Electric fields	
Static electricity	Charge can be transferred by friction, contact, and induction.

Electric Charge (pages 600–601)

1. Is the following sentence true or false? In an atom, negatively charged electrons surround a positively charged nucleus. _____

2. Is the following sentence true or false? If a neutral atom gains one or more electrons, it becomes a positively charged ion. _____

Electric Forces (page 601)

3. Circle the letter of each sentence that is true about electric force.

   a. Like charges attract and opposite charges repel.
   b. Electric force is the attraction or repulsion between electrically charged objects.
   c. Electric force is inversely proportional to the amount of charge.

4. Which are stronger inside an atom, electric forces or gravitational

forces? _____

5. Is the following sentence true or false? Electric forces cause friction and

other contact forces. _____

Electric Fields (page 602)

6. A charge's electric field is the effect the charge has on

_____ in the space around it.

7. Circle the letters of the factors that the strength of an electric field
depends on.

a. whether the charge is positive or negative

b. the amount of charge that produces the field

c. the distance from the charge

Static Electricity and Charging (pages 602–603)

8. Static electricity is the study of the _____.

9. Is the following sentence true or false? Charge can be transferred

by friction, by contact, and by induction. _____

10. What is the law of conservation of charge? _____

_____

11. Circle the letter of the correct answer. A charge transfer between objects
that touch each other is called _____.

a. charging by induction

b. charging by contact

c. static discharge

12. Circle the letter of each sentence that is true about charging.

a. When you rub a balloon on your hair, your hair loses electrons and
becomes positively charged.

b. Static charges cannot move.

c. Induction occurs when charge is transferred without contact between
materials.

Static Discharge (page 603)

13. Is the following sentence true or false? Static discharge occurs when a
pathway through which charges can move forms suddenly.

_____

Chapter 20   Electricity

Section 20.2 Electric Current and Ohm's Law
(pages 604–607)

This section discusses electric current, resistance, and voltage. It also uses Ohm's law to explain how voltage, current, and resistance are related.

Reading Strategy (page 604)

Predicting Before you read, write a prediction of what electric current is in the table below. After you read, if your prediction was incorrect or incomplete, write what electric current actually is. For more information on this Reading Strategy, see the **Reading and Study Skills** in the **Skills and Reference Handbook** at the end of your textbook.

Electric Current	
Electric Current Probably Means	**Electric Current Actually Means**

Electric Current (page 604)

1. What is electric current? _____

_____

2. Use the words in the box to complete the following table about electric current.

Two directions	Flashlight
One direction	Home or school

Electric Current		
Type of Current	**How Charge Flows**	**Examples**
Direct		
Alternating		

Conductors and Insulators (page 605)

3. What is an electrical conductor? _____

_____

4. What is an electrical insulator? _____

_____

5. Is the following sentence true or false? Metals are good conductors

because they do not have freely moving electrons. _____

Chapter 20   Electricity

Match each material to the category of a conductor or insulator.

	Material		Category
_____	**6.** Copper		**a.** conductor
_____	**7.** Plastic		**b.** insulator
_____	**8.** Rubber		
_____	**9.** Silver		
_____	**10.** Wood		

Resistance (page 605)

11. Circle the letter of each factor that affects a material's resistance.

    a. its length

    b. its temperature

    c. its thickness

12. What is a superconductor? _____

_____

Voltage (page 606)

Match each term to its definition.

	Definition		Term
_____	**13.** A device that converts chemical energy to electrical energy		**a.** flow of charge
_____	**14.** Requires a complete loop		**b.** voltage
_____	**15.** The difference in electrical potential energy between two places in an electric field		**c.** battery

16. Is the following sentence true or false? Three common voltage sources

are batteries, solar cells, and generators. _____

Ohm's Law (page 607)

17. Is the following sentence true or false? According to Ohm's law, the voltage in a circuit equals the product of the energy and the resistance.

_____

18. Is the following sentence true or false? Doubling the resistance in a circuit will halve the current if voltage is held constant.

_____

Chapter 20   Electricity

Section 20.3 Electric Circuits
(pages 609–613)

This section describes circuit diagrams and types of circuits. It also explains calculation of electric power and electric energy and discusses electrical safety.

Reading Strategy (page 609)

Relating Text and Visuals As you read about household circuits, complete the table by listing three things the diagram in Figure 13 helps you understand about circuits. For more information on this Reading Strategy, see the **Reading and Study Skills** in the **Skills and Reference Handbook** at the end of your textbook.

Understanding a Circuit Diagram
What Can Be Seen in the Circuit Diagram?
Wire bringing current from outside
Separate circuit for the lights

Circuit Diagrams (pages 609–610)

1. Circuit diagrams use _____ to represent parts of a circuit, including a source of electrical energy and devices that are run by the electrical energy.

Match each symbol to what it indicates on a circuit diagram.

Symbol	What Symbol Indicates
_____ **2.** +	a. The direction of current
_____ **3.** –	b. A negative terminal
_____ **4.** ⟶	c. A positive terminal

Series Circuits (page 610)

5. Is the following sentence true or false? In a series circuit, if one element stops functioning, then none of the elements can operate.

_____

Parallel Circuits (page 610)

6. Is the following sentence true or false? Circuits in a home are rarely wired in parallel. _____

7. If one light goes out in a parallel circuit, the rest of the lights

_____ .

Power and Energy Calculations (pages 611–612)

8. The rate at which electrical energy is converted to another form of

energy is called _____.

9. Circle the letter of each measure of power.

    a. joule per second

    b. coulomb

    c. watt

10. Is the following sentence true or false? Electric power is calculated by

multiplying current times voltage. _____

11. The unit of energy usually used by electric power companies is the

_____. Circle the correct term.

    joules/s   kilowatt-hour   watts/hour

Electrical Safety (pages 612–613)

12. Circle the letters of what could happen if the current in a wire exceeds
the circuit's safety limit.

    a. The wire could get cooler.

    b. A fuse could blow.

    c. A fire could start.

13. The transfer of excess charge through a conductor to Earth is called

_____.

14. Use the words in the box to complete the following table about
equipment used to prevent electrical accidents. You may use terms more
than once.

fuse	insulation	circuit breaker
three-pronged plug	grounding wire	

Equipment to Prevent Current Overload	Equipment to Protect People From Shock	Equipment to Prevent Short Circuits
a. _____	c. _____	f. _____
b. _____	d. _____	
	e. _____	

Chapter 20   Electricity

Section 20.4 Electronic Devices
(pages 618–622)

This section discusses how various electronic devices operate and what they are used for.

Reading Strategy (page 618)

Summarizing Copy the table on a separate sheet of paper. As you read, complete the table to summarize what you learned about solid-state components. For more information on this Reading Strategy, see the **Reading and Study Skills** in the **Skills and Reference Handbook** at the end of your textbook.

Solid-State Components		
Solid-State Component	**Description**	**Uses**
Diode	Electrons flow from an n-type to a p-type semiconductor.	
Transistor		Switch, amplifier
Integrated circuit		

Electronic Signals (pages 618–619)

Match each term to its definition.

Definition

_____ **1.** Information sent as patterns in the controlled flow of electrons through a circuit

_____ **2.** The science of using electric current to process or transmit information

_____ **3.** A smoothly varying signal produced by continuously changing the voltage or current in a circuit

_____ **4.** A signal that encodes information as a string of ones and zeros

Term

a. electronics

b. analog signal

c. electronic signal

d. digital signal

Chapter 20   Electricity

Vacuum Tubes (page 619)

5. Circle the letter of each item that is true about vacuum tubes.

   a. can change alternating current to direct current

   b. never burn out

   c. can increase the strength of a signal

Semiconductors (page 621)

6. What is a semiconductor? _____

_____

7. Circle the letter of each sentence that is true about a p-type semiconductor.

   a. It can be made by adding a trace amount of boron to silicon.

   b. Electrons are attracted to positively charged holes at each boron atom.

   c. As the electrons jump from hole to hole, it looks like a flow of positive charge.

8. Is the following sentence true or false? In an n-type semiconductor,

   weakly bound electrons can conduct a current. _____

Solid-State Components (pages 621–622)

Match each term to its definition.

Term	Definition
_____ 9. diode	a. A solid-state component with three layers of semiconductors
_____ 10. transistor	
_____ 11. integrated circuit	b. A thin slice of silicon that contains many solid-state components
	c. A solid-state component that combines an n-type and p-type semiconductor

Communications Technology (page 622)

12. Circle the letter of the reasons to use microchips in communication devices.

   a. Microchips make them smaller.

   b. Microchips use less energy than vacuum tubes.

   c. Microchips can run without power if necessary.

Chapter 20   Electricity

WordWise

Match each definition with the correct term in the grid and then write its number under the appropriate term. When you have filled in all the boxes, add up the numbers in each column, row, and the two diagonals.

What is surprising about the sums? _____

Definitions

1. A switch that opens when current in a circuit is too high
2. A thin slice of silicon that contains many solid-state components
3. Material through which charge can easily flow
4. A circuit in which the charge has only one path through which it can flow
5. An electric circuit with two or more paths through which charge can flow
6. The attraction or repulsion between electrically charged objects
7. Charge transfer without contact between materials
8. Material through which a charge cannot easily flow
9. A continuous flow of electric charge

			Diagonal = _____
integrated circuit	induction	electric force	= _____
_____	_____	_____	
electric current	parallel circuit	circuit breaker	= _____
_____	_____	_____	
series circuit	electrical conductor	electrical insulator	= _____
_____	_____	_____	
= _____	= _____	= _____	Diagonal = _____

Chapter 20   Electricity

Power, Voltage, and Current

The power rating on an electric soldering iron is 40.0 watts. If the soldering iron is connected to a 120-volt line, how much current does it use?

**Math Skill:
Formulas and
Equations**

You may want to read more about this **Math Skill** in the **Skills and Reference Handbook** at the end of your textbook.

1. Read and Understand

What information are you given in the problem?

Power = P = 40.0 watts

Voltage = V = 120 volts

2. Plan and Solve

What unknown are you trying to calculate?

Current = I = ?

What formula contains the given quantities and the unknown?

$$P = I \times V; I = \frac{P}{V}$$

Replace each variable with its known value.

$$I = \frac{40.0 \text{ watts}}{120 \text{ volts}} = 0.33 \text{ amps}$$

3. Look Back and Check

Is your answer reasonable?

The answer is reasonable, because a soldering iron needs a relatively low current to generate heat.

Math Practice

On a separate sheet of paper, solve the following problems.

1. A steam cleaner has a power rating of 1100 watts. If the cleaner is connected to a 120-volt line, what current does it use?

2. A coffee maker uses 10.0 amps of current from a 120-volt line. How much power does it use?

Chapter 21 Magnetism

Summary

21.1 Magnets and Magnetic Fields

- **Magnetic force** is the force a magnet exerts on another magnet, on iron or a similar metal, or on moving charges.

- **Like magnetic poles repel one another, and opposite magnetic poles attract one another.**
  - All magnets have two **magnetic poles**, regions where the magnet's force is strongest.

- **A magnetic field, which is strongest near a magnet's poles, will either attract or repel another magnet that enters the field.**
  - The area surrounding Earth that is influenced by a giant magnetic field is the **magnetosphere**.

- **When a material is magnetized, most of its magnetic domains are aligned.**
  - A **magnetic domain** is a region that has a very large number of atoms with aligned magnetic fields.
  - A **ferromagnetic material,** such as iron, can be magnetized because it contains magnetic domains.

21.2 Electromagnetism

- Electricity and magnetism are different aspects of a single force known as the **electromagnetic force.**
- The electric force results from charged particles. The magnetic force usually results from the movement of electrons in an atom.

- **Moving electric charges create a magnetic field.**
  - A coil of wire carrying a current produces a magnetic field. The coil acts like a bar magnet. Each end of the coil is a pole. A coil of current-carrying wire that produces a magnetic field is called a **solenoid.**

- **Changing the current in an electromagnet controls the strength and direction of its magnetic field.**
  - An **electromagnet** is a solenoid with a ferromagnetic core.

- **Electromagnetic devices such as galvanometers, electric motors, and loudspeakers change electrical energy into mechanical energy.**
  - A **galvanometer** is a device that uses a solenoid to measure small amounts of current.

- An **electric motor** is a device that uses an electromagnet to turn an axle.
- A loudspeaker reproduces sounds.

21.3 Electrical Energy Generation and Transmission

◉ **According to Faraday's law, a voltage is induced in a conductor by a changing magnetic field.**

- **Electromagnetic induction** is the process of generating a current by moving an electrical conductor relative to a magnetic field.

◉ **The two types of generators are AC generators and DC generators.**

- A **generator** is a device that converts mechanical energy into electrical energy by rotating a coil of wire in a magnetic field.
- AC generators produce alternating current. DC generators produce direct current.

◉ **A transformer changes voltage and current by inducing a changing magnetic field in one coil. This changing field then induces an alternating current in a nearby coil with a different number of turns.**

- A **transformer** is a device that increases or decreases the voltage and current of two linked AC circuits.
- Power lines carry power from power plants to homes. The voltage is very high in the lines. The voltage must be lowered before it enters homes.

◉ **Most of the electrical energy generated in the United States is produced using coal as an energy source. Some other sources are water (hydroelectric), nuclear energy, wind, natural gas, and petroleum.**

- A turbine uses the energy from one of these six sources to produce electricity.
- A **turbine** is a device with fanlike blades that turn when pushed, for example, by water or steam.

Chapter 21   Magnetism

Section 21.1 Magnets and Magnetic Fields
(pages 630–633)

This section describes magnetic forces and magnetic fields. It discusses characteristics of magnetic materials.

Reading Strategy (page 630)

Using Prior Knowledge Before you read, copy the diagram below and add what you already know about magnets to the diagram. After you read, revise the diagram based on what you learned. For more information on this Reading Strategy, see the **Reading and Study Skills** in the **Skills and Reference Handbook** at the end of your textbook.

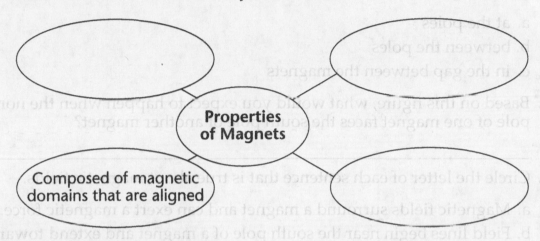

Properties of Magnets

Composed of magnetic domains that are aligned

Magnetic Forces (page 630)

1. Is the following sentence true or false? Magnetic force can be exerted on moving charges, as well as on iron or on another magnet. _____

2. Circle the letter of the correct answer. Where is the magnetic force strongest around a magnet?

   a. the north pole

   b. the south pole

   c. both poles

3. Circle the letter of each sentence that is true about magnetic force.

   a. Two magnets that approach each other may attract or repel.

   b. Magnetic forces do not vary with distance.

   c. Magnetic forces act over a distance.

Chapter 21   Magnetism

Magnetic Fields (pages 631–632)

For questions 4 and 5, refer to the figure below.

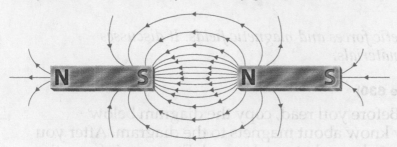

4. Circle the letter of the phrase that describes where the magnetic field is the strongest.

   a. at the poles

   b. between the poles

   c. in the gap between the magnets

5. Based on this figure, what would you expect to happen when the north pole of one magnet faces the south pole of another magnet?

   _____

6. Circle the letter of each sentence that is true about magnetic fields.

   a. Magnetic fields surround a magnet and can exert a magnetic force.

   b. Field lines begin near the south pole of a magnet and extend toward the north pole.

   c. Iron filings are most attracted to areas where the field is strongest.

7. The area that is influenced by the magnetic field surrounding Earth is called the _____. Circle the best answer.

   atmosphere   ionosphere   magnetosphere

Magnetic Materials (pages 632–633)

Match each term with its description.

	Description	Term
_____	8. Can be magnetized because it has many domains	a. ferromagnetic material
_____	9. Has randomly oriented domains	b. magnetic domain
_____	10. Has many atoms with aligned magnetic fields	c. nonmagnetized material

Chapter 21   Magnetism

Section 21.2 Electromagnetism
(pages 635–639)

This section describes how electricity and magnetism are related. It discusses uses of solenoids and electromagnetic devices, and describes how these devices work.

Reading Strategy (page 635)

Identifying Main Ideas Copy the table on a separate sheet of paper. As you read, write the main idea of the text that follows each topic in the table. For more information on this Reading Strategy, see the **Reading and Study Skills** in the **Skills and Reference Handbook** at the end of your textbook.

Electromagnetism	
Topic	**Main Idea**
Electricity and magnetism	Electricity and magnetism are different aspects of a single force known as the electromagnetic force.
Direction of magnetic fields	
Direction of electric currents	
Solenoids and electromagnets	
Electromagnetic devices	

Electricity and Magnetism (pages 635–636)

1. Electricity and magnetism are different aspects of a single force known as the _____ force.

2. Is the following sentence true or false? Moving electric charges create a magnetic field. _____

3. Is the following sentence true or false? The vibrating charges that produce an electromagnetic wave also create a magnetic field.

   _____

4. A charge moving in a magnetic field will be deflected in a direction that is _____ to both the magnetic field and to the velocity of the charge. Circle the correct answer.

   opposed   parallel   perpendicular

Chapter 21 Magnetism

Solenoids and Electromagnets (pages 637–638)

5. A coil of current-carrying wire that produces a magnetic field is called a(n) _____. Circle the best answer.

   ferromagnet   galvanometer   solenoid

6. What is an electromagnet? _____
   _____

7. Circle the letter of each sentence that is true about electromagnets.

   a. Placing an iron rod in a solenoid reduces the strength of its magnetic field.

   b. Devices that utilize electromagnets include doorbells and telephones.

   c. A magnetic field can be turned on and off with an electromagnet.

8. Circle the letter of each factor that determines the strength of an electromagnet.

   a. type of ferromagnetic core

   b. number of turns in the solenoid coil

   c. current in the solenoid

9. Is the following sentence true or false? Decreasing the current in the

   solenoid decreases the strength of an electromagnet. _____

Electromagnetic Devices (pages 638–639)

10. Use the words in the box below to fill in the blanks. Electromagnetic

    devices change _____ energy into _____ energy.

chemical	mechanical
electrical	potential

11. Use the words in the box to complete the table about electromagnetic devices.

Electric motor Galvanometer Loudspeaker	Description	Device
	Uses electromagnets to convert electrical signals into sound waves	
	Uses a rotating electromagnet to turn an axle	
	Uses an electromagnet to measure small amounts of current	

Chapter 21   Magnetism

Section 21.3 Electrical Energy Generation and Transmission
(pages 642–647)

This section describes how electricity is generated and transmitted for human use. It also describes how generators and transformers function.

Reading Strategy (page 642)

Sequencing As you read the section, complete the flowchart to show how a step-up transformer works. Then make a similar flowchart for a step-down transformer. For more information on this Reading Strategy, see the **Reading and Study Skills** in the **Skills and Reference Handbook** at the end of your textbook.

Step-up Transformers

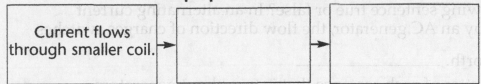

Generating Electric Current (pages 642–643)

1. Circle the letter for the name of the process of generating a current by moving an electrical conductor relative to a magnetic field.

   a. electromagnetic force

   b. electromagnetic field

   c. electromagnetic induction

2. Electrical charges can easily flow through materials known as _____. Circle the correct answer.

   conductors   generators   magnets

3. Circle the letter of the correct answer. According to Faraday's law, electric current can be induced in a conductor by _____.

   a. a static magnetic field

   b. moving the conductor

   c. a changing magnetic field

4. Is the following sentence true or false? Moving a magnet relative to a coil of wire induces a current in the wire if the coil is part of a complete circuit. _____

Generators (pages 643–644)

5. Use the words in the box to fill in the blanks. A generator converts

   _____ energy into _____ energy.

chemical	mechanical
electrical	potential

6. Circle the letter that best describes how most of the electrical energy used in homes and businesses is produced.

   a. with DC generators

   b. using AC generators at large power plants

   c. by rotating a magnetic field around a coil of wire

7. Is the following sentence true or false? In an alternating current produced by an AC generator, the flow direction of charges switches

   back and forth. _____

8. Circle the letter of each sentence that is true about generators.

   a. Small generators can produce enough electricity for a small business.

   b. DC generators produce current that flows back and forth.

   c. Most modern power plants use DC generators.

Transformers (pages 644–645)

9. A device that increases or decreases voltage and current of two linked

   AC circuits is called a(n) _____.

10. Use the words in the box to fill in the blanks. To change voltage and current, a transformer induces a changing magnetic field in one coil,

    which then induces a(n) _____ in a nearby coil with

    _____ number of turns.

AC current	the same
DC current	a different

Electrical Energy for Your Home (pages 646–647)

11. Name at least three sources used to produce electrical energy in

    the United States. _____

    _____

Chapter 21   Magnetism

WordWise

Use the clues and the words below to help you write the vocabulary terms from the chapter in the blanks. Then find and circle the terms in the puzzle. The terms may occur vertically, horizontally, or diagonally. Some terms may be spelled backwards.

domain	galvanometer	generator
ferromagnetic	magnetic pole	magnetosphere
transformer	turbine	solenoid

```
f  g  d  e  l  o  p  c  i  t  e  n  g  a  m
e  a  a  t  s  o  r  m  e  v  r  p  e  a  b
r  r  q  l  z  f  f  r  e  r  e  v  g  c  t
r  c  i  u  v  t  t  c  h  n  g  n  r  r  r
o  s  d  o  m  a  i  n  i  u  e  t  a  o  a
m  o  u  b  p  l  n  b  k  t  n  u  u  f  n
a  l  t  y  o  i  r  o  o  n  e  r  m  t  s
g  e  k  p  o  u  d  s  m  a  r  b  i  n  f
n  n  k  a  t  p  p  o  i  e  a  i  c  a  o
e  o  g  o  y  h  z  a  v  b  t  n  s  y  r
t  i  e  e  e  h  n  j  n  m  o  e  m  o  m
i  d  i  r  j  u  e  r  t  c  r  f  r  u  e
c  t  e  z  z  w  y  n  r  p  e  r  j  b  r
```

Clues	Hidden Words
Region where a magnetic field is strongest	_____
Nickel is a(n) _____ material.	_____
Current-carrying wire with a loop in it	_____
Uses an electromagnet to measure small amounts of current	_____
Device with fanlike blades that converts energy from various sources to electrical energy	_____
Area influenced by Earth's magnetic field	_____
Converts mechanical energy into electrical energy	_____
Aligned magnetic fields	_____
Step-down or step-up	_____

Chapter 21   Magnetism

Calculating Voltage

A step-down transformer has a primary coil with
500 turns of wire, and a secondary coil with 50 turns.
If the input voltage is 120 V, what is the output voltage?

**Math Skill:
Ratios and
Proportions**

You may want to read
more about this **Math
Skill** in the **Skills and
Reference Handbook**
at the end of your
textbook.

1. Read and Understand

What information are you given?

Input Voltage = 120 V

Primary Coil: 500 turns

Secondary Coil: 50 turns

2. Plan and Solve

What unknown are you trying to calculate?

Output Voltage = ?

What formula contains the given quantities and the unknown?

$$\frac{\text{Secondary Coil turns}}{\text{Primary Coil turns}} = \frac{\text{Output Voltage}}{\text{Input Voltage}}$$

Replace each variable with its known value.

$$\frac{50 \text{ turns}}{500 \text{ turns}} = \frac{\text{Output Voltage}}{120 \text{ V}}$$

$$\text{Output Voltage} = \frac{50 \text{ turns}}{500 \text{ turns}} \times 120 \text{ V} = 12 \text{ V}$$

3. Look Back and Check

Is your answer reasonable?

The ratio of secondary to primary turns is 1 : 10. 12 V is one tenth of
120 V, so the answer is reasonable.

Math Practice

On a separate sheet of paper, solve the following problems.

1. The input voltage from a substation is 7200 V, and the output voltage to a
   home is 240 V. What is the ratio of turns for the secondary to primary
   coils in the step-down transformer?

2. A step-down transformer has 200 turns of wire in its primary coil. How
   many turns are in the secondary coil if the input voltage = 120 V, and the
   output voltage = 6 V?

Chapter 22 Earth's Interior

Summary

22.1 Earth's Structure

👉 **Geology is the study of planet Earth, including its composition and structure.**

- Scientists who study Earth and the processes that have shaped Earth over time are called **geologists.**
- **Uniformitarianism** is the idea that the geologic processes that operate today also operated in the past.

👉 **Earth can be divided into three main layers—the crust, mantle, and core—based on the materials that make up each layer.**

- The rocky outer layer of Earth is the **crust.**
- Much of the crust is made up of **silicates,** rocks made of compounds of silicon and oxygen.
- Beneath the crust is the **mantle,** a thick layer of hot but solid rock.
- The **lithosphere** is a layer of relatively cool, rigid rock that includes the uppermost part of the mantle as well as Earth's crust.
- Beneath the lithosphere in the mantle is the **asthenosphere,** a layer of softer, weaker rock that can flow slowly.
- Beneath the asthenosphere is the stronger lower part of the mantle called the **mesosphere.**
- Beneath the mantle is the **core,** a large sphere of metal that occupies Earth's center.

22.2 Minerals

👉 **A mineral is a naturally occurring, inorganic solid with a crystal structure and a characteristic chemical composition.**

- A **rock** is a solid combination of minerals or mineral materials.
- Minerals are **inorganic,** meaning that living things did not produce them.

👉 **The properties by which minerals can be identified include their crystal structure, color, streak, luster, density, hardness, fracture, and cleavage.**

- Crystal structure refers to the shape of a mineral's crystal.
- Some minerals have a characteristic color. Many are not always the same color.
- The color of a mineral's powder is known as its **streak.** The color of a mineral's streak may be different than the color of the mineral itself.
- The **luster** of a mineral is the way in which its surface reflects light.
- Density is the amount of mass in a given volume of a material.

- **Hardness** is the resistance of a mineral to scratching.
- The **fracture** of a mineral is how the mineral breaks.
- **Cleavage** is a mineral's tendency to split along regular, well-defined planes.

22.3 Rocks and the Rock Cycle

Rocks are classified into three major groups—igneous, sedimentary, and metamorphic—based on how they form.

Igneous rock forms when molten material cools and solidifies either inside Earth or at the surface.

- **Igneous** rock forms from magma.
- **Magma** is a mixture of molten rock and gases. It forms underground.
- Magma that flows out of volcanoes is called **lava.**
- An igneous rock that forms underground from hardened magma is called an **intrusive rock.**
- An igneous rock that forms at Earth's surface is called an **extrusive rock.**

Geologists classify sedimentary rocks into three main groups according to how they form: clastic rocks, chemical rocks, and organic rocks.

- Sedimentary rocks that form from the broken fragments of other rocks are called **clastic rocks.**
- Chemical rocks form from dissolved minerals. When the water evaporates, the minerals are left behind.
- Organic rocks form from the shells and bones of dead animals.
- **Sediment** consists of small, solid pieces of material that comes from rocks or living things.
- **Sedimentary rock** forms over time as sediment is squeezed and cemented together.

Metamorphic rock forms when a rock is transformed by heat, pressure, or chemical reactions. Most metamorphic rocks form under high temperatures and pressures deep underground.

- **Metamorphic** rock forms from other rocks.
- Metamorphic rocks with crystals arranged in parallel layers are **foliated rocks.**

In the rock cycle, forces within Earth and at the surface cause rocks to change form.

- The **rock cycle** is a series of repeating processes in which rocks continuously change from one type to another.

22.4 Plate Tectonics

◖ **The theory of plate tectonics explains the formation and movement of Earth's plates.**

- **Plate tectonics** is the theory that pieces of Earth's lithosphere, called plates, move about slowly on top of the asthenosphere.

◖ **Wegener hypothesized that the continents were once joined in a single supercontinent, which then broke into pieces that moved apart.**

- All the land surface of Earth once formed a single supercontinent, named **Pangaea**. Later, Pangaea broke into pieces that moved apart.
- The continents move slowly across Earth's surface in a process called **continental drift**.

◖ **Sea-floor spreading creates new oceanic crust at mid-ocean ridges. Subduction destroys old oceanic crust at subduction zones.**

- The **mid-ocean ridge** is a chain of underwater mountains.
- A huge crack in the crust lies all along the mid-ocean ridge. When pieces of ocean floor move slowly apart on each side of the crack, it is called **sea-floor spreading**.
- As sea-floor spreading occurs, old oceanic plates sink into the mantle in the process of **subduction**.
- As a plate sinks through a subduction zone, it bends, forming a depression in the ocean floor called a **trench**.

◖ **Plate motions are the visible part of the process of mantle convection.**

◖ **There are three types of plate boundaries: divergent boundaries, convergent boundaries, and transform boundaries.**

- Plates move away from each other along a **divergent boundary**. Magma rises and forms new rock at the gap between divergent plates.
- Plates come together, or collide, at a **convergent boundary.** The denser plate may slide under the other plate and sink into the mantle. Sometimes the two plates buckle at the edges and create mountain ranges.
- At a **transform boundary,** plates slide past each other, moving in opposite directions.

◖ **Geologists found that most mountains form along plate boundaries.**

22.5 Earthquakes

- An **earthquake** is a movement of Earth's lithosphere. Earthquakes occur when rocks in the lithosphere suddenly shift, releasing stored energy.
- A small portion of the energy released during an earthquake is carried by vibrations called **seismic waves**.
- A **tsunami** is a large sea wave generated by an underwater earthquake, volcano, or landslide.

☟ **As tectonic plates move, they cause stress in the crust, which in turn produces faults and folds.**

- **Stress** is a force that squeezes rocks together, stretches or pulls them apart, or pushes them in different directions.
- A **fault** is a break in a mass of rock along which movement occurs.
- A **fold** is a bend in layers of rock.

☟ **Earthquakes occur because stress forces have exceeded the strength of rock.**

- The location beneath Earth's surface where an earthquake begins is the **focus**.
- The location on Earth's surface directly above the focus is the **epicenter**.
- Earthquakes produce three main types of seismic waves: P waves, S waves, and surface waves.
- **P waves** are longitudinal waves similar to sound waves. **S waves** are transverse waves, similar to electromagnetic radiation. **Surface waves** develop when seismic waves reach Earth's surface.

☟ **To measure earthquakes and pinpoint their epicenters, geologist record seismic waves using seismographs.**

- A device that can detect and record seismic waves is a **seismograph**.

☟ **Most earthquakes are concentrated along plate boundaries, where many faults are found.**

22.6 Volcanoes

☟ **Under certain conditions, small amounts of mantle rock can melt, forming liquid magma. The magma rises upward through the crust, erupting at the surface as a volcano.**

- A **volcano** is a mountain that forms when magma reaches the surface.
- Before an eruption, magma often collects in a pocket called a **magma chamber**.
- Magma rises to the surface in a narrow, vertical channel called a **pipe**.

- An opening in the ground where magma escapes to the surface is called a **vent.**
- At the top of the central vent in most volcanoes is a bowl-shaped pit called a **crater.**
- A **caldera** is a huge depression at the top of a volcano.

⊙ **Volcanoes erupt explosively or quietly, depending on the characteristics of the magma.**

- Thin magma flows easily. It causes quiet eruptions.
- Thick magma resists flowing. It can clog a volcanic pipe until great pressure builds up in the volcano. Finally, the volcano erupts with an explosion.

⊙ **Most volcanoes occur along plate boundaries or at hot spots in the crust.**

- A **hot spot** is a region where hot rock extends from deep within the mantle to the surface.

⊙ **The three major types of volcano are shield volcanoes, cinder cones, and composite volcanoes.**

- A quiet eruption of low-viscosity lava produces a wide, flat volcano called a **shield volcano.**
- If an eruption is entirely ash and cinders, the result will be a small, steep-sided volcano called a **cinder cone.**
- A **composite volcano** forms from explosive eruptions of lava and ash.

⊙ **Igneous features formed by magma include batholiths, sills, dikes, and volcanic necks.**

- A **batholith** is the largest type of intrusive igneous rock mass.
- Magma sometimes squeezes into a crack between layers of rock and then hardens. If the crack is parallel to existing rock layers, the magma hardens into a structure called a **sill.** If the crack cuts across rock layers, the hardened magma forms a **dike.**
- When magma hardens in a volcano's pipe, a structure called a **volcanic neck** may form.

Chapter 22   Earth's Interior

Section 22.1 Earth's Structure
(pages 660–663)

This section explains what geologists study. It describes the main layers of Earth.

Reading Strategy (page 660)

Building Vocabulary Copy the table on a separate sheet of paper and add more rows as needed. As you read the section, define each vocabulary term in your own words. For more information on this Reading Strategy, see the **Reading and Study Skills** in the **Skills and Reference Handbook** at the end of your textbook.

Earth's Structure	
Vocabulary Term	**Definition**
Geologist	A scientist who studies Earth and the processes that have shaped Earth over time
Uniformitarianism	
Crust	

The Science of Geology (pages 660–661)

1. The study of planet Earth, including its composition and structure, is called _____.

2. Is the following sentence true or false? People who study Earth and the processes that have shaped Earth over time are called geologists.

   _____

3. What is uniformitarianism? _____

   _____

   _____

A Cross Section of Earth (pages 661–663)

4. Circle the letter of the best answer. Scientists divide Earth's interior into the crust, mantle, and core based on the _____.

   a. thickness of each layer

   b. materials in each layer

   c. density of each layer

5. Much of Earth's crust is made up of _____. Circle the correct answer.

   igneous rock   metamorphic rock   silicates

Chapter 22   Earth's Interior

Match each type of crust to its characteristics. Each type of crust will have more than one characteristic.

Crust

_____ **6.** oceanic crust

_____ **7.** continental crust

Characteristic

a. Averages 7 kilometers in thickness

b. Averages 40 kilometers in thickness

c. Makes up the ocean floor

d. Makes up the continents

8. Circle the letters of each sentence that is true about Earth's mantle.

a. It is the thickest layer of Earth.

b. It is divided into layers based on the physical properties of rock.

c. It is less dense than the crust.

9. Is the following sentence true or false? Rock flows slowly in the

asthenosphere. _____

10. The stronger, lower part of the mantle is the _____. Circle the correct answer.

asthenosphere   lithosphere   mesosphere

11. Is the following sentence true or false? The outer core of Earth is liquid.

_____

12. Use the words in the box to label the main layers of Earth's interior in the diagram.

Crust	Mantle
Inner core	Outer core

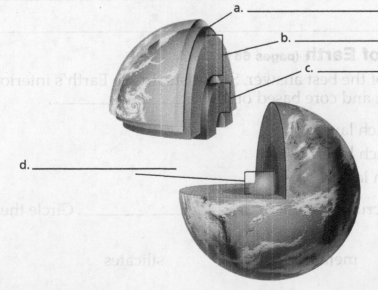

a. _____

b. _____

c. _____

d. _____

Section 22.2 Minerals
(pages 664–669)

This section describes minerals and rocks found on Earth and their different properties.

Reading Strategy (page 664)

Outlining Copy the outline on a separate sheet of paper and add more lines as needed. Before you read, make an outline of this section. Use the green headings as main topics and the blue headings as subtopics. As you read, add supporting details. For more information on this Reading Strategy, see the **Reading and Study Skills** in the **Skills and Reference Handbook** at the end of your textbook.

Minerals
I. Minerals and Rocks
II. The Properties of Minerals
A. Crystal Structure
B. _____
C. Streak
D. _____

Minerals and Rocks (page 665)

1. A solid combination of minerals or mineral materials is a(n)

   _____.

2. Is the following sentence true or false? A mineral is a naturally occurring, inorganic solid with a crystal structure and a characteristic

   chemical composition. _____

3. A material is called _____ if it is not produced from a living thing.

4. Circle the letters of sentences that are true about minerals.

   a. Within each mineral, chemical composition is nearly constant.
   b. Minerals are organic.
   c. Minerals are the building blocks of rocks.

The Properties of Minerals (pages 666–669)

5. Is the following sentence true or false? Minerals such as sulfur can

   sometimes be identified by color. _____

Chapter 22   Earth's Interior

6. Is the following sentence true or false? The color of a mineral's streak

   is not always the same color as the mineral. _____

7. Circle the letter of the correct answer. The density of a mineral depends
   on its _____.

   a. chemical composition

   b. crystalline structure

   c. hardness

8. Use the words and phrases in the box to complete the table about the
   properties by which minerals can be identified.

Fracture	The way in which a mineral's surface reflects light
Streak	How a mineral breaks
Density	The resistance of a mineral to scratching

Minerals and Properties	
Property	**Description**
Crystal structure	The particular geometric shape that the atoms of a mineral are arranged in
	The color of a mineral's powder
Luster	
	A mineral's mass divided by its volume
Hardness	
Cleavage	A type of fracture where a mineral splits along regular, well-defined, flat surfaces where the bonds are weakest

Match each mineral to its property.

Mineral

_____ 9. calcite

_____ 10. magnetite

_____ 11. fluorite

Property

a. Gives off visible light under
   an ultraviolet light

b. Is attracted by a magnet

c. Easily dissolved by acids

Section 22.3 Rocks and the Rock Cycle
(pages 670–675)

This section describes how rocks are classified. It also explains how rocks change form in the rock cycle.

Reading Strategy (page 670)

Comparing and Contrasting After you read, compare groups of rocks by completing the table. For more information on this Reading Strategy, see the **Reading and Study Skills** in the **Skills and Reference Handbook** at the end of your textbook.

Groups of Rocks		
Rock Group	**Formed by**	**Example**
Igneous		
Sedimentary		Sandstone
Metamorphic	Heat and pressure	

Classifying Rocks (page 670)

1. Circle the letters of the major groups into which rocks are classified.

   a. sedimentary

   b. igneous

   c. metamorphic

2. Circle the letter of the correct answer. Scientists divide rocks into groups based on _____.

   a. where they appear

   b. how they form

   c. their chemical composition

Igneous Rock (page 671)

Match each type of igneous rock to its characteristics. Each type of rock will have more than one characteristic.

Igneous Rock	Characteristic
_____ 3. intrusive rock	a. Forms underground
_____ 4. extrusive rock	b. Forms at Earth's surface
	c. Cools quickly
	d. Cools slowly

Chapter 22 Earth's Interior

5. A rock that forms from magma is called a(n) _____.

6. What is lava? _____

Sedimentary Rock (pages 672–673)

7. The process of _____ breaks down rock at Earth's surface. Circle the correct answer.

   metamorphism   sedimentation   weathering

8. Circle the groups into which geologists classify sedimentary rocks.

   a. foliated rocks
   b. organic rocks
   c. chemical rocks

9. Sedimentary rocks formed from broken fragments of other rocks are called _____ rocks. Circle the correct answer.

   clastic   chemical   foliated

Metamorphic Rock (page 674)

10. Circle the letters of the ways a rock can be transformed into a metamorphic rock.

    a. by heat
    b. by pressure
    c. by chemical reaction

11. Where do most metamorphic rocks form? Circle the correct answer.

    in volcanoes   underwater   underground

12. Metamorphic rocks with crystals arranged in parallel bands or layers are called _____ rocks. Circle the correct answer.

    chemical   clastic   foliated

The Rock Cycle (pages 674–675)

13. Circle the letters of the sentences that are true about the rock cycle.

    a. A metamorphic rock that melts and cools to form a new rock becomes an igneous rock.
    b. In the rock cycle, rocks may wear away, undergo metamorphism, or melt and form new igneous rock.
    c. The rock cycle is a series of processes in which rocks change from one type to another continuously.

Chapter 22   Earth's Interior

Section 22.4 Plate Tectonics
(pages 676–683)

This section describes the theory of plate tectonics. It also examines sea-floor spreading, plate boundaries, and mountain building.

Reading Strategy (page 676)

Previewing Before you read this section, rewrite the headings as how, why, and what questions about plate tectonics. As you read, write answers to the questions. For more information on this Reading Strategy, see the **Reading and Study Skills** in the **Skills and Reference Handbook** at the end of your textbook.

Plate Tectonics
Questions on Plate Tectonics
What is the hypothesis of continental drift?

1. Is the following sentence true or false? According to the theory of plate tectonics, Earth's plates move about quickly on top of the crust.

   _____

2. Circle the letters of the characteristics of Earth's plates that the theory of plate tectonics explains.

   a. composition

   b. formation

   c. movement

Continental Drift (page 677)

3. Define Pangaea. _____

   _____

4. The process by which the continents move slowly across Earth's surface

   is called _____.

Sea-floor Spreading (pages 678–679)

5. Is the following sentence true or false? The theory of sea-floor spreading explains why rocks of the ocean floor are youngest near the mid-ocean

   ridge. _____

6. Is the following sentence true or false? Old oceanic plates sink into the mantle at mid-ocean ridges in a process called subduction.

    _____

7. The process called _____ destroys old oceanic crust at subduction zones.

The Theory of Plate Tectonics (pages 679–680)

8. Is the following sentence true or false? The concept of sea-floor spreading supports the theory of plate tectonics by providing a way for the pieces of Earth's crust to move. _____

9. Heat from Earth's interior causes convection currents in Earth's _____. Circle the correct answer.

    crust   mantle   sea floor

10. Circle the sentences that are true about the theory of plate tectonics.

    a. The ocean floor sinks back into the mantle at subduction zones.

    b. The heat that drives convection currents comes from solar energy.

    c. Hot rock rises at mid-ocean ridges, cools, and spreads out as sea floor.

Plate Boundaries (pages 681–682)

11. Identify each type of plate boundary. Use these words: *convergent, divergent, transform.*

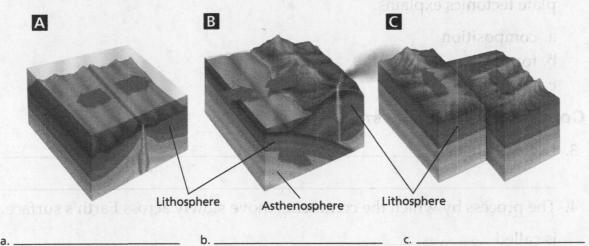

a. _____   b. _____   c. _____

Mountain Building (page 683)

12. Is the following sentence true or false? Most mountains form along

    plate boundaries. _____

Section 22.5 Earthquakes
(pages 684–689)

This section explains what earthquakes are, their causes, and their effects.

Reading Strategy (page 684)

Building Vocabulary Copy the table on a separate sheet of paper and add more rows as needed. As you read, define each term for this section in your own words. For more information on this Reading Strategy, see the **Reading and Study Skills** in the **Skills and Reference Handbook** at the end of your textbook.

Earthquake Terms	
Vocabulary Terms	**Definitions**
Earthquake	A movement of Earth's lithosphere that occurs when rocks in the lithosphere suddenly shift, releasing energy
Seismic waves	
Stress	

Stress in Earth's Crust (page 685)

1. Circle the letters of the ways that stress can affect rocks.

   a. It can squeeze them together.

   b. It can stretch or pull them apart.

   c. It can push them in different directions.

2. Is the following sentence true or false? Stress from moving tectonic plates produces faults and folds in Earth's crust. _____

Match each result of stress to its characteristics. Each result will have more than one characteristic.

Result of Stress	Characteristic
_____ 3. fault	a. A bend in layers of rock
_____ 4. fold	b. Many occur along plate boundaries
	c. A break in a mass of rock where movement happens
	d. Forms where rocks are squeezed but do not break

Chapter 22   Earth's Interior

Earthquakes and Seismic Waves (pages 686–687)

5. Is the following sentence true or false? The location underground where

an earthquake begins is called the focus. _____

6. Define epicenter. _____

_____

7. Circle the sentences that are true about the physics of earthquakes.

   a. Stress builds in areas where rocks along fault lines snag and remain locked.

   b. Potential energy is transformed into kinetic energy in the form of seismic waves.

   c. Potential energy increases as rocks break and move.

Match each type of seismic wave to its characteristic.

Seismic Waves	Characteristic
_____ **8.** P waves	**a.** Transverse waves that cannot travel through liquids
_____ **9.** S waves	**b.** Slow moving wave that develops when seismic waves reach Earth's surface
_____ **10.** surface waves	**c.** Longitudinal waves similar to sound waves that cause particles in the material to vibrate in the direction of the waves' motion

Measuring Earthquakes (page 687)

11. What devices do geologists use to record seismic waves? Circle the correct answer.

    Richter scale   seismograph   wave meter

Seismographic Data (page 689)

12. Most earthquakes are concentrated along _____.

13. Is the following sentence true or false? Some earthquakes will occur in

    the interior of plates. _____

Chapter 22   Earth's Interior

Section 22.6 Volcanoes
(pages 690–696)

This section describes volcanoes, how they form, and the different ways they erupt. It also describes the different types of volcanoes and other features created by magma.

Reading Strategy (page 690)

Sequencing As you read, complete the flowchart to show how a volcano forms. For more information on this Reading Strategy, see the **Reading and Study Skills** in the **Skills and Reference Handbook** at the end of your textbook.

Formation of a Volcano

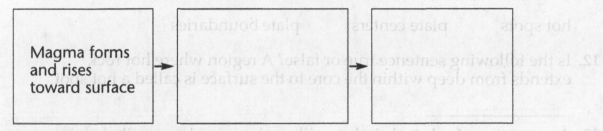

Formation of a Volcano (page 691)

1. Is the following sentence true or false? Liquid magma is formed when small amounts of mantle rock melt. _____

2. Describe how a volcano forms. _____

   _____

3. Magma collects in a pocket called the _____ before a volcanic eruption.

Match each feature of a volcano to its correct description.

Feature	Description
_____ **4.** pipe	**a.** A narrow, vertical channel where magma rises to the surface
_____ **5.** vent	**b.** An opening in the ground where magma escapes to the surface
_____ **6.** crater	
_____ **7.** magma chamber	**c.** A huge depression created if the shell of the magma chamber collapses
_____ **8.** caldera	**d.** A bowl-shaped pit at the top of a volcano
	e. A pocket where the magma collects

Chapter 22   Earth's Interior

Quiet and Explosive Eruptions (page 692)

9. Is the following sentence true or false? How easily magma flows depends on its viscosity. _____

10. Circle the letter of the factors that determine the viscosity of magma.

    a. depth
    b. water content
    c. silica content

Location and Types of Volcanoes (pages 693–695)

11. Where do most volcanoes occur? Circle the correct answers.

    hot spots   plate centers   plate boundaries

12. Is the following sentence true or false? A region where hot rock extends from deep within the core to the surface is called a hot spot.

    _____

13. An eruption of ash and cinders will produce a volcano called a(n)

    _____.

14. Is the following sentence true or false? A composite volcano is formed

    from an explosive eruption of lava and ash. _____

Other Igneous Features (page 696)

15. Circle the letters of the igneous features that are formed by magma.

    a. dikes
    b. sills
    c. volcanic necks

16. Define batholith. _____

    _____

17. Is the following sentence true or false? A crack that has filled with magma and hardens parallel to existing rock layers is called a dike.

    _____

Chapter 22   Earth's Interior

WordWise

Use the clues and the words in the box below to help you write the vocabulary terms from the chapter in the blanks. Use the circled letter in each term to find the hidden vocabulary word.

caldera	convergent boundary	fold
cleavage	core	rock
continental drift	earthquake	volcano

Clues

1. A solid combination of minerals or mineral materials
2. The central layer of Earth
3. A type of fracture in which a mineral tends to split along regular, well-defined planes
4. A movement of Earth's lithosphere that occurs when rocks shift suddenly, releasing stored energy
5. A region where plates collide
6. A mountain that forms when magma reaches the surface
7. A bend in layers of rock
8. Wegener's hypothesis in which continents move slowly across Earth's surface

Vocabulary Terms

1. Ⓞ _ _ _

2. _ Ⓞ _ _

3. Ⓞ _ _ _ _ _ _ _

4. _ _ _ _ _ _ _ Ⓞ _

5. Ⓞ _ _ _ _ _ _ _ _ Ⓞ _

6. _ _ _ Ⓞ _ _ _

7. _ _ Ⓞ _

8. _ _ _ _ _ _ _ Ⓞ _ _ _ _ _

Hidden Word: _ _ _ _ _ _ _ _ _

Definition: _____

_____

Chapter 22   Earth's Interior

Calculating Wavelength and Frequency

Math Skill:
Line Graphs

You may want to read more about this **Math Skill** in the **Skills and Reference Handbook** at the end of your textbook.

An earthquake occurs 1000 km from seismograph station B. What is the difference in time between the arrivals of the first P wave and the first S wave at station B?

1. Read and Understand

What information are you given in the problem?

Station B is 1000 km from where an earthquake occurred.

2. Plan and Solve

What does the question ask you to find?

The difference in time between the arrivals of the first P wave and the first S wave at station B

Find how long it took the first P wave to reach station B. Follow the 1000-km line up to the P wave curve.

2 minutes

Find how long it took the first S wave to reach station B. Follow the 1000-km line up to the S wave curve.

4 minutes

Subtract the amount of time it took the P wave to travel to station B from the amount of time it took the S wave to travel to station B.

4 minutes − 2 minutes = 2 minutes

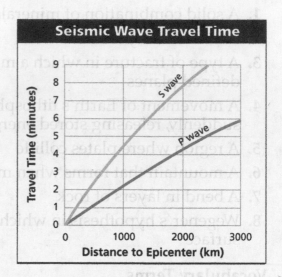

Seismic Wave Travel Time

3. Look Back and Check

Is your answer reasonable?   Yes, because S waves move slower than P waves.

Math Practice

On a separate sheet of paper, solve the following problems. Use the graph.

1. An earthquake occurs 500 km from seismograph station B. What is the difference in time between the arrivals of the first P waves and the first S waves?

2. Station C is 2000 km from the epicenter of the earthquake. If P waves arrived there at 4:37 a.m., when did the earthquake occur?

Chapter 23 Earth's Surface

Summary

23.1 Fresh Water

- Most of Earth's liquid fresh water is in the form of **groundwater**, the water found underground within cracks in rocks and between particles of soil.

- The water cycle is made up of several processes, including evaporation, transpiration, condensation, precipitation, and the eventual return of flowing water to the ocean.

  - The **water cycle** is the continuous movement of water all over Earth.
  - Evaporation occurs when sunlight heats water and changes it into water vapor in the atmosphere.
  - The leaves of trees and other plants release water vapor in a process called **transpiration.**
  - Condensation occurs when water droplets or ice crystals condense on small particles in the air.
  - Precipitation occurs when water droplets or ice crystals fall from clouds to the ground.
  - A **glacier** is a large mass of moving ice and snow on land.

- A small portion of Earth's fresh water is located in the atmosphere, streams, and lakes. Most is located in groundwater and glaciers.

  - **Runoff** is water that flows over Earth's surface after it rains.
  - A major river has many smaller streams, called **tributaries,** that flow into it. Tributaries collect runoff and channel it into rivers.
  - The area of land that contributes water to a river system is called a **watershed.**
  - The **saturated zone** is a region where groundwater fills all the tiny spaces in soil and rocks.
  - The top of the saturated zone is the **water table.**
  - A rock is **permeable** if water can easily pass through it.
  - A permeable rock layer that is saturated with water is called an **aquifer.**
  - Rocks are **impermeable** if water cannot easily pass through them.

23.2 Weathering and Mass Movement

- Erosion acts through weathering, the force of gravity, and the movement of streams, groundwater, glaciers, wind, and waves.

  - **Erosion** is the process that wears down and carries away rock and soil.

There are two forms of weathering: mechanical and chemical. They cause rocks to disintegrate or decompose.

- **Weathering** is the process by which rocks are chemically altered or physically broken down into fragments at or near Earth's surface.
- **Mechanical weathering** physically breaks rock into smaller fragments.
- **Abrasion** is mechanical weathering that occurs when rocks scrape or grind against one another.
- **Chemical weathering** dissolves rock. Water is the main agent of chemical weathering.

The rate at which mechanical and chemical weathering take place depends on three main factors: temperature, the availability of water, and the type of rock.

Through the process of mass movement, gravity moves loose material down a slope.

- **Mass movement** is the downward movement of rock and soil due to gravity.
- A landslide is a rapid movement of rock and soil down a slope.
- A mudflow is a rapid movement of wet soil and other fine sediment down a slope.
- Creep is a gradual movement of soil down a slope.
- Slumping is a sudden movement of an entire layer of soil or rock down a slope.

23.3 Water Shapes the Land

- **Deposition** is the process in which sediment is laid down in new locations.

A stream's ability to erode depends mainly on its speed.

- The process of particles bouncing along a stream bottom is called **saltation**.
- The speed of the stream determines the size and amount of sediment it can carry.

Water erosion forms V-shaped valleys, waterfalls, meanders, and oxbow lakes.

- A V-shaped valley is a deep, narrow valley with steep sides. A V-shaped valley forms where a stream flows rapidly down a steep slope.
- A waterfall is a sharp drop in a streambed that causes the water to fall from a higher level to a lower level.
- A **flood plain** is the flat area along a stream that is entirely covered with water only during times of flood.

- A loop-like bend in a river is called a **meander.** It forms where a river has a curve.
- An **oxbow lake** is a curved lake near a river. It forms when an old meander is cut off from the rest of the river.

Features deposited by flowing water include alluvial fans and deltas.

- A fan-shaped deposit of sediment on land is an **alluvial fan.** It forms where a stream flows out of mountains and onto a plain.
- A **delta** is a mass of sediment deposited where a river enters a large body of water.

The processes of chemical weathering cause much groundwater erosion, including the formation of caves and sinkholes.

- A cave is an empty passage in rock that is left behind when the water table drops.
- Water that drips from a cave ceiling may form an icicle-like formation called a **stalactite.**
- If the water drips down to the floor, a pillar of minerals called a **stalagmite** forms.
- A **sinkhole** is a hole in the ground that forms when a portion of ground suddenly collapses.

23.4 Glaciers and Wind

Glaciers form in places where more snow falls than melts or sublimates.

- A **continental glacier** is a thick sheet of ice that covers a huge area, such as a continent or large island.
- A glacier that occurs in a high mountain valley is a **valley glacier.**
- Glaciers erode rock through abrasion and plucking.
- In **plucking,** glacial ice widens cracks in bedrock beneath the glacier. Pieces of loosened rock are then frozen to the bottom of the glacier, which carries them away.

Glaciers cause many distinctive features in the landscape, including cirques, horns, U-shaped valleys, and glacial lakes.

- **Cirques** are large bowl-shaped valleys carved by glaciers out of a mountainside.
- A horn is a pyramid-shaped peak. It forms when several cirques develop around the top of a mountain.
- A U-shaped valley is a V-shaped valley that has been widened by a glacier.
- A glacial lake forms when a natural depression is eroded and enlarged by a moving continental glacier.

☞ **When a glacier melts, it deposits its load of sediment, creating a variety of landforms.**

- Glacial sediment is called **till.**
- The till forms **moraines,** mounds of sediment at the downhill end of the glacier and along its sides.
- Drumlins are long mounds of till.
- Erratics are boulders that a glacier has carried away from their place of origin.

☞ **Wind erodes the land by deflation and abrasion.**

- **Deflation** occurs when wind carries away loose surface material.
- Abrasion occurs when the wind blows sand against rocks.

☞ **Features deposited by wind include sand dunes and loess deposits.**

- **Dunes** are deposits formed from windblown sand.
- Deposits formed from windblown dust are called **loess.**

23.5 The Restless Oceans

- Most of Earth's water exists as salt water in the oceans.
- **Salinity** is the proportion of dissolved salts in water.
- The **continental shelf** is a gently sloping plain that forms an apron of shallow water along the edge of a continent.

☞ **Light and temperature decrease with depth, whereas pressure increases.**

☞ **Winds blowing across the surface of the ocean cause the continuous flow of surface currents.**

- A **surface current** is a large stream of ocean water that moves continuously in about the same path.

☞ **Deep ocean currents are caused by differences in the density of ocean water.**

- Because deep ocean currents are affected by density, they are called **density currents.**

☞ **In upwelling, winds blow warm surface water aside. This allows cold water from the deep ocean to rise and take the place of the warmer water.**

- The movement of water from the deep ocean to the surface is called **upwelling.**

○ **Two physical processes, hydraulic action and abrasion, are responsible for much wave erosion.**

- **Hydraulic action** occurs when waves pound on cracks in rock. The pressure of repeated pounding enlarges the cracks.
- **Longshore drift** is the process in which ocean waves gradually move sand along a shore by repeated erosion and deposition.

23.6 Earth's History

○ **Geologists use the law of superposition to determine the relative ages of sedimentary rocks from the sequence of rock layers and the fossils within each layer.**

- The **relative age** of a rock is its age compared to the ages of other rocks above or below it in a sequence of rock layers.
- The **law of superposition** states that if rock layers are undisturbed, younger rocks lie above older rocks, and the oldest rocks are at the bottom.
- **Fossils** are the preserved remains or traces of once living things.
- An **extinct** organism is one that no longer exists.
- The fossils of extinct organisms that are easily identified, occurred over a large area, and lived during a well-defined period of time are called **index fossils.** These fossils help geologists determine the relative age of sedimentary rocks.

○ **Geologists use radioactive dating to determine the absolute ages of rocks.**

- A rock's **absolute age** is the time that has passed since the rock formed.

○ **The geologic time scale is based on the relative ages of rock layers and the use of radioactive dating to find the absolute ages of rocks.**

○ **The major divisions of Earth's history are Precambrian time and the Paleozoic, Mesozoic, and Cenozoic Eras.**

- An **era** is one major stage in Earth's history.
- An era is divided into smaller units called **periods.**
- Some eras are marked by mass extinctions. A **mass extinction** is an event when many kinds of organisms became extinct within a relatively short time.

Chapter 23   Earth's Surface

Section 23.1 Fresh Water
(pages 704–708)

This section describes where water is found on Earth. It also explains the water cycle.

Reading Strategy (page 704)

Building Vocabulary Copy the table on a separate sheet of paper. As you read, add terms and definitions from this section to the table. For more information on this Reading Strategy, see the **Reading and Study Skills** in the **Skills and Reference Handbook** at the end of your textbook.

Earth's Fresh Water	
Vocabulary Term	**Definition**
Groundwater	Fresh water found underground among particles of rock and soil
Water cycle	
Transpiration	

1. Water found underground in soil and within cracks in rocks

   is called _____.

The Water Cycle (pages 705–706)

2. Define the water cycle. _____

_____

Match each process with its correct description.

Description	**Process**
_____ 3. When water droplets or ice crystals fall to the ground	a. evaporation
_____ 4. When a liquid changes into a gas	b. transpiration
_____ 5. The process that forms clouds	c. condensation
_____ 6. When a plant's leaves release water	d. precipitation

7. A glacier is a large mass of moving ice and _____.

Chapter 23   Earth's Surface

Fresh Water (pages 706–708)

8. Circle the letters that contain portions of Earth's fresh water.

   a. streams

   b. the atmosphere

   c. the oceans

9. Use the words in the box to fill in the blanks. Most of Earth's fresh

   water is located in _____ and _____.

glaciers	lakes
groundwater	rivers

10. What is runoff? _____

11. A smaller stream that flows into a river is called a(n) _____.
    Circle the best answer.

    rivulet   tributary   watershed

12. Circle the letters of the sentences that are true about watersheds.

    a. Watersheds are areas of land that contribute water to a river system.

    b. Watersheds are always large.

    c. The Mississippi River watershed drains most of the central United
       States.

13. Is the following sentence true or false? Ponds usually form in large,

    deep depressions, but lakes form in smaller depressions. _____

14. An area underground where the pore spaces are entirely filled with

    water is called the _____.

15. Is the following sentence true or false? The water table is found at the

    bottom of the saturated zone. _____

16. Water cannot pass through _____ rocks. Circle the correct
    answer.

    igneous   impermeable   permeable

17. Circle the letters of the sentences that are true about aquifers.

    a. They are permeable rock layers that are saturated with water.

    b. They are recharged or refilled as rainwater seeps into them.

    c. They are often made of shale and unbroken granite.

Chapter 23   Earth's Surface

Section 23.2 Weathering and Mass Movement
(pages 709–712)

This section describes how land is changed by weathering and erosion. It also discusses mass movement.

Reading Strategy (page 709)

Concept Map As you read, complete the concept map showing the key factors that affect the rate of weathering. For more information on this Reading Strategy, see the **Reading and Study Skills** in the **Skills and Reference Handbook** at the end of your textbook.

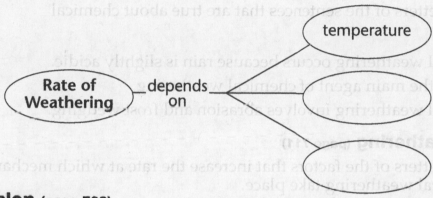

Erosion (page 709)

1. The process that wears down and carries away rock and soil is called

   _____.

2. Circle the letters of the sentences that are true about erosion.

   a. It acts through hoodoos.

   b. It acts through weathering.

   c. It acts through the force of gravity.

3. Is the following sentence true or false? The end product of erosion

   is sediment. _____

Weathering (pages 710–711)

4. Circle the letters of the sentences that are true about weathering.

   a. It can be mechanical.

   b. It can be chemical.

   c. It only breaks down soft rocks.

Chapter 23   Earth's Surface

5. Circle the letters of the sentences that are true about mechanical weathering.

   a. It occurs through frost wedging.

   b. It occurs from acidic rain.

   c. It occurs through abrasion.

6. Is the following sentence true or false? Abrasion happens when rocks scrape against each other. _____

7. In the process of chemical weathering, rock is broken down by _____.

8. Circle the letters of the sentences that are true about chemical weathering.

   a. Chemical weathering occurs because rain is slightly acidic.

   b. Water is the main agent of chemical weathering.

   c. Chemical weathering involves abrasion and frost wedging.

Rates of Weathering (page 711)

9. Circle the letters of the factors that increase the rate at which mechanical and chemical weathering take place.

   a. abundant rainfall

   b. low temperatures

   c. rocks with calcite

Mass Movement (page 712)

10. In mass movement, rocks and soil move downhill because of _____.

Match each type of mass movement with its correct description.

Description	Mass Movement
_____ 11. Rapid mass movement of soil and other sediment mixed with water	a. slumping
_____ 12. The rapid movement of large amounts of rock and soil	b. mudflow
_____ 13. Weak layers of soil or rock suddenly moving down a slope as a single unit	c. landslide

Chapter 23   Earth's Surface

Section 23.3 Water Shapes the Land
(pages 713–717)

This section describes how water erodes the land. It also describes features created by water erosion and water deposition.

Reading Strategy (page 713)

Concept Map As you read, complete the concept map showing how moving water shapes the land. For more information on this Reading Strategy, see the **Reading and Study Skills** in the **Skills and Reference Handbook** at the end of your textbook.

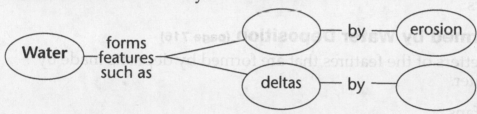

1. The process through which sediment is laid down in new locations is called _____. Circle the correct answer.

   deposition   erosion   saltation

Running Water Erodes the Land (pages 714–715)

Match each method by which sediment is transported in streams with its correct description.

Description	Method of Transportation
_____ 2. Dissolved sediment is carried this way.	a. in suspension
_____ 3. Large boulders can be moved this way during floods.	b. in solution
_____ 4. Tiny sediment grains move along with the water in a stream.	c. by saltation
_____ 5. Large particles bounce along the bottom of a stream.	d. by pushing or rolling

6. What does a stream's ability to erode mainly depend on? Circle the correct answer.

   depth   sediment load   speed

Features Formed by Water Erosion (pages 715–716)

7. A(n) _____ valley is formed by a fast-moving stream.

Chapter 23   Earth's Surface

8. A flat area alongside a stream or river that is covered by water only during times of flood is called a(n) _____.

9. Is the following sentence true or false? Oxbow lakes form when an old meander is cut off from the rest of a river. _____

10. Circle the letters of features that are formed by water erosion.

    a. oxbow lakes
    b. V-shaped valleys
    c. meanders

Features Formed by Water Deposition (page 716)

11. Circle the letters of the features that are formed by deposits made by flowing water.

    a. alluvial fans
    b. deltas
    c. sinkholes

12. A fan-shaped deposit of sediment found on land is called a(n)

    _____.

13. Is the following sentence true or false? Deltas are masses of sediment that form where rivers enter large bodies of water. _____

Groundwater Erosion (page 717)

14. _____ weathering causes groundwater erosion. Circle the correct answer.

    Chemical   Mechanical   Physical

15. Circle the letters of the features that are formed by groundwater erosion.

    a. caves
    b. sinkholes
    c. waterfalls

16. Circle the letter of the correct answer. What is the difference between stalactites and stalagmites?

    a. They appear in different types of caves.
    b. Stalactites grow down; stalagmites grow up.
    c. Stalagmites form before stalactites do.

Chapter 23   Earth's Surface

Section 23.4 Glaciers and Wind
(pages 719–724)

This section describes how glaciers form and how landscape features are created. It also describes wind erosion and deposition.

Reading Strategy (page 719)

Sequencing As you read, complete the flowchart to show how a glacier forms and moves, and how it erodes and deposits sediment. For more information on this Reading Strategy, see the **Reading and Study Skills** in the **Skills and Reference Handbook** at the end of your textbook.

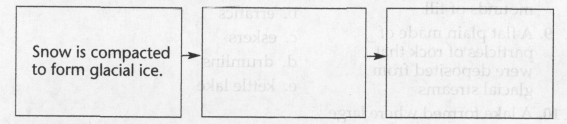

Snow is compacted to form glacial ice.

How Glaciers Form and Move (page 719)

1. Glaciers form in places where snow melts _____ than it falls.

Match the type of glacier to its description.

Description	Glacier Type
_____ 2. Found in high mountain valleys	a. valley glacier
_____ 3. Covers a continent or large island	b. continental glacier

Glacial Erosion and Deposition (pages 720–722)

4. Circle the letters of the sentences that are true about glacial erosion.

   a. Glacial ice widens cracks in bedrock beneath a glacier.

   b. As a glacier moves, it gently brushes the rocks and soil underneath it.

   c. Rocks stuck to the bottoms and sides of a glacier act like sandpaper, scraping rock and soil.

5. Circle the letters of the distinctive features caused by glacial erosion.

   a. cirque

   b. horn

   c. V-shaped valley

Chapter 23   Earth's Surface

6. Large bowl-shaped valleys carved high on a mountainside are called

_____.

7. Mounds of sediment at the downhill end of a glacier are called
_____. Circle the correct answer.

drumlin   morraine   till

Match each feature formed by glacial deposition to its correct description.

Description

_____ **8.** Long teardrop-shaped
mounds of till

_____ **9.** A flat plain made of
particles of rock that
were deposited from
glacial streams

_____ **10.** A lake formed where large
blocks of glacial ice become
buried and melt

_____ **11.** Ridges made from sand and
gravel that were deposited
in the bed of a glacial stream

_____ **12.** Boulders that a glacier has
carried away from their
place of origin

Feature Formed

a. outwash plain

b. erratics

c. eskers

d. drumlins

e. kettle lake

Wind Erosion and Deposition (pages 723–724)

13. Circle the letters of the ways that wind erodes the land.

a. abrasion

b. deflation

c. inflation

14. Is the following sentence true or false? Deflation happens when the

wind picks up and carries away loose surface material. _____

15. Circle the letters of the features deposited by wind.

a. cirques

b. sand dunes

c. loess deposits

16. Is the following sentence true or false? Deposits formed from

windblown dust are called loess deposits. _____

Chapter 23   Earth's Surface

Section 23.5 The Restless Oceans
(pages 725–729)

This section describes the oceans and ocean currents. It also describes water erosion and deposition in the oceans.

Reading Strategy (page 725)

Relating Cause and Effect Copy the table on a separate sheet of paper. After you read, complete the table to compare ways that ocean water can move. For more information on this Reading Strategy, see the **Reading and Study Skills** in the **Skills and Reference Handbook** at the end of your textbook.

Ways Ocean Water Moves		
Movement Type	**Causes**	**Effects**
Surface current	Winds	Warm water generally flows away from the equator along the east side of continents; cold water generally flows away from polar regions along the west side of continents.
Density current		
Upwelling		
Longshore drift		

Exploring the Ocean (pages 725–726)

1. Is the following sentence true or false? Salt is removed from the ocean by animals and plants and through deposition as sediment.

   _____

2. Circle the letters of the conditions that decrease with the ocean's depth.

   a. pressure

   b. light

   c. temperature

3. What is the continental shelf? _____

   _____

Chapter 23   Earth's Surface

Ocean Currents (pages 726–728)

Match each type of ocean current with its correct description.

Description

_____ **4.** A current responsible for a slow mixing of water between the surface and deeper ocean

_____ **5.** Movement of water from the deep ocean to the surface

_____ **6.** A large stream of ocean water that moves continuously in about the same path near the surface

Ocean Current

a. surface current

b. density current

c. upwelling

7. What does each letter in the diagram below represent? Use the terms in the box to fill in the blanks

Cold water upwelling	Surface wind
Density current	Warm surface water
Surface current	

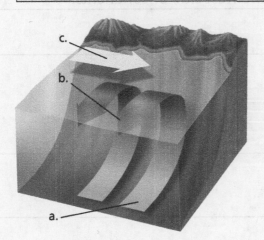

a. _____   b. _____   c. _____

Wave Erosion and Deposition (pages 728–729)

8. Circle the letters of the sentences that are true about hydraulic action.

   a. Hydraulic action causes no changes to earth's coastlines.

   b. Waves compress air as they slam into cracked rocks.

   c. Pressure from waves causes cracks in rocks to get bigger.

9. Is the following sentence true or false? The process that moves sand

along a shore is called hydraulic action. _____

Chapter 23   Earth's Surface

Section 23.6 Earth's History
(pages 732–738)

This section explains how scientists determine the age of rocks and how they use these methods to develop a time line for the history of Earth. It also describes the four major divisions of Earth history.

Reading Strategy (page 732)

Previewing Before you read, examine Figures 34 and 36 to help you understand geologic time. Write at least two questions about them in the table. As you read, write answers to your questions. For more information on this Reading Strategy, see the **Reading and Study Skills** in the **Skills and Reference Handbook** at the end of your textbook.

Questions on Geologic Time

1. What are fossils? _____

_____

Determining the Age of Rocks (pages 732–734)

2. Is the following sentence true or false? The relative age of a rock is its

age compared to the ages of rocks above or below it. _____

3. Circle the letter that identifies the direction in which layers of sedimentary rocks form.

a. vertically

b. horizontally

c. diagonally

4. Circle the letter of the sentence that is true about the law of superposition.

a. Younger rocks lie above older rocks if the layers are undisturbed.

b. Older rocks lie above younger rocks if the layers are undisturbed.

c. Rock layers are never disturbed.

Chapter 23   Earth's Surface

5. Organize and write the letters of the layers of rock in the diagram from oldest to youngest. If two rock layers are the same age, write them as a pair. _____

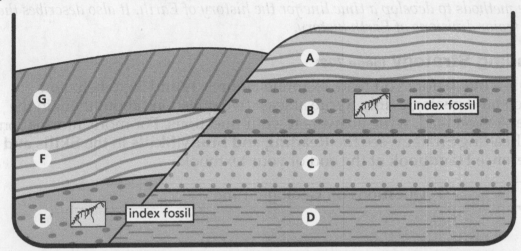

6. Circle the letters of the sentences that are true about index fossils.

   a. They can be easily identified.

   b. They help to determine the relative ages of rocks.

   c. The organisms that formed them occurred over a large area.

A Brief History of Earth (pages 734–738)

7. What is a mass extinction? _____

_____

Match each division of Earth's history to its correct description.

Description	Time
_____ 8. Dinosaurs appeared.	a. Precambrian time
_____ 9. Fishes and other animals first developed in the oceans.	b. Mesozoic Era
	c. Cenozoic Era
_____ 10. Humans first appeared in Africa.	d. Paleozoic Era
_____ 11. Earth was formed.	

WordWise

Use the clues and the words below to help you write the vocabulary terms from the chapter in the blanks. Then find and circle the terms in the puzzle. The terms may occur vertically, horizontally, or diagonally.

deposition	period
loess	fossil
transpiration	runoff
deflation	

```
t  l  o  e  s  s  k  d  r
r  w  f  a  d  u  o  l  u
a  d  q  t  w  i  d  m  j
n  p  t  h  r  p  e  p  d
s  g  i  e  a  q  p  y  e
p  j  p  r  u  n  o  f  f
i  b  x  i  a  b  s  c  l
r  t  c  n  s  f  i  p  a
a  z  y  g  q  a  t  j  t
t  x  f  o  s  s  i  l  i
i  i  o  p  d  f  o  g  o
o  l  o  e  m  k  n  c  n
n  r  q  n  i  g  f  s  d
```

Clues	Hidden Words
When water is released from the leaves of plants	_____
Water that flows over Earth's surface	_____
The process through which sediment is laid down in new locations	_____
When wind picks up and carries away loose surface material	_____
Deposits formed from windblown dust	_____
A preserved remain or trace of a once living thing	_____
A smaller unit of an era	_____

Chapter 23   Earth's Surface

Exploring Radioactive Dating

A fossil contains 100.0 milligrams of thorium-232, which has a half-life of 14.0 billion years. How much thorium-232 will remain after 3 half-lives?

Math Skill: Fractions
You may want to read more about this **Math Skill** in the **Skills and Reference Handbook** at the end of your textbook.

1. Read and Understand

How many milligrams of thorium-232 does the fossil contain?

100.0 milligrams

What is the half-life of thorium-232?   14.0 billion years

What are you asked to find?   the amount of thorium-232 that will remain in the fossil after 3 half-lives

2. Plan and Solve

During a half-life, $\frac{1}{2}$ of the original amount of a radioisotope decays.
To find the amount of thorium-232 left in the fossil after 3 half-lives, begin by multiplying $\frac{1}{2}$ 3 times.

$$\frac{1}{2} \times \frac{1}{2} \times \frac{1}{2} = \frac{1}{8}$$

This is the fraction of thorium-232 that will be left in the fossil after 3 half-lives. Multiply this fraction by the original amount of thorium-232 to find the amount of thorium-232 that will remain.

$$100.0 \text{ milligrams} \times \frac{1}{8} = 12.5 \text{ milligrams}$$

3. Look Back and Check

Is your answer reasonable?

To check your answer, divide the number of milligrams in the fossil after 3 half-lives by the fraction of thorium-232 left after 3 half-lives. Your answer should equal the original amount of thorium-232 in the fossil, 100.0 milligrams.

Math Practice

On a separate sheet of paper, solve the following problems.

1. A fossil contains 40.0 milligrams of uranium-238, which has a half-life of 4.5 billion years. How much uranium-238 will remain after two half-lives?

2. How long will it take for 50.0 milligrams of thorium-232 in a rock to decay to 25.0 milligrams?

Chapter 24 Weather and Climate

Summary

24.1 The Atmosphere

☞ **The atmosphere forms a protective boundary between Earth and space and provides conditions that are suitable for life.**

- The **atmosphere** is the layer of gases that surround Earth.

☞ **Earth's atmosphere is a mixture of nitrogen, oxygen, water vapor, and many other gases, in which tiny solid and liquid particles are suspended.**

☞ **As altitude increases, air pressure and density decrease.**

- The atmosphere has weight because of Earth's gravity. **Air pressure** is the force exerted by the weight of a column of air on a surface.
- A **barometer** measures air pressure.

☞ **The four layers of the atmosphere are the troposphere, the stratosphere, the mesosphere, and the thermosphere.**

- The **troposphere** is the lowest layer of Earth's atmosphere. Most weather takes place in the troposphere.
- **Weather** is the condition of the atmosphere in a particular place at a particular time.
- The **stratosphere** extends from an altitude of about 12 kilometers to about 50 kilometers.
- The upper stratosphere is warmer than the lower stratosphere because of the presence of the **ozone layer**, a region of high ozone concentration.
- The **mesosphere** begins at an altitude of about 50 kilometers and extends to about 80 kilometers.
- The outermost layer of the atmosphere, the **thermosphere**, begins at an altitude of about 80 kilometers and extends outward into space.
- The **ionosphere** is a region of charged particles in the lower thermosphere.
- An **aurora** is a colorful display of light in the ionosphere. It is produced when charged particles from the sun are attracted to Earth's magnetic poles.

24.2 The Sun and the Seasons

☞ **Earth moves in two major ways: rotation and revolution.**

- The spinning of Earth on its axis is called **rotation**.
- **Revolution** is the movement of one body in space around another.

☞ **Scientists use lines of latitude to mark out three different types of regions within which temperatures are generally similar: the tropic, temperate, and polar zones.**

- Between the latitudes of 23.5° south and 23.5° north is the **tropic zone,** where Earth is generally warm.
- From 23.5° north to 66.5° north and from 23.5° south to 66.5° south are the **temperate zones,** which are generally cooler than the tropics.
- From 66.5° north to the North Pole and from 66.5° south to the South Pole are the **polar zones,** which are generally cold.

☞ **The seasons are caused by the tilt of Earth's axis as it moves around the sun.**

- A **solstice** occurs on the two days each year when the sun is directly overhead at latitude 23.5° north or 23.5° south.
- At an **equinox,** neither hemisphere is tilted toward the sun, and the lengths of daylight and of darkness are approximately equal.

24.3 Solar Energy and Winds

☞ **Some solar energy that reaches Earth's atmosphere is reflected back, some is absorbed by the atmosphere, and some is absorbed by Earth's surface.**

- Certain gases in the atmosphere radiate absorbed infrared radiation back to Earth's surface, warming the lower atmosphere in a process called the **greenhouse effect.**

☞ **Energy is transferred within the troposphere in three ways: radiation, convection, and conduction.**

- Much of the sun's radiation reaches Earth's surface, where it heats the land and water. Land and water radiate heat back into the atmosphere.
- Convection moves heat through the troposphere.
- The conduction process transfers heat from land and water directly to the few meters of air nearest Earth's surface.

☞ **Winds are caused by differences in air pressure.**

- **Wind** is the mainly horizontal movement of air.

☞ **The breezes that occur where land meets a large body of water are examples of local winds.**

- A **local wind** is a wind that blows over a short distance.
- **Sea breezes** blow during the day from the ocean to the land.
- **Land breezes** blow during the night from the land to the ocean.

☞ **Trade winds, westerlies, and polar easterlies are examples of global winds.**

- Winds that blow over long distances from a specific direction are **global winds.** They are caused by unequal heating of Earth's surface.
- The curving effect of Earth's rotation is called the **Coriolis effect.**
- **Monsoons** are global winds that are characterized by seasonal reversal of direction.
- A **jet stream** is a belt of high-speed wind in the upper troposphere.

24.4 Water in the Atmosphere

☞ **Water vapor typically condenses as dew, frost, clouds, or fog.**

- The amount of water vapor in the air is called **humidity.**
- **Relative humidity** is the ratio of the amount of water vapor in the air to the maximum amount of water vapor that can exist at that temperature.
- The temperature at which air becomes saturated with humidity is its **dew point.**

☞ **Clouds form as warm, moist air rises and water vapor condenses in the atmosphere.**

- A **cloud** is a dense, visible mass of tiny water droplets or ice crystals that are suspended in the atmosphere.

☞ **There are three basic cloud forms: stratus, cumulus, and cirrus.**

- **Fog** is a cloud that is near or touching the ground.
- **Stratus clouds** are flat layers of clouds that cover much or all of the sky.
- **Cumulus clouds** are puffy white clouds that look like piles of cotton balls with flat bottoms.
- **Cirrus clouds** are thin, white, wispy clouds, often with a feathery or veil-like appearance.

☞ **The most common types of precipitation are rain, snow, hail, sleet, and freezing rain.**

- Precipitation occurs when water droplets or ice crystals in clouds fall to the ground.

24.5 Weather Patterns

☞ **An air mass forms when a large body of air becomes fairly stationary over a region of Earth's surface or as air moves over a large, uniform region like an ocean.**

- An **air mass** is a large body of air that has about the same temperature and moisture content throughout.

◯ **There are four types of fronts: cold fronts, warm fronts, stationary fronts, and occluded fronts.**

- The sharply defined boundary that forms when two unlike air masses meet is called a **front.**
- A **cold front** occurs when a cold air mass overtakes a warm air mass. Cold fronts usually produce high winds and heavy precipitation.
- A **warm front** occurs when a warm air mass overtakes a cold air mass. Warm fronts usually produce steady rain.
- A **stationary front** forms when two unlike air masses have formed a boundary but neither is moving. Stationary fronts usually produce clouds and steady precipitation for several days.
- An **occluded front** forms when a warm air mass is caught between two cooler air masses. Occluded fronts usually produce cloudy skies and precipitation.

◯ **Cyclones are associated with clouds, precipitation, and stormy weather.**

- A weather system with a center of low air pressure is called a **cyclone.**

◯ **The weather associated with an anticyclone includes clear skies, very little precipitation, and generally calm conditions.**

- A weather system with a center of high air pressure is called an **anticyclone.**

◯ **Thunderstorms form when columns of air rise within a cumulonimbus cloud.**

- A **thunderstorm** is a small weather system that includes thunder and lightning.
- **Lightning** is a sudden electrical discharge in the atmosphere.
- **Thunder** is the sound produced by rapidly expanding air along the path of a lightning discharge.

◯ **A tornado forms when a vertical cylinder of rotating air develops in a thunderstorm.**

- A **tornado** is a small but intense windstorm. It forms a spinning column of air that touches the ground.
- A **hurricane** is a large tropical cyclone with winds of at least 119 kilometers per hour. Hurricanes form over warm ocean water.

24.6 Predicting the Weather

◯ **Meteorologists use many technologies to help predict the weather, including Doppler radar, automated weather stations, weather satellites, and high-speed computers.**

- **Meteorologists** are scientists who study weather.

☞ **Weather maps typically show predicted temperatures and include sun or cloud symbols to indicate cloud cover. They have drawings of rain or snow to show areas of precipitation.**

- An **isotherm** is a line on a map that connects points of equal air temperature.
- An **isobar** is a line that connects points of equal air pressure.

24.7 Climate

☞ **Climate is a description of the pattern of weather over many years.**

- **Climate** is the long-term weather conditions of a place or region.

☞ **The two main factors that determine a region's climate are temperature and precipitation.**

☞ **Factors that affect a region's temperature include its latitude, distance from large bodies of water, ocean currents, and altitude.**

☞ **Factors that affect a region's precipitation include its latitude, the distribution of air pressure systems and global winds, and the existence of a mountain barrier.**

- A **desert** is an extremely dry region, receiving less than 25 centimeters of rain per year.

☞ **Climates change over the long term, and they vary somewhat over the short term.**

- **Ice ages** were periods when climates were colder than usual and glaciers covered a large portion of Earth's surface.
- A climate variation that happens every three to eight years is **El Niño**, the periodic warming of water in the central and eastern Pacific Ocean.

☞ **One cause of climate change is the addition of carbon dioxide and other greenhouse gases into the atmosphere.**

- **Global warming** is a rise in the temperature of the atmosphere caused by the greenhouse effect.

Chapter 24   Weather and Climate

Section 24.1 The Atmosphere
(pages 746–751)

This section describes Earth's atmosphere, its composition, and its different layers. It also explains air pressure and the effects of altitude on air pressure.

Reading Strategy (page 746)

Relating Text and Diagrams As you read, refer to Figure 5 and the text to complete the table on the layers of the atmosphere. For more information on this Reading Strategy, see the **Reading and Study Skills** in the **Skills and Reference Handbook** at the end of your textbook.

Layers of the Atmosphere		
Layer	Altitude Range	Temperature Change
Troposphere		
	12–50 km	
	50-80 km	
Thermosphere		Temperature increases rapidly with altitude.

Earth's Protective Layer (page 747)

1. Is the following sentence true or false? The layer of gases that surrounds

   Earth is called the atmosphere. _____

2. Circle the letter of each sentence that is true. How does the atmosphere make Earth's temperatures suitable for life?

   a. The atmosphere forms a protective layer around Earth.

   b. The atmosphere provides all elements necessary for life.

   c. The atmosphere provides conditions suitable for life.

Composition of the Atmosphere (page 747)

3. Is the following sentence true or false? The composition of the atmosphere changes every few kilometers as you move away

   from Earth. _____

4. Circle the letters of the two most abundant gases in Earth's atmosphere.

   a. carbon dioxide   b. nitrogen   c. oxygen

5. Is the following sentence true or false? Both water droplets and solid

   particles are suspended in the atmosphere. _____

Chapter 24   Weather and Climate

Air Pressure (page 748)

6. What is air pressure? _____

_____

7. As altitude increases, air pressure and density _____.

8. Circle the letter of the instrument used to measure air pressure.

   a. a thermometer

   b. a barometer

   c. a psychrometer

Layers of the Atmosphere (pages 749–751)

9. Is the following sentence true or false? Weather is the average condition of the atmosphere in a particular place over a period of

   many years. _____

10. The ozone layer is a region of high ozone concentration in the

    _____.

11. Is the following sentence true or false? Infrared radiation in sunlight is

    absorbed by ozone before it reaches Earth. _____

12. Is the following sentence true or false? The temperature of the outer

    thermosphere is quite high. _____

Match the layer of the atmosphere with a characteristic that would best describe it.

	Layer of the Atmosphere	Characteristic
_____ 13.	troposphere	a. Contains the ozone layer
_____ 14.	stratosphere	b. The outermost layer of the atmosphere
_____ 15.	mesosphere	c. The layer where most meteoroids burn up
_____ 16.	thermosphere	d. The layer where most weather occurs

17. What is the ionosphere? _____

_____

18. When charged particles from the sun are attracted to Earth's magnetic poles, a(n) _____ may appear. Circle the correct answer.

   aurora   ionosphere   ozone layer

Chapter 24 Weather and Climate

Section 24.2 The Sun and the Seasons
(pages 752–754)

This section describes the two major ways Earth moves. It also explains what causes the seasons.

Reading Strategy (page 752)

Building Vocabulary Copy the table on a separate sheet of paper. As you read, complete it by defining each vocabulary term from the section. For more information on this Reading Strategy, see the **Reading and Study Skills** in the **Skills and Reference Handbook** at the end of your textbook.

Vocabulary Term	Definition
Rotation	
Revolution	

1. Circle the two major ways that Earth moves.

orbit   revolution   rotation

2. The spinning of Earth on its axis, called _____, causes day and night. Circle the correct answer.

orbit   revolution   rotation

3. Is the following sentence true or false? It takes Earth one year to complete one rotation. _____

4. Earth completes a full revolution around the sun in _____ days.

Earth's Latitude Zones (pages 752–753)

5. What is latitude? _____

6. Circle the letter that identifies the latitude of the North Pole.

a. 70° north

b. 80° south

c. 90° north

Chapter 24   Weather and Climate

7. Is the following sentence true or false? Scientists use lines of latitude to

mark out three different types of regions on Earth. _____

Match each type of region to its latitude.

Region	Latitude
_____ **8.** temperate zone	**a.** Falls between latitudes of 23.5° south and 23.5° north
_____ **9.** tropic zone	**b.** From 66.5° north to the North Pole, and 66.5° south to the South Pole
_____ **10.** polar zone	**c.** From 23.5° north to 66.5° north, and 23.5° south to 66.5° south

The Seasons (pages 753–754)

11. The _____ are caused by the tilt of Earth's axis as it moves around the sun.

12. Circle the letter of each sentence that is true about a solstice.

   a. A solstice occurs when the sun is directly above the North Pole.

   b. A solstice occurs when the sun is directly above the latitude 66.5° north or 66.5° south.

   c. A solstice occurs when the sun is directly above the latitude 23.5° north or 23.5° south.

13. Is the following sentence true or false? When the winter solstice begins in the Northern Hemisphere, the Southern Hemisphere is tilted toward

the sun. _____

14. Is the following sentence true or false? Earth is closer to the sun when it is summer than when it is winter in the Northern Hemisphere.

_____

15. Circle the letter that identifies the season that begins with the vernal equinox.

   a. summer

   b. spring

   c. autumn

Chapter 24   Weather and Climate

Section 24.3 Solar Energy and Winds
(pages 755–759)

This section explains what happens to solar energy that reaches Earth's atmosphere and how it is transferred within the troposphere. It also describes the different winds on Earth and what causes them.

Reading Strategy (page 755)

Comparing and Contrasting After you read, complete the table to compare and contrast sea and land breezes. For more information on this Reading Strategy, see the **Reading and Study Skills** in the **Skills and Reference Handbook** at the end of your textbook.

Sea and Land Breezes		
	Day or Night?	**Direction of Air Movement**
Sea breeze		Cool air moves toward land.
Land breeze		

Energy in the Atmosphere (page 755)

1. Circle the letter of each sentence that describes what happens to the solar energy that reaches Earth's atmosphere.

   a. It is reflected back into space.

   b. The atmosphere absorbs it.

   c. Earth's surface absorbs it.

2. Is the following sentence true or false? The atmosphere is heated

   mainly by energy that is reradiated by Earth's surface. _____

3. Use the words in the box to name the type of energy transfer in the troposphere that each type of arrow on the diagram represents.

convection	radiation
precipitation	conduction

   a. _____   b. _____   c. _____

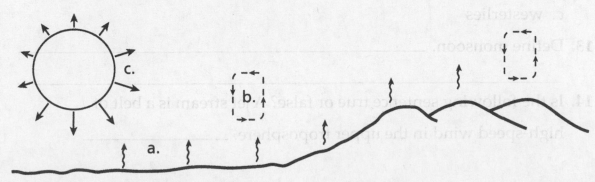

Chapter 24   Weather and Climate

4. The process where certain gases in the atmosphere radiate absorbed energy back to Earth's surface, warming the lower atmosphere, is called the _____.

Wind (page 757)

5. Is the following sentence true or false? Air flows from areas of high pressure to areas of low pressure. _____

6. Is the following sentence true or false? The equal heating of Earth's surface causes differences in air pressure. _____

7. When air warms, expands, and becomes less dense, does it rise or fall? _____

Local Winds (page 757)

8. Is the following sentence true or false? A local wind blows over a long distance. _____

9. Circle the letter of each example of a local wind.

   a. a sea breeze

   b. a trade wind

   c. a land breeze

10. Would you expect to find a land breeze on the beach during the day or during the night? _____

Global Winds (pages 758–759)

11. Is the following sentence true or false? Winds that blow over short distances from a specific direction are global winds. _____

12. Circle the letter of each global wind.

   a. polar easterlies

   b. tradewinds

   c. westerlies

13. Define monsoon. _____
_____.

14. Is the following sentence true or false? A jet stream is a belt of high-speed wind in the upper troposphere. _____

Section 24.4 Water in the Atmosphere
(pages 760–764)

This section discusses the water in the atmosphere. It explains the effect water has on processes in the atmosphere such as cloud formation and precipitation.

Reading Strategy (page 760)

Sequencing As you read, complete the flowchart to show how a cloud forms. For more information on this Reading Strategy, see the **Reading and Study Skills** in the **Skills and Reference Handbook** at the end of your textbook.

Cloud Formation

Warm, moist air rises. → □ → □ → Water vapor condenses on small solid particles in the air.

Humidity (pages 760–761)

1. The amount of water vapor in the air is called _____.

2. Is the following sentence true or false? The ratio of the amount of water vapor in the air to the amount of water vapor the air can hold at that

   temperature is relative humidity. _____

3. What is the dew point? _____

4. What can water vapor condense into? Circle all the possible products.

   dew   fog   frost

Cloud Formation (page 761)

5. What is a cloud? _____

   _____

6. Circle the letter of the best answer. Clouds may form when moist air rises and the temperature cools below the _____.

   a. land temperature

   b. dew point

   c. relative humidity

7. Besides water vapor, what must be present for a cloud to form? Circle the best answer.

   ice crystals   ions   solid particles

Chapter 24   Weather and Climate

Classifying Clouds (pages 762–763)

8. Is the following sentence true or false? Flat layers of clouds that cover

   much of the sky are stratus clouds. _____

9. Is the following sentence true or false? Altostratus clouds are

   low-level clouds similar to fog. _____

10. Circle the letter of the cloud form that is puffy and white with a flat
    bottom.

    a. stratus

    b. altostratus

    c. cumulus

11. What do cirrus clouds look like? _____

    _____

12. Circle the letter of each type of cloud you often see on sunny days.

    a. cumulonimbus

    b. cumulus

    c. cirrus

Match each cloud to its description.

Cloud	Description
_____ 13. cumulus	a. Thin, high-altitude clouds that generally produce no rain
_____ 14. cirrus	b. "Fair-weather clouds" that look like piles of cotton balls
_____ 15. altostratus	c. Middle-level clouds that can produce light rain

Forms of Precipitation (page 764)

16. Name three of the five most common types of precipitation.

    _____

17. Is the following sentence true or false? Snow is precipitation in the form

    of ice crystals. _____

18. Rain that freezes as it falls is called _____. Circle the correct
    answer.

    hail   freezing rain   sleet

Section 24.5 Weather Patterns
(pages 765–771)

This section describes the weather patterns on Earth. It explains how air masses form and create fronts, low- and high-pressure systems, and storms.

Reading Strategy (page 765)

Outlining Complete the outline with information from the section. Use the green headings as the main topics and the blue headings as subtopics. As you read, add supporting details to the subheadings. For more information on this Reading Strategy, see the **Reading and Study Skills** in the **Skills and Reference Handbook** at the end of your textbook.

Weather Patterns
I. Air Masses
II. Fronts
A. Cold fronts occur when a cold air mass overtakes a warm air mass.
B.
C.
D. Occluded fronts occur when a warm air mass is caught between two cooler air masses.

Air Masses (pages 765–766)

1. A large body of air that has fairly uniform physical properties such as temperature and moisture content at any given altitude is a(n)

   _____.

Match the classifications of air masses to where they form.

Classification of Air Mass	Where It Forms
_____ 2. maritime	a. Where it is very warm
_____ 3. tropical	b. Over water transpiration
_____ 4. polar	c. Over land
_____ 5. continental	d. Where it is very cold

Fronts (pages 767–768)

6. Circle the letters of the weather conditions often associated with cold fronts.

   a. large amounts of precipitation

   b. clear skies

   c. severe thunderstorms

Chapter 24   Weather and Climate

Match each front to the way it forms.

Front	How It Forms
_____ 7. cold front	a. A warm air mass is caught between two cooler air masses.
_____ 8. warm front	b. A warm air mass overtakes a cold air mass.
_____ 9. stationary front	c. A cold air mass overtakes a warm air mass.
_____ 10. occluded front	d. Two unlike air masses have formed a boundary and neither is moving.

Low- and High-Pressure Systems (page 769)

11. A weather system around a center of low pressure is called a(n) _____. Circle the correct answer.

    anticyclone   cyclone   front

12. Circle the letter of each weather condition associated with cyclones.

    a. precipitation

    b. clear skies

    c. stormy weather

13. Is the following sentence true or false? An anticyclone is a weather system with a swirling center of low pressure. _____

Storms (pages 770–771)

14. Is the following sentence true or false? A thunderstorm is a small weather system with thunder and lightning. _____

15. Circle the letter of each characteristic of a thunderstorm.

    a. strong winds and heavy rain or hail

    b. only occurs on cool days

    c. thunder and lightning

16. Is the following sentence true or false? A tornado is a small, intense windstorm in the shape of a rotating column that touches the ground.

_____

Chapter 24   Weather and Climate

Section 24.6 Predicting the Weather
(pages 774–777)

This section explains some of the technology meteorologists use to predict the weather. It also explains some of the symbols found on weather maps.

Reading Strategy (page 774)

Identifying the Main Idea As you read the text, write the main idea for each heading of this section in the table. For more information on this Reading Strategy, see the **Reading and Study Skills** in the **Skills and Reference Handbook** at the end of your textbook.

Heading	Main Idea
Weather forecasting	
Weather maps	

Weather Forecasting (pages 774–776)

1. What is meteorology? _____

2. Circle the letters of the technologies that help meteorologists predict the weather.

   a. Automated weather stations

   b. High-speed computers

   c. Weather satellites

3. With Doppler radar, _____ are bounced off particles of precipitation in moving storms. Circle the correct answer.

   light waves   microwaves   radio waves

4. Scientists can calculate a storm's _____ by calculating how much the frequency of Doppler radar waves changes. Circle the correct answer.

   duration   intensity   speed

5. Circle the types of weather data that can be collected by a typical weather station.

   temperature   precipitation   wind speed

6. Meteorologists use high-speed computers to analyze data and create short- and long-term _____.

7. Meteorologists can accurately forecast the movement of large weather systems for a period of _____ days.

Chapter 24   Weather and Climate

Weather Maps (pages 776–777)

8. Circle the letter of each type of information that a typical weather map shows.

   a. temperatures

   b. mountain altitudes

   c. symbols for cloud cover

9. Is the following sentence true or false? Weather maps often include symbols for fronts and areas of high and low pressure.

   _____

Look at the weather map and the key to answer questions 10–12.

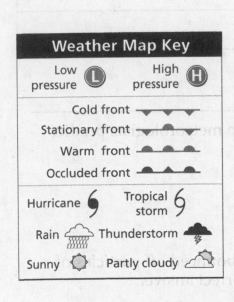

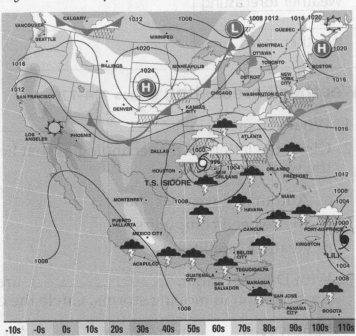

10. What type of front is shown near Calgary, Canada? _____

11. What are the weather conditions in Los Angeles? _____

12. What is the highest air pressure shown on the map? _____

13. A line on a map that connects points of equal air temperatures is called a(n) _____. Circle the correct answer.

    isobar   isomer   isotherm

14. Is the following sentence true or false? An isobar is a line that connects

    points of unequal air pressure. _____

Chapter 24   Weather and Climate

Section 24.7 Climate
(pages 778–782)

This section describes climate and climate changes. It also describes factors that affect the patterns of temperature and precipitation of a region.

Reading Strategy (page 778)

Building Vocabulary As you read, complete the concept map with terms from this section. For more information on this Reading Strategy, see the **Reading and Study Skills** in the **Skills and Reference Handbook** at the end of your textbook.

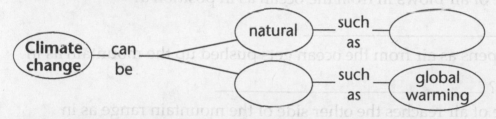

1. What is climate? _____

Classifying Climates (pages 778–779)

2. Circle the letter of the climate group that is determined mostly by altitude.

   a. Tropical rainy   b. Dry   c. Highlands

3. Circle the letters of the two main factors that determine a region's climate.

   a. elevation   b. temperature   c. precipitation

Factors Affecting Temperature (pages 779–780)

4. Circle the letter of the factors that influence the temperature of coastal regions.

   a. altitude

   b. large bodies of water

   c. ocean currents

Factors Affecting Precipitation (page 780)

5. Circle the letter of each factor that can affect a region's precipitation.

   a. the existence of a mountain barrier

   b. latitude

   c. distribution of global winds

Chapter 24   Weather and Climate

Use the diagram below to answer Questions 6–8.

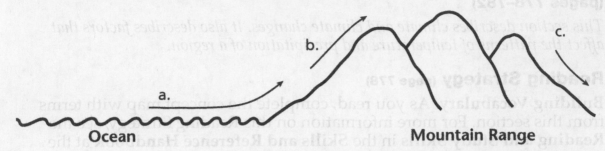

Ocean   **Mountain Range**

6. What type of air blows in from the ocean as in position a?

   _____

7. What happens as air from the ocean gets pushed up the mountain as in

   position b? _____

8. What type of air reaches the other side of the mountain range as in

   position c? _____

Natural Climate Change (page 781)

9. Is the following sentence true or false? The climate of a region never

   changes. _____

10. Circle the letters of two factors that may contribute to changes
    in climate.

    a. human activities

    b. animal activities

    c. natural forces

11. Glaciers covered a portion of Earth's surface and temperatures were

    colder than usual during _____.

12. Is the following sentence true or false? El Niño is the periodic cooling

    of water in the central and eastern Atlantic Ocean. _____

Global Warming (page 782)

13. The addition of _____ and certain other gases to the
    atmosphere may cause global warming. Circle the correct answer.

    carbon dioxide   nitrogen   water vapor

14. The process called _____ refers to an increase in the
    worldwide temperature of the lower atmosphere.

WordWise

Complete the sentences by using one of the vocabulary terms from Chapter 24.

atmosphere	air pressure	troposphere
rotation	equinox	dew point
sea breeze	climate	isotherm
air mass	thunder	

The lower-most layer of the atmosphere is called the _____.

A description of the pattern of weather over many years in a place or region is its _____.

A time when neither hemisphere is tilted toward the sun and lengths of daylight and sunlight are approximately equal is called a(n)

_____.

A large body of air that has fairly uniform physical properties such as temperature and moisture content at any given altitude is a(n)

_____.

The layer of gases that surrounds Earth is called the _____.

The spinning of Earth on its axis is called its _____.

A local wind that blows from sea to land is a(n) _____.

A line on a map that connects points of equal air temperature is called a(n) _____.

The force exerted by the weight of a column of air on a surface is called _____.

The temperature at which air becomes saturated is its _____.

The sound produced by rapidly expanding air along the path of a lightning discharge is called _____.

Chapter 24   Weather and Climate

Calculating Volume of Gases

**Math Skill:
Percents and
Decimals**

You may want to read
more about this **Math
Skill** in the **Skills and
Reference Handbook**
at the end of your
textbook.

About 78% of the volume of dry air is composed of
nitrogen. About how much nitrogen would there be in
a 500 m³ volume of dry air?

1. Read and Understand

What information are you given in the problem?
   Dry air = 78% nitrogen

2. Plan and Solve

What unknown are you trying to calculate?
   500 m³ volume of dry air contains ___?___ m³ of nitrogen

Convert the percent of nitrogen in dry air (78%) to a decimal.
*Move the decimal point in 78% two places to the left and drop the
percent sign.*   = 0.78

*To find the amount of nitrogen in a 500 m³ volume of dry air, multiply 500 by
the decimal conversion of 78%.* $0.78 \times 500 \text{ m}^3 = 390 \text{ m}^3$

About how much nitrogen will a 500 m³ volume of dry air have?
   500 m³ volume of dry air contains about 390 m³ nitrogen

3. Look Back and Check

*To check your answer, find what percent of 500 m³ your answer is. To do this,
first divide your answer by 500.*

$$\frac{390 \text{ m}^3}{500 \text{ m}^3} = 0.78$$

*Then, convert the decimal to a percent by moving the decimal point two places to
the right and placing a percent symbol after the number. If the percent is the
same as the percentage of nitrogen found in dry air, your answer is correct.*

   0.78 becomes 78%

Math Practice

On a separate sheet of paper, solve the following problems.

1. Helium makes up 0.00052% of dry air. About how much helium would
    there be in a 10,000 m³ volume of dry air?

2. A 500 m³ volume of dry air contains 0.185 m³ of carbon dioxide. What
    percent of this sample of air is made up of carbon dioxide?

Chapter 25 The Solar System

Summary

25.1 Exploring the Solar System

👄 **In a geocentric model, Earth is stationary while objects in the sky move around it.**

- In ancient times, people believed Earth was at the center of the universe. Since *geo* is the Greek word for "Earth," such a model of thinking is called a **geocentric** model.

👄 **In a heliocentric model, Earth and the other planets revolve around the sun.**

- The Greek astronomer Aristarchus developed the **heliocentric** model.

👄 **Gravity and inertia combine to keep the planets in orbit around the sun.**

- The plane of Earth's orbit is the **ecliptic plane.**

👄 **Our solar system consists of the sun, the planets, their moons, and a variety of smaller objects that mostly revolve in the same plane around the sun.**

- A **moon** is a relatively small natural body in space that revolves around a planet.
- One **astronomical unit** (AU) equals the average distance from Earth to the sun—about 150 million kilometers.

👄 **Modern technology, including complex telescopes, piloted spacecraft, and space probes, has allowed scientists to explore the solar system.**

- A **space probe** is a spacecraft without people on board. It carries scientific instruments into space and sends data back to Earth.
- Telescopes in space have provided new views of the solar system.

25.2 The Earth-Moon System

👄 **The lack of an atmosphere allows the moon's surface temperature to vary tremendously.**

👄 **The major surface features of the moon are maria, highlands, and craters.**

- **Maria** are low, flat plains formed by ancient lunar lava flows.
- **Highlands** are rough, mountainous regions. They cover most of the moon.
- **Craters** are round dents in the surface caused by meteoroids hitting the moon.
- **Meteoroids** are chunks of rock that move through the solar system.

◓ Scientists hypothesize that the moon formed after an enormous collision early in Earth's history.

◓ The moon's phases are caused by changes in the relative positions of the moon, sun, and Earth as the moon revolves around Earth.

- The different shapes of the moon visible from Earth are called **phases.** They depend on how much of the sunlit portion of the moon is facing Earth.

◓ A solar eclipse occurs when the moon casts a shadow on a portion of Earth's surface.

- An **eclipse** occurs when an object in space, such as the moon, casts a shadow on another object in space, such as Earth.
- The small cone-shaped **umbra** is the darkest part of the moon's shadow.
- Surrounding the umbra is the larger **penumbra,** a region of shadow that is less dark than the umbra.

◓ A lunar eclipse occurs when Earth casts a shadow on the moon.

◓ Tides are caused mainly by differences in the moon's gravitational pull on Earth.

- **Tides** are the regular rise and fall of ocean waters.
- Most coastal areas have two high tides and two low tides each day.
- The **spring tide** occurs when the change between daily high and low tides is the greatest.
- The **neap tide** occurs when the change between daily high and low tides is the smallest.

25.3 The Inner Solar System

◓ The four inner planets are all relatively small and dense, and have rocky surfaces. Like Earth, they all have a crust, mantle, and iron core.

- The **terrestrial planets** are similar in structure to Earth.
- The inner planets are Mercury, Venus, Earth, and Mars.

◓ Mercury is the smallest of the terrestrial planets, and the closest planet to the sun.

◓ Venus's thick atmosphere is composed mostly of carbon dioxide, which traps heat and raises the planet's temperature.

◓ Earth's surface has a suitable atmosphere and temperature range for water to exist as a liquid.

💭 **Mars shows evidence of once having a great deal of liquid surface water.**

- Beyond Mars is a belt of asteroids that orbit the sun.

💭 **Scientists now hypothesize that asteroids are remnants of the early solar system that never came together to form a planet.**

- **Asteroids** are small, rocky bodies that orbit around the sun and range in diameter from about 1 kilometer to 500 kilometers.
- The region where asteroids are found is called the **asteroid belt**.

25.4 The Outer Solar System

💭 **The four gas giants are thought to have small, dense cores, and thick atmospheres that are mostly hydrogen and helium.**

- The gas giants are Jupiter, Saturn, Uranus, and Neptune. These planets are cold and distant from the sun.
- The **gas giants** are planets made mainly of hydrogen and helium.
- The gas giants have many moons. Each giant is surrounded by rings.
- A **ring** is a disk made of many small particles of rock and ice in orbit around a planet.

💭 **Jupiter is the largest and most massive planet in our solar system.**

💭 **Saturn's rings are the largest and most visible from Earth.**

💭 **The axis of Uranus's rotation is tilted more than 90°.**

💭 **Neptune's bluish color comes from the methane in its atmosphere.**

💭 **A dwarf planet, like a planet, is spherical and orbits the sun directly. But unlike a planet, a dwarf planet has not cleared the neighborhood around its orbit.**

- The dwarf planet Pluto is much smaller than the gas giants. Its orbit is very elliptical, and it has a very tilted axis.

💭 **Comets are dusty pieces of ice and rock that partially vaporize when they pass near the sun. Meteoroids are pieces of rock, usually less than a few hundred meters in size, that travel through the solar system.**

💭 **Most of the objects in the Kuiper belt lie in a doughnut-shaped region close to the ecliptic.**

- Objects in the **Kuiper belt** are mostly made of ice, dust, and rock.

💭 **Beyond the Kuiper belt lies a great reservoir of comets called the Oort cloud.**

- The **Oort cloud** is a very sparse sphere of comets surrounding the sun and planets.

25.5 The Origin of the Solar System

◗ **The nebular theory states that the solar system formed from a rotating cloud of dust and gas.**

- A large, thin cloud of dust and gas is called a **solar nebula.**
- When the solar nebula flattened out, it formed a large disk-shaped cloud of dust and gas called a **protoplanetary disk.**
- **Planetesimals** were asteroid-like bodies that formed in the protoplanetary disk.
- Planetesimals grew by **accretion,** the process of adding mass by colliding with other planetesimals.
- The planetesimals eventually combined to form planets.

◗ **The terrestrial planets are relatively small and rocky. In part, that is because the inner solar system was too hot during their formation for ice-forming compounds to condense.**

◗ **The gas giants are large and have low densities because the outer solar system was cool enough for ice-forming compounds to condense.**

Chapter 25   The Solar System

Section 25.1 Exploring the Solar System
(pages 790–794)

This section explores early models of our solar system. It describes the components of the solar system and scientific exploration of the solar system.

Reading Strategy (page 790)

Comparing and Contrasting After you read, compare the geocentric and heliocentric systems by completing the table below. For more information on this Reading Strategy, see the **Reading and Study Skills** in the **Skills and Reference Handbook** at the end of your textbook.

Solar System Models		
	Location of Earth	**Location of Sun**	**Developer(s) of Theory**
Geocentric System	Center of universe		Ancient Greeks, Ptolemy
Heliocentric System			Aristarchus, Copernicus

Models of the Solar System (pages 790–791)

1. Is the following sentence true or false? In the Northern Hemisphere, the stars appear to circle around the North Star. _____

2. Many ancient Greeks thought _____ was the center of the universe. Circle the correct answer.

    Earth   the moon   the sun

3. Circle the letter of each sentence that is true about a geocentric model.

    a. Earth is stationary at the center.
    b. Objects in the sky move around Earth.
    c. The sun is the center of the solar system.

4. Name the center of the solar system in a heliocentric model.

    _____

5. Is the following sentence true or false? The first heliocentric model was widely accepted by most ancient Greeks. _____

6. Is the following sentence true or false? The sun, moon, and stars appear to move because Earth is rotating on its axis. _____

Chapter 25   The Solar System

Planetary Orbits (page 792)

7. Planets move around the sun in orbits that are in the shape of a(n) _____. Circle the correct answer.

   circle   rectangle   ellipse

8. The plane containing Earth's orbit is called the _____.

9. Circle the letter of the factors that combine to keep the planets in orbit around the sun.

   a. gravity
   b. inertia
   c. mass

Components of the Solar System (pages 792–793)

10. Circle the letters that identify objects in our solar system.

    a. planets
    b. the stars other than the sun
    c. the sun

11. Is the following sentence true or false? All of the planets have moons.

    _____

12. Unlike the sun, planets and moons do not produce their own _____. Circle the best answer.

    atmosphere   light   orbit

13. Is the following sentence true or false? The sun's mass is smaller than

    the combined mass of the rest of the solar system. _____

Exploring the Solar System (pages 793–794)

14. Circle the letters of types of modern technology that scientists use to explore the solar system.

    a. Complex telescopes
    b. Piloted spacecraft
    c. Weather balloons

15. An unpiloted vehicle that sends data back to Earth is called a(n) _____. Circle the correct answers.

    Hubble telescope   space probe   space station

Chapter 25   The Solar System

Section 25.2 The Earth-Moon System
(pages 796–801)

This section describes Earth's moon, how it was formed, and its phases. It also explains solar and lunar eclipses and tides on Earth.

Reading Strategy (page 796)

Building Vocabulary As you read, complete the concept map with terms from this section. Make similar concept maps for eclipses and tides. For more information on this Reading Strategy, see the **Reading and Study Skills** in the **Skills and Reference Handbook** at the end of your textbook.

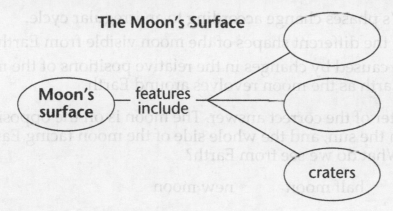

The Moon's Surface

Earth's Moon (pages 796–797)

1. Circle the letter of the sentence that describes how the moon's lack of an atmosphere affects its temperatures.

   a. Its internal temperature is fairly steady.

   b. Its surface temperature is about 130°C.

   c. Its surface temperature varies greatly.

Surface Features (page 797)

2. Circle the letter of each major surface feature of the moon.

   a. highlands

   b. maria

   c. seas

Match each lunar surface feature with its correct description.

Description	Surface Feature
_____ 3. A round depression caused by a meteoroid	a. maria
_____ 4. Low, flat plains formed by ancient lava flows	b. crater
_____ 5. A rough, mountainous region	c. highland

Chapter 25   The Solar System

Formation of the Moon (page 798)

6. Circle the letter of the event that scientists think led to the creation of the moon.

    a. a collision between Earth and Mars

    b. the collapse of a cloud of debris

    c. a collision between Earth and a large object

Phases of the Moon (pages 798–799)

7. Circle the letter of each sentence that is true about phases of the moon.

    a. The moon's phases change according to an irregular cycle.

    b. Phases are the different shapes of the moon visible from Earth.

    c. Phases are caused by changes in the relative positions of the moon, sun, and Earth as the moon revolves around Earth.

8. Circle the letter of the correct answer. The moon is on the opposite side of Earth from the sun, and the whole side of the moon facing Earth is lit by the sun. What do we see from Earth?

    full moon   half moon   new moon

Eclipses (pages 799–800)

9. When the shadow of a planet or moon falls on another body in space,

    a(n) _____ occurs.

10. Look at the diagram showing a solar eclipse. Label the parts, using the following terms: *moon*, *penumbra*, and *umbra*.

    a. _____   b. _____   c. _____

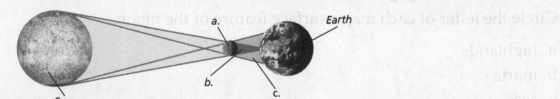

Solar Eclipse

Sun   Earth

a.

b.

c.

Tides on Earth (page 801)

11. Circle the letter of the best answer. Tides are caused by differences in _____ on Earth.

    a. the moon's gravitational pull

    b. the sun's gravitational pull

    c. gravitational pull of the sun and the moon

Chapter 25   The Solar System

Section 25.3 The Inner Solar System
(pages 803–809)

This section describes the terrestrial planets found in the inner solar system.

Reading Strategy (page 803)

Summarizing Copy the table on a separate sheet of paper. Write all the headings for the section in the table. Write a brief summary of the text for each heading. For more information on this Reading Strategy, see the **Reading and Study Skills** in the **Skills and Reference Handbook** at the end of your textbook.

> **The Terrestrial Planets**
>
> I. The Terrestrial Planets
> - Four planets closest to the sun
> - Small, dense, with rocky surfaces
>
> II.
>   a.
>
> III. Venus
>   b. Thick atmosphere, very hot surface, many volcanoes

The Terrestrial Planets (pages 803–804)

1. Identify the four terrestrial planets.

   a. _____   b. _____

   c. _____   d. _____

2. Circle the letter of each sentence that is true about the terrestrial planets.

   a. They are all relatively small and dense.

   b. They all have rocky surfaces.

   c. They all have a crust, mantle, and iron core.

Mercury (pages 804–805)

3. Circle the letter of each sentence that is true about Mercury.

   a. It is the closest planet to the sun.

   b. It is the smallest of the terrestrial planets.

   c. It is the slowest-moving planet.

Chapter 25   The Solar System

Venus (page 805)

4. Circle the letter of each sentence that is true. What effect does carbon dioxide in Venus's atmosphere have?

   a. It traps heat.

   b. It creates acidic clouds.

   c. It raises Venus's temperature.

Earth (pages 805–806)

5. Circle the letter of each sentence that is true about Earth.

   a. Its core has cooled down to the point where it is geologically dead.

   b. It supports millions of different species of living things.

   c. It has a suitable atmosphere and temperature for liquid water to exist.

Mars (pages 807–808)

6. Circle the letter of each sentence that is true about Mars.

   a. The largest volcano in the solar system is on Mars.

   b. Iron-rich rocks on Mars's surface give it a reddish color.

   c. It has a thick atmosphere that keeps the planet warm.

7. Is the following sentence true or false? Mars shows evidence of once having liquid surface water. _____

Asteroids (page 809)

8. Small, rocky bodies in space are called _____.

9. Circle the letter of each sentence that is true about asteroids.

   a. Most small asteroids have irregular forms.

   b. The asteroid belt formed when a giant planet was shattered by a collision with a meteoroid.

   c. Most asteroids are less than 1 kilometer in diameter.

Chapter 25   The Solar System

Section 25.4 The Outer Solar System
(pages 810–815)

This section describes the planets in the outer solar system. It also describes the dwarf planet Pluto, comets and meteoroids, and the edge of the solar system.

Reading Strategy (page 810)

Summarizing Copy the table on a separate sheet of paper. Fill in the table as you read to summarize the characteristics of the outer planets. For more information on this Reading Strategy, see the **Reading and Study Skills** in the **Skills and Reference Handbook** at the end of your textbook.

The Outer Planets	
Outer Planets	**Characteristics**
Jupiter	Largest; most mass; most moons; Great Red Spot
Saturn	
	Atmosphere contains methane; at least eight moons

Gas Giants (page 811)

1. Circle the letter of each sentence that is true about Jupiter, Saturn, Uranus, and Neptune compared to the terrestrial planets.

   a. Their years are shorter than the terrestrial planets.

   b. They are colder than the terrestrial planets.

   c. They are much larger than the terrestrial planets.

2. Circle the letter of each sentence that is true about the gas giants.

   a. Their cores are small and dense.

   b. They are made mostly of hydrogen.

   c. Their atmospheres are mostly hydrogen and helium.

Jupiter (pages 811–812)

3. Circle the letter of each sentence that is true about Jupiter.

   a. Jupiter has about 63 moons.

   b. Scientists hypothesize that Jupiter could support life.

   c. Jupiter is the most massive planet in the solar system.

Chapter 25   The Solar System

Saturn (pages 812–813)

4. Saturn has the largest and most visible _____ in the solar system. Circle the correct answer.

   moons   rings   storms

5. Is the following sentence true or false? Saturn has the largest atmosphere and the lowest average density of all the planets in the solar system. _____

Uranus (page 813)

6. Circle the letter of each sentence that is true about Uranus.

   a. It has lots of methane in its atmosphere.

   b. Its axis is tilted more than 90°.

   c. It has no rings.

Neptune (page 814)

7. Is the following sentence true or false? Neptune gets its distinctive blue-green appearance from large amounts of methane in its atmosphere.

   _____

Dwarf Planets (page 814)

8. Circle the letter of each sentence that is true about dwarf planets.

   a. They orbit the sun directly.

   b. They are too massive to attract neighboring debris.

   c. Pluto is a dwarf planet.

Comets and Meteoroids (page 815)

9. A(n) _____ is made of ice and rock that partially vaporizes when it passes near the sun.

10. Chunks of rock, usually less than a few hundred meters in size, that travel through the solar system are called _____.

The Edge of the Solar System (page 815)

11. What is the Kuiper belt? _____

   _____

12. What objects are found in the Oort cloud? Circle the correct answer.

   asteroids   comets   planetoids

Chapter 25   The Solar System

Section 25.5 The Origin of the Solar System
(pages 818–820)

This section explains a theory of how the solar system originated. It also describes how this theory explains the composition and size of the planets.

Reading Strategy (page 818)

Identifying Main Ideas As you read, write the main idea for each topic. For more information on this Reading Strategy, see the **Reading and Study Skills** in the **Skills and Reference Handbook** at the end of your textbook.

Theories on the Origin of the Solar System	
Topic	Main Idea
The nebular theory	
Formation of the protoplanetary disk	
Planetesimals and protoplanets	
Composition and size of the planets	The temperatures in the early solar system were very high near the sun and much lower in the outer system. These temperatures affected which materials condensed to form planets.

The Nebular Theory (pages 818–819)

1. Circle the letter of each sentence that is true about the nebular theory.

   a. The solar nebula formed from the remnants of previous stars.

   b. As the solar nebula contracted, it began to spin more slowly.

   c. The solar system formed from a rotating cloud of dust and gas.

2. Define a solar nebula. _____

   _____

3. Is the following sentence true or false? Most planets and moons are revolving now in the direction that the protoplanetary disk was

   spinning. _____

Chapter 25   The Solar System

4. Circle the letter of each sentence that is true about the formation of the protoplanetary disk.

   a. The disk was densest in the center and thinner toward the edges.

   b. At the center of the disk, nuclear reactions fused hydrogen and helium and the sun was formed.

   c. Nearly all of the mass of the solar nebula became concentrated near the outer edge of the disk.

5. Define planetesimals. _____
   _____

6. Put the following events about the formation of planetesimals and protoplanets in correct order. Number the events 1–5 in the order that they occurred.

   _____ Balls of gas and dust collided and grew larger.

   _____ Planetesimals became large enough to exert gravity on nearby objects.

   _____ Planetesimals grew by accretion.

   _____ Protoplanets joined to form the current planets in a series of collisions.

   _____ Planetesimals grew into protoplanets.

Composition and Size of the Planets (page 820)

7. Circle the letter of each reason that the terrestrial planets are small and rocky.

   a. At low pressures, cooling materials can change from a gas directly into a solid.

   b. Ice-forming materials vaporize at high temperatures.

   c. Rock-forming materials condense at high temperatures.

8. Circle the letter of each sentence that is true about the formation of the gas giants.

   a. The gravity of the gas giants decreased as they grew larger.

   b. Ice-forming material could condense in the outer solar system.

   c. The planets grew large and were able to capture hydrogen and helium from nearby space.

Chapter 25   The Solar System

WordWise

Use the clues and the list of vocabulary words from Chapter 25 to complete this crossword puzzle.

eclipse	asteroids	comets
meteoroid	geocentric	tides
planetesimals	ring	maria
moon		

Clues across:

3. A model where Earth is stationary while objects in the sky move around it

4. A small natural body in space that revolves around a planet

6. Asteroid-like bodies that eventually combined to form planets

9. The regular rise and fall of ocean waters

10. A chunk of rock that moves through the solar system

Clues down:

1. The event that occurs when the shadow of one body in space falls on another

2. Dusty pieces of ice and rock that partially vaporize when they pass near the sun

5. Small, rocky bodies that travel through the solar system

7. Low, flat plains on the moon

8. A disk made of many small particles of rock and ice in orbit around a planet

Calculating Distances Between Objects in Space

Math Skill:
Conversion Factors

You may want to read more about this **Math Skill** in the **Skills and Reference Handbook** at the end of your textbook.

Jupiter is, on average, 5.2 astronomical units (AU) from the sun. About how many kilometers is Jupiter from the sun?

1. Read and Understand

What information are you given?

Jupiter's distance = 5.2 AU from the sun

2. Plan and Solve

What are you asked to find?

Jupiter's distance = ? kilometers from the sun

How many kilometers are in one AU?

149,598,000 kilometers

Write a conversion factor that can be used to change AU to kilometers.

$$\frac{149{,}598{,}000 \text{ km}}{1 \text{ AU}}$$

Multiply the distance from the sun to Jupiter in AU by the conversion factor.

$$5.2 \text{ AU} \times \frac{149{,}598{,}000 \text{ km}}{1 \text{ AU}} = 780 \text{ million km}$$

Jupiter's distance = 780 million km from the sun

3. Look Back and Check

Is your answer reasonable?

To check your answer, convert the distance between the sun and Jupiter in kilometers back to AU.

$$\frac{780{,}000{,}000 \text{ km}}{149{,}598{,}000 \text{ km/AU}} = 5.2 \text{ AU}$$

Math Practice

On a separate sheet of paper, solve the following problems.

1. Pluto is an average distance of 39.5 AU from the sun. How many kilometers from the sun is Pluto?

2. Mercury is 58.3×10^6 km from the sun on average. How many AU is Mercury from the sun?

Chapter 26 Exploring the Universe

Summary

26.1 The Sun

☀ The sun's energy is produced in its central region by the fusion of hydrogen nuclei into helium nuclei.

☀ The sun remains stable because the inward pull of gravity balances the outward push of thermal pressure from nuclear fusion.

☀ The sun's interior consists of the core, the radiation zone, and the convection zone.

- The sun's **core** is its central region, where nuclear fusion occurs.
- The **radiation zone** is the middle layer of the sun's interior. It is a region of gas under pressure.
- The **convection zone** is the outer layer of the sun's interior.

☀ The sun's atmosphere consists of three layers: the photosphere, the chromosphere, and the corona.

- The **photosphere** is the innermost layer of the sun's atmosphere. It is the visible surface of the sun.
- The **chromosphere** is the middle layer of the sun's atmosphere. It is hotter than the photosphere.
- The **corona** is the outermost layer of the sun's atmosphere. The gases here are very thin. It gradually thins into the solar wind.
- The **solar wind** is a stream of electrically charged particles. The stream flows outward from the sun through the solar system.

☀ Features of the sun's atmosphere include sunspots, prominences, and solar flares.

- **Sunspots** are relatively cool areas in the photosphere. They look like dark spots on the sun's surface.
- **Prominences** are huge loops of gas that erupt from sunspot regions.
- **Solar flares** are sudden bursts of energy released from the sun.

26.2 Stars

- A **star** is large, glowing ball of gas in space. It produces energy through nuclear fusion in its core.
- A **light-year** is the distance that light travels in a vacuum in a year, which is about 9.5 trillion kilometers.

- Astronomers measure the parallax of nearby stars to determine their distance from Earth.

  - The apparent change in position of an object with respect to a distant background is called **parallax.**

- Astronomers classify stars by their color, size, and brightness. Other important properties of stars include their chemical composition and mass.

  - The brightness of a star as it appears from Earth is called its **apparent brightness.**
  - **Absolute brightness** is how bright a star really is.

- Most stars have a chemical makeup that is similar to the sun, with hydrogen and helium together making up 96 to 99.9 percent of the star's mass.

  - Each star has its own spectrum. **Absorption lines** in the spectrum show where light has been absorbed. These lines are used to identify different elements in the star.

- H-R diagrams are used to estimate the sizes of stars and their distances, and to infer how stars change over time.

  - An **H-R diagram** is a graph of the surface temperature, or color, and absolute brightness of a sample of stars.
  - The diagonal band on an H-R diagram is called the **main sequence.**
  - The very bright stars at the upper right of the H-R diagram are called **supergiants.**
  - Just below the supergiants are the **giants.** These are large, bright stars that are smaller and fainter than supergiants.
  - A **white dwarf** is the small, dense remains of a low- or medium-mass star. White dwarfs are dim but hot.

26.3 Life Cycles of Stars

- A star is formed when a contracting cloud of gas and dust becomes so dense and hot that nuclear fusion begins.

  - A **nebula** is a large cloud of gas and dust spread out over space.
  - A contracting cloud of gas and dust with enough mass to form a star is called a **protostar.**

⬤ **A star's mass determines the star's place on the main sequence and how long it will stay there.**

- High-mass stars burn more brightly and use up fuel quickly. They do not last as long as low- or medium-mass stars.
- High-mass stars become red supergiants. Low- or medium-mass stars become red giants.

⬤ **The dwindling supply of fuel in a star's core ultimately leads to the star's death as a white dwarf, neutron star, or black hole.**

- White dwarfs are surrounded by a glowing cloud of gas, called a **planetary nebula.**
- As fusion slows in a high-mass star, the outer layers collapse. This collapse produces a **supernova,** an explosion so violent that the dying star becomes more brilliant than an entire galaxy.
- The dense core that remains after the explosion is called a **neutron star.** When a spinning neutron star appears to give off strong pulses of radio waves, it is called a **pulsar.**
- If a star is very massive, it may collapse beyond the neutron-star stage, into a black hole. A **black hole** is an object with such strong gravity that light cannot escape from it.

26.4 Groups of Stars

- A group of stars that appears to form a pattern as seen from Earth is called a **constellation.**

⬤ **Astronomers have determined that more than half of all stars are members of star systems.**

- A **star system** is a group of two or more stars that are held together by gravity.
- A star system with two stars is called a **binary star.**

⬤ **There are three basic kinds of star clusters: open clusters, associations, and globular clusters.**

- Open clusters are loose groupings of stars. They often contain bright supergiants.
- Associations are temporary groupings of bright, young stars.
- **Globular clusters** are large groups of older stars.

☞ **Astronomers classify galaxies into four main types: spiral, barred-spiral, elliptical, and irregular.**

- A **galaxy** is a huge group of individual stars, star systems, star clusters, dust, and gas bound together by gravity.
- **Spiral galaxies** have a bulge of stars at the center. They have arms extending outward like a pinwheel.
- **Barred-spiral galaxies** have a bar through the center with the arms extending outward from the bar on either side.
- **Elliptical galaxies** are spherical or oval. They do not have arms.
- **Irregular galaxies** come in many shapes. They look disorganized.
- **Quasars** are the enormously bright centers of distant, young galaxies.

26.5 The Expanding Universe

☞ **The observed red shift in the spectra of galaxies shows that the universe is expanding.**

- The light from most galaxies undergoes a **red shift.** Their light is shifted toward the red wavelengths. Galaxies that are more distant from Earth have greater red shifts.
- **Hubble's law** says that the speed at which a galaxy is moving away is proportional to its distance from us.

☞ **Astronomers theorize that the universe came into being at a single moment, in an event called the big bang.**

- The **big bang theory** states that the universe began in an instant, billions of years ago, in an enormous explosion.
- The universe expanded quickly and cooled down after the big bang.

☞ **The existence of cosmic microwave background radiation and the red shift in the spectra of distant galaxies strongly support the big bang theory.**

☞ **Dark matter cannot be seen directly, but its presence can be detected by observing its gravitational effects on visible matter.**

- **Dark matter** is matter that does not give off radiation.

Chapter 26   Exploring the Universe

Section 26.1 The Sun
(pages 828–833)

This section describes how the sun produces energy. It also describes the sun's interior and atmosphere.

Reading Strategy (page 828)

Building Vocabulary Copy the table on a separate sheet of paper and add more lines as needed. As you read, write a definition of each vocabulary term in your own words. For more information on this Reading Strategy, see the **Reading and Study Skills** in the **Skills and Reference Handbook** at the end of your textbook.

The Sun	
Vocabulary Term	**Definition**
Core	The central region of the sun where fusion occurs
Radiation zone	
Convection zone	

Energy from the Sun (pages 828–829)

1. What is the source of the energy that reaches Earth from the sun?

   a. chemical reaction

   b. electromagnetic radiation

   c. combustion

2. Circle the letter of each sentence that is true about nuclear fusion in the sun.

   a. Less massive nuclei combine into more massive nuclei.

   b. Fusion is a type of chemical reaction.

   c. Hydrogen nuclei fuse into helium nuclei.

Forces in Balance (page 829)

3. For the sun to be stable, inward and outward forces within it must be in

   _____.

4. Is the following sentence true or false? The sun remains stable because the inward pull of gravity balances the outward push of thermal

   pressure from nuclear fission. _____

Chapter 26 Exploring the Universe

The Sun's Interior (pages 830–831)

5. List the layers of the sun's interior shown on the diagram. Use the following terms: *core, convection zone, radiation zone.*

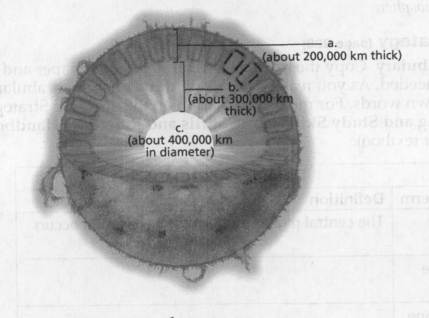

a. (about 200,000 km thick)

b. (about 300,000 km thick)

c. (about 400,000 km in diameter)

a. _____   b. _____   c. _____

The Sun's Atmosphere (page 831)

6. Circle the letter of each layer of the sun's atmosphere.

    a. photosphere

    b. chromosphere

    c. corona

Features of the Sun's Atmosphere (pages 832–833)

Match each description to a feature of the sun's atmosphere.

Description	Feature of Sun's Atmosphere
_____ 7. Spectacular features of the sun's atmosphere that occur near sunspots	a. solar flares
_____ 8. Areas of gas in the atmosphere that are cooler than surrounding areas	b. prominences
_____ 9. Sudden releases of energy that produce X-rays and hurl charged particles into space	c. sunspots

Chapter 26   Exploring the Universe

Section 26.2 Stars
(pages 834–839)

This section discusses how scientists classify stars. It also describes other important properties of stars.

Reading Strategy (page 834)

Using Prior Knowledge Add what you already know about stars to the concept map. After you read, complete your concept map, adding more ovals as needed. For more information on this Reading Strategy, see the **Reading and Study Skills** in the **Skills and Reference Handbook** at the end of your textbook.

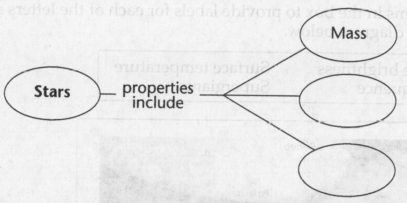

Distances to the Stars (pages 834–836)

1. Circle the letter of each sentence that is true about a light-year.

   a. It is a typical unit of measure for distances on Earth.

   b. It is a distance of about 9.5 trillion kilometers.

   c. It is the distance that light travels in a vacuum in a year.

2. Is the following sentence true or false? Parallax is the apparent change in position of an object with respect to a distant background.

   _____

Properties of Stars (pages 836–837)

3. Circle the letter of each property that astronomers use to classify stars.

   a. brightness

   b. distance

   c. color

4. Is the following sentence true or false? The brightness of a star as it appears from Earth is called its absolute brightness. _____

Chapter 26   Exploring the Universe

5. Circle the elements that make up most of the mass of most stars.

helium   hydrogen   iron

The Hertzsprung-Russell Diagram (pages 838–839)

6. Circle the letter of each way that Hertzsprung-Russell (H-R) diagrams might be used.

    a. to study distant planets

    b. to determine a star's absolute brightness

    c. to determine a star's surface temperature or color

7. Use the terms in the box to provide labels for each of the letters shown on the H-R diagram below.

Absolute brightness	Surface temperature
Main sequence	Supergiants

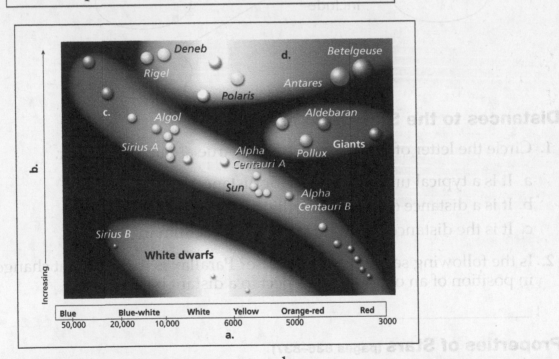

a. _____   b. _____

c. _____   d. _____

8. Circle the letter(s) of each sentence that is true about supergiants.

    a. They are found at the upper right of the H-R diagram.

    b. They are much brighter than main sequence stars of the same temperature.

    c. They are smaller and fainter than giants.

Chapter 26   Exploring the Universe

Section 26.3 Life Cycles of Stars
(pages 840–844)

This section explains how stars form, their adult stages, and how they die.

Reading Strategy (page 840)

Sequencing Copy the flowchart on a separate sheet of paper. As you read, extend and complete it to show how a low-mass star evolves. For more information on this Reading Strategy, see the **Reading and Study Skills** in the **Skills and Reference Handbook** at the end of your textbook.

Evolution of a Low-Mass Star

How Stars Form (pages 840–841)

1. A large cloud of dust and gas spread out over a large volume of space is called a(n) _____. Circle the correct answer.

   nebula   protostar   star

2. Circle the letter of each sentence that is true about a protostar.

   a. Nuclear fusion is taking place within it.
   b. It has enough mass to form a star.
   c. Its internal pressure and temperature continue to rise as it contracts.

3. Number the events from 1 to 3 to show how a star is formed.

   _____ Nuclear fusion begins.
   _____ A protostar contracts.
   _____ The contracting dust and gas get dense and hot.

Adult Stars (page 841)

4. Circle the letter of each true sentence about adult main-sequence stars.

   a. High-mass stars become the bluest and brightest main-sequence stars.
   b. Yellow stars like the sun are in the middle of the main sequence.
   c. Red stars are the hottest and brightest of all visible stars.

Chapter 26   Exploring the Universe

The Death of a Star (pages 842–844)

5. Is the following sentence true or false? The final stages of a star's life

   depend on its mass. _____

6. Circle the letter of each sentence that is true about the death of low-mass and medium-mass stars.

   a. The cores of the stars shrink and only their atmospheres remain.

   b. They remain in the giant stage until their supplies of helium and hydrogen are gone and there are no other elements to fuse.

   c. The energy coming from the stars' interiors decreases and the stars eventually collapse.

7. Match the stages in the evolution of a low-mass star with the letters in the diagram below.

   _____ Black dwarf   _____ Protostar

   _____ White dwarf   _____ Planetary nebula

   _____ Nebula   _____ Main sequence star

EVOLUTION OF STARS   Later stages of a low-mass star

a.   b.   c.   Red giant   d.   e.   f.

8. Is the following sentence true or false? A high-mass star dies quickly

   because it consumes fuel rapidly. _____

Match each final stage of a high-mass star to its correct description.

Description	Final Stage of a High-Mass Star
_____ 9. Surface gravity is so great that nothing can escape from it	a. pulsar
_____ 10. A spinning neutron star that gives off strong pulses of radio waves	b. black hole
_____ 11. The remnant of a high-mass star that has exploded as a supernova, which begins to spin more and more rapidly as it contracts	c. neutron star

Chapter 26   Exploring the Universe

Section 26.4 Groups of Stars
(pages 846–849)

This section describes star systems, star clusters, and galaxies.

Reading Strategy (page 846)

Comparing and Contrasting After you read, compare types of star clusters by completing the table. For more information on this Reading Strategy, see the **Reading and Study Skills** in the **Skills and Reference Handbook** at the end of your textbook.

Types of Star Clusters		
Cluster Type	**Appearance**	**Age and Type of Stars**
Open cluster	Disorganized, loose appearance	
		Bright, young stars
Globular cluster	Spherical, densely packed	

1. Is the following sentence true or false? Constellations are important to

astronomy because they help to form a map of the sky. _____

Star Systems (pages 846–847)

2. A group of two or more stars that are held together by gravity is called

a(n) _____.

3. Is the following sentence true or false? Astronomers have concluded that more than half of all stars are members of groups of two or more

stars. _____

Star Clusters (page 847)

Match each basic kind of star cluster to its description.

Description	**Star Cluster**
_____ **4.** A loose grouping of no more than a few thousand stars that are well spread out	a. globular cluster
	b. open cluster
_____ **5.** Loose groupings of bright, young stars	c. associations
_____ **6.** A large group of older stars	

Chapter 26   Exploring the Universe

7. Is the following sentence true or false? Astronomers estimate that the oldest globular clusters are at least 20 billion years old.

_____

Galaxies (pages 848–849)

8. A huge group of individual stars, star systems, star clusters, dust, and gas bound together by gravity is called a(n) _____.

9. Our galaxy is called the _____.

10. Is the following sentence true or false? The arms of spiral galaxies contain very little gas and dust. _____

11. Circle the letter of each sentence that is true about elliptical galaxies.

a. They usually contain only old stars.

b. They typically have lots of dust and gas.

c. They come in a wide range of sizes.

12. A(n) _____ galaxy has a disorganized appearance and is typically smaller than other types of galaxies.

Match each type of galaxy to its description.

Description

_____ 13. Spherical or oval, no spiral arms, and usually contains only old stars

_____ 14. Bulge of stars at the center with arms extending outward like a pinwheel

_____ 15. Composed of many young stars, comes in many shapes, and has a disorganized appearance

_____ 16. Has a bar through the center with arms extending outward from the bar on either side

Galaxy

a. barred-spiral galaxy

b. elliptical galaxy

c. spiral galaxy

d. irregular galaxy

17. Is the following sentence true or false? The Milky Way appears as a band from Earth because we are looking at it edgewise. _____

18. The enormously bright centers of distant galaxies are called _____. Circle the correct answer.

nebulas   quasars   supernovas

Chapter 26   Exploring the Universe

Section 26.5 The Expanding Universe
(pages 852–855)

This section describes Hubble's law. It also explains the big bang theory.

Reading Strategy (page 852)

Previewing Before reading, examine Figure 26 and write at least two questions to help you understand the information in it. As you read, write answers to your questions. For more information on this Reading Strategy, see the **Reading and Study Skills** in the **Skills and Reference Handbook** at the end of your textbook.

The Evolution of the Universe
Questions on the Evolution of the Universe

Hubble's Law (pages 852–853)

1. Is the following sentence true or false? The apparent change in frequency and wavelength of a wave as it moves towards or away from

   an observer is known as the Doppler effect. _____

2. Circle the letter of each sentence that is true about spectra of stars or galaxies.

   a. As a star or galaxy circles the Earth, the lines in its spectrum shift toward the middle of the spectrum.

   b. As a star moves toward Earth, the lines in its spectrum undergo a blue shift.

   c. As a star or galaxy moves away from Earth, the lines in its spectrum undergo a red shift.

3. State Hubble's law. _____

   _____

4. Is the following sentence true or false? The most distant galaxies that can be seen from Earth are moving away at more than 90% of the speed

   of light. _____

Chapter 26   Exploring the Universe

5. Circle the letter of the sentence that gives the meaning of the observed red shift in the spectra of galaxies.

   a. The universe is contracting.

   b. The universe started with a bang.

   c. The universe is expanding.

The Big Bang Theory (page 854)

6. Circle the letter of each sentence that is true according to the big bang theory.

   a. The matter and energy in the universe was once concentrated in a very hot region smaller than a sentence period.

   b. The universe began billions of years ago with an enormous explosion.

   c. The matter and energy in the universe has taken billions of years to form.

7. Circle the letter of each piece of evidence that supports the big bang theory.

   a. The existence of cosmic microwave background radiation

   b. The red shift in the spectra of distant galaxies

   c. The fact that the sun is about 20 billion years old

8. Circle the letter of the correct answer. Recent measurements of the microwave background radiation have led astronomers to estimate that the universe is how old?

   a. 2.7 billion years

   b. 13.7 billion years

   c. 43.7 billion years

Continued Expansion (page 855)

9. Circle the letter of each sentence that is true about dark matter.

   a. It does not give off radiation.

   b. It can be measured using the Doppler effect.

   c. It can be detected by observing how its gravity affects visible matter.

10. Circle all the reasons that make the amount of dark matter important to the shape of the universe.

   a. It affects what galaxies look like.

   b. It determines whether the universe will keep expanding.

   c. It affects the mass of visible matter.

Chapter 26   Exploring the Universe

WordWise

Use the clues and the words below to help you write the vocabulary terms from the chapter in the blanks. Use the circled letter in each word to find the hidden word.

neutron star	parallax	solar flare
star	light-year	supergiants
black hole	photosphere	nebula

Clues

Vocabulary Terms

What is the surface layer of the sun?

Ⓞ _ _ _ _ _ _ _ _ _ _

What is a dramatic eruption on the sun that produces X-rays and hurls charged particles into space at nearly the speed of light?

_ _ _ _ _ Ⓞ _ _ _ _ _

What is the dense remnant of a high-mass star that has exploded as a supernova?

_ _ _ _ _ _ Ⓞ _ _ _ _ _

What is the distance that light travels in a vacuum in a year?

_ _ _ _ _ Ⓞ - _ _ _ _

What is an object whose surface gravity is so great that nothing, not even light, can escape from it?

_ _ _ _ _ _ Ⓞ _ _ _

What are the very bright stars at the upper right of the H-R diagram?

Ⓞ _ _ _ _ _ _ _ _ _ _

What is a large glowing ball of gas in space?

_ Ⓞ _ _

What is a large cloud of gas and dust spread out over a large volume of space?

_ _ _ _ _ Ⓞ

What is the apparent change in position of an object with respect to a distant background?

_ _ _ Ⓞ _ _ _ _

Hidden Word: _ _ _ _ _ _ _ _ _ _ _

Definition: _____

_____

Chapter 26   Exploring the Universe

Calculating Distances to Stars

Math Skill:
Exponents

You may want to read more about this **Math Skill** in the **Skills and Reference Handbook** at the end of your textbook.

A star is 3.6×10^{19} kilometers from Earth. How many light-years is this?

1. Read and Understand

How many kilometers from Earth is the star?

Star = 3.6×10^{19} kilometers from Earth

What are you asked to find?

Star = ? light-years from Earth

2. Plan and Solve

Write the number of kilometers in a light-year using scientific notation.

9.5×10^{12} kilometers

To find the number of light-years the star is from Earth, divide its distance by the number of kilometers in a light-year.

$$\frac{3.6 \times 10^{19} \text{ kilometers}}{9.5 \times 10^{12} \text{ kilometers}} = 0.38 \times 10^{7} \text{ light-years} = 3.8 \times 10^{6} \text{ light-years}$$

3. Look Back and Check

Is your answer reasonable?

To check your answer, multiply the number of light-years away the star is by the number of kilometers in a light-year. Remember to add the exponents when you multiply. Your answer should be the distance from Earth to the star in kilometers.

3.6×10^{19} kilometers

Math Practice

On a separate sheet of paper, solve the following problems.

1. A star is 8.6×10^{14} kilometers from Earth. How many light-years away is the star? Round your answer to the nearest tenth.

2. The star Proximi Centauri is about 4.3 light-years from Earth. How many kilometers from Earth is it?